RADIO WAR

THE SECRET ESPIONAGE WAR OF
THE RADIO SECURITY SERVICE
1938-1946

Dr DAVID ABRUTAT

FONTHILL

... a team of brilliance unparalleled anywhere in the intelligence machine.

Patrick Reilly, Assistant to Head of MI6 Stewart Menzies

... it would be well to try to achieve a little more recognition for the now diminishing group of radio amateurs who made a unique and seemingly invaluable contribution to British and Allied intelligence during the Second World War.

Edward Hancocks, Radio Security Service Voluntary Interceptor (VI)

Fonthill Media Language Policy

Fonthill Media publishes in the international English language market. One language edition is published worldwide. As there are minor differences in spelling and presentation, especially with regard to American English and British English, a policy is necessary to define which form of English to use. The Fonthill Policy is to use the form of English native to the author. Dr David Abrutat was born and educated in the UK; therefore British English has been adopted in this publication.

Fonthill Media Limited
Fonthill Media LLC
www.fonthillmedia.com
office@fonthillmedia.com

First published in the United Kingdom and the United States of America 2019

British Library Cataloguing in Publication Data:
A catalogue record for this book is available from the British Library

Copyright © Dr David Abrutat 2019

ISBN 978-1-78155-759-4

Typeset in 10pt on 13pt Sabon
Printed and bound in England

Foreword

The story of Bletchley Park is now familiar to many: its tales of intellectual brilliance and painstaking slog, of code-busting and large-scale analysis, of individual triumphs and team-based breakthroughs.

We think instinctively of the Government Code and Cipher School, the direct predecessor of Government Communications Headquarters, or GCHQ as it is commonly known. Yet periodically we are treated to some new ingredient of its history that develops our understanding of the pivotal role played in the run-up to and through the Second World War, illuminations that continue to shed light on both signals intelligence (SIGINT) and communications security and that have sustained relevance even in today's world of the World Wide Web.

Now Dr David Abrutat presents us with a complementary narrative, for once not with Bletchley Park at its core but as a customer and partner, even perhaps at times a competitor in some sense: the story of the Radio Security Service with another park—Hanslope Park—as one of its listening posts, but with its HQ at Arkley, outside Barnet.

The work carried out in the RSS shines a light on subsequent, even modern, SIGINT tradecraft: the elaborate, patient construction of the overall mosaic that eventually depicts the intelligence-derived picture—recalling the essence of GCHQ's work on the Warsaw Pact during the Cold War; the discovery, discrimination, and assimilation of fragments of communication methods and content—chiming with the modern-day counter-terrorism mission carried out by GCHQ and its sister agencies.

That professional craft of the 1930s and '40s has been handed down over generations to the intelligence collectors and analysts of today.

So in itself, the RSS was every bit as much a forerunner to GCHQ as GC&CS. As Dr Abrutat describes, the RSS contribution was such that the skill and dedication of the volunteer radio interceptors led to GC&CS coming to the conclusion that full-time professionals were needed for the task of discovering, logging, and, in due course, analysing the networks used for communication to illicit agents.

This study offers a tantalising glimpse of the 'third letter I' mission as developed and pursued by GCHQ—the initial 'I' standing for illicit: this is a mission that finds scant mention in the official histories, with the various American government releases in the mid-1990s around the historic VENONA work representing the sum of official releases on the subject.

It is striking that the very attributes, cherished and preserved at a time of existential threat to these islands, are precisely the same as those now at the heart of the intelligence effort that strives to keep us safe from today's adversaries, eight decades later.

I commend *Radio War* to all students of the strategic, operational, and tactical difference that intelligence can make in conflict and in what passes for peacetime.

Sir Iain Lobban, KCMG, CB
GCHQ 1983–2014 and Director GCHQ 2008–2014

Acknowledgements

Thanks go to Stan Ames; Bob King; Gardner Crawley and his mother, Helena Crawley; Bill Peek, and his brothers; Ray Fautley; George Busby; Mike Griffiths; David White; Tony Comer, Jock Bruce, and the archivists at GCHQ; staff at TNA and IWM Archives; Paul J. Cort-Wright; Edwina Holden, John Shere, and Neville Cullingford at the Royal Observer Corps (ROC) Archives; BT Archives Manager James Elder; ex-GCHQ Director Sir Iain Lobban, KCMG, CB; Oliver House and Michael Hughes; Elizabeth Bruton; Ray Wright; Jo Carter at Carterworks Ltd; Gill Clark; Jeanette and Michael Chamberlain; and Martyn Baker, the National Radio Centre (NRC) Coordinator at Bletchley and RSGB. I dedicate this book to my parents who have been my source of inspiration throughout my life.

CONTENTS

List of Abbreviations

AORG:	Army Operations Research Group
ATS:	Auxiliary Territorial Service
AU:	Amplifier Unit
BBC:	British Broadcasting Corporation
BCRA:	*Bureau Central de Renseignements et d'Action*
BEF:	British Expeditionary Force
BFO:	Beat Frequency Oscillator
BP:	Bletchley Park
BRS:	British Receiving Station
BTM:	British Tabulating Machine company
CBME:	Combined Bureau Middle East
CCO:	Chief of Combined Operations
CH:	Chain Home (radar)
CHIS:	Covert Human Intelligence Source
CI:	Counter-Intelligence
CIC:	Combined Intelligence Committee
CID:	Committee for Imperial Defence
CO:	Commanding Officer
COHQ:	Combined Operations Headquarters
CP:	Command Post
CSDIC:	Combined Services Detailed Interrogation Centre
C/S:	Call sign
CWR:	Civilian Wireless Reserve
DASD:	*Deutschen Amateur-Sende und Empfangsdienstes*
DASV:	*Deutscher Amateur Sende und Empfangs Verein*
DF:	Direction Finding
DFTV:	*Deutsche Funktechnische Verband*

DMI:	Director of Military Intelligence
DDMI:	Deputy Director of Military Intelligence
DNI:	Director Naval Intelligence
FBI:	Federal Bureau of Investigations
FCC:	Federal Communications Commission
FRUMEL:	Fleet Radio Unit in Melbourne
FUSAG:	First United States Army Group
GAF:	German Air Force
GCC:	Government Communications Centre
GCHQ:	Government Communications Headquarters
GCVRS:	Government Communications Voluntary Radio Service
GC&CS:	Government Code & Cipher School
GHQ:	General Headquarters
GPO:	General Post Office
GS:	General Search
GSIS:	German Secret Intelligence Service
GVRO:	Group Voluntary Radio Operator
HFDF:	High Frequency Direction Finding
HG:	Home Guard
HUMINT:	Human Intelligence
HVRO:	Honoraria Voluntary Radio Operator
IDET:	Italian Detachment
ISK:	Intelligence Services Knox
ISLD:	Inter-Service Liaison Department
ISOS:	Intelligence Services Oliver Strachey
IWIO:	Illicit Wireless Intercept Organisation
JCS:	Joint Chiefs of Staff
JIC:	Joint Intelligence Committee
JIS:	Joint Intelligence Staff
JNCO:	Junior Non-Commissioned Officer
KFV:	*Kriegs Funkverkehr*
LVF:	*Légion des volontaires français*
MERS:	Middle East Radio Security
MEW:	Ministry of Economic Warfare
MF:	Medium Frequency
MI:	Military Intelligence
MI5:	British Security Service
MI6:	Secret Intelligence Service (also SIS)
NCO:	Non-Commissioned Officer
NID:	Naval Intelligence Division
OIC:	Officer in Charge
OKH/GdNA:	*Oberkommando des Heeres, General der Nachrichtenaufklärung*

OKW:	*Oberkommando der Wehrmacht*
OKW/Chi:	*Oberkommando der Wehrmacht/Chiffrier Abteilung*
ORBAT:	Order of Battle
OSS:	Office for Strategic Services
OTP:	One Time Pads
PID:	Political Intelligence Department (cover name for the Political Warfare Executive)
PMWR:	Polish Military Wireless Research (Unit)
POW:	Prisoner of War
PVRO:	Part-Time Voluntary Radio Operator
PWD:	Psychological Warfare Division (SHAEF)
PWE:	Political Warfare Executive
PWIS:	Prisoner of War Interrogation Section
RADAR:	Radio Detection and Ranging
RAF:	Royal Air Force
RAF:	Royal Air Force Voluntary Radio Service
RCA:	Radio Corporation of America
RCM:	Radio Countermeasures
REME:	Royal Electrical and Mechanical Engineers
RIS:	Radio Intelligence Section
RM:	Royal Marines
RN:	Royal Navy
RNR:	Royal Naval Reserve
RNVR:	Royal Naval Volunteer Reserve
RNWAR:	Royal Naval Wireless Auxiliary Reserve
RO:	Radio Operator or Regional Officer
ROC:	Royal Observer Corps
RSC:	Radio Security Committee or Company
RSGB:	Radio Society of Great Britain
RSIC:	Radio Security Intelligence Conference
RSS:	Radio Security Service
RU:	Research Unit
SCIU:	Special Counter Intelligence Unit
SCU:	Special Communications Unit
SD:	*Sicherheitsdienst*
SE:	Security Executive
SFHQ:	Special Forces Headquarters
SHAEF:	Supreme Headquarters Allied Expeditionary Force
SIGINT:	Signals Intelligence
SIME:	Security Intelligence Middle East
SIPO:	*Sicherheitspolizei*
SIS:	Secret Intelligence Service

SLO:	Special Liaison Officer
SLS:	Special Listening Service/Section
SLU:	Special Liaison Unit
SNCO:	Senior Non-Commissioned Officer
SO:	Special Operations
SOE:	Special Operations Executive
SSB:	Secret Service Bureau
STS:	Special Training Schools
SWL:	Short Wave Listener
SWOPS:	Special Wireless Operators
TA:	Territorial Army
T/A:	Traffic Analysis
TAF:	Tactical Air Force
TICOM:	Target Intelligence Committee
TIS:	Theatre Intelligence Section
TOI:	Time of Intercept
TP:	Teleprinter
TRE:	Telecommunications Research Establishment
USAAF:	United States of America Air Force
VI:	Voluntary Interceptor
VRO:	Voluntary Radio Operator
WD:	War Department
WNV:	*Wehrmachts Nachrichten Verbinden*
WOYG:	War Office 'Y' Group
WRNS:	Women's Royal Naval Service (informally Wrens)
W/T:	Wireless Telegraphy
WU:	Wireless Unit

Introduction

During the Second World War, across the expanse of our country, teams of amateur radio enthusiasts were recruited to take part in one of the most innovative projects in the intelligence community. Working out of their sheds, attics, and bedrooms, they monitored the wireless networks of the German and other Axis Intelligence services. Alongside their full-time operator colleagues, they quickly became one of the most significant sources of signals traffic for Bletchley Park. The organisation was to become known as the Radio Security Service. This is a remarkable story of dedication to duty, technical skills, and service for the country. It was also a reflection of a time-honoured British tradition of improvisation.

Much has been made over the significant role that Bletchley Park made to the Allied war effort during the Second World War. This was first exposed in 1974 with the release of *The Ultra Secret* by Frederick Winterbotham, closely followed in 1982 when one of the key Bletchley codebreakers, Gordon Welchman, ignored the ban on releasing information on Ultra traffic (the code name for the wartime signals intelligence derived from deciphered German wireless transmissions) with his published work *The Hut 6 Story*.

Few of the books on GCHQ since Welchman's have included any insight into the role the Radio Security Service (RSS) was to play in intercepting German Intelligence services signals, which were to be a significant proportion of intercepted German traffic. The successful decryption of enciphered sensitive German traffic was dependent on accurate interception by the skilled wireless operators of the RSS, General Post Office (GPO), and the military 'Y' services. Ultra was often an output from analysis of distinct cipher message strings (referred to as 'cribs') and frequently the operational mistakes by German wireless operators.

Ultra was Churchill's most valuable source of intelligence. During the Second World War, it was closely protected. It was a huge part of the Bletchley Park intelligence machine. On average, around 15,000 messages were being passed every week from the RSS to the Government Code and Cipher School (GC&CS), which was around 20 per cent of the total messages being handled at Bletchley. It was intelligence collection on an industrial scale. The RSS was to build and maintain the most complete reference resource of radio signals in the world.

The idea behind the RSS was borne out of a need to track down enemy agent transmissions in Britain before the Second World War began. The concept could be traced back to the early stages of the First World War. This was to rely on skilled radio operators who had the skills and experience to interpret weak Morse signals, build their own wireless equipment, and understand the vagaries of the radio spectrum.

The full Second World War history of the RSS and its relationship to the GC&CS at Bletchley Park, MI5, MI6, and MI8c is complex, and building a coherent story has been challenged by the restrictions of the Official Secrets Act, which up until recently has restricted any of the RSS operators from formally publishing any accounts of their roles and work during the war. There is still of cloak of secrecy that prevails, even in the surviving veterans of the unit. It was not until 1979 when a BBC East researcher, Paul Cort-Wright, produced a documentary for the BBC called *The Secret Listeners*, which exposed the work of the Voluntary Interceptors of the RSS.

MI5 was to work very closely with the RSS during the Second World War on the infamous Double-Cross System derived by John Masterman, Chairman of the Twenty (XX) Committee. The RSS would intercept the wireless traffic and, working with GC&CS, decipher the coded messages used by the German intelligence services. This gave MI5 a tipoff and the ability to arrest any incoming German spies bound for Britain as they landed on the coastline or via parachute. MI5's 'B' Branch would then screen these detained agents and attempt to turn them to work for the Allies as double agents and help British intelligence broadcast false messages back to their German controllers. It was a master stroke and one that was to significantly change the course of the war.

The RSS was integral to the Double-Cross System. They would be responsible for agent identification and knowledge of their pending arrival in Britain. The wireless operators would also monitor how far their disinformation was accepted within the German Intelligence command structures.

At its height, the RSS (according to Hinsley and Simkin—*British Intelligence in the Second World War: Volume 4*) had a total manifest of 2,094 staff, which would include ninety-eight officers, 1,317 operators, eighty-three engineers, 471 administrative personnel, and 125 civilian clerks, as well as some 1,200 Voluntary Interceptors. The number of VIs is estimated to be much higher, in the region of 1,500–1,700 in number. In total, the RSS at its peak would number around 3,500. All told, the whole of the British SIGINT machine at the height of the war would gainfully employ over 50,000 people across the RSS, GPO, GC&CS, and the military 'Y' service sites.

During the Second World War, German intelligence had deployed wireless teams throughout occupied Europe. Agents had even been deployed to mainland Britain to spy on British military activity. The monitoring and reporting of their wireless transmissions was to fall to the military 'Y' service teams and to a small, secretive, and largely unknown unit manned almost exclusively by volunteers.

The Voluntary Interceptors (VI), as they became known, would spend hours every day at home monitoring the short-wave frequencies for often-faint and difficult-to-copy signals transmitted by these German secret intelligence services. Without interceptors like the RSS, Bletchley would not have existed. It grew from its small niche pre-war activities to identify and locate illicit wireless transmissions from German agents operating in Britain to one of the most significant intelligence services of the war, and it quickly evolved into a global organisation capable of unravelling the operations of the German Intelligence Services wherever in the world they were active.

Much of the story has been lost to the march of time, but what I have tried to accomplish is a mix of historical facts and personal accounts from those involved with the RSS during the war. I have left it to the people to quote themselves. Throughout the text, I have often included the known call signs of the radio amateurs, as a sequence of numbers and letters that act as an identifier on a radio network.

Their story has never truly been written and had scant attention from military historians. *Radio War* focuses on the secret world of wireless espionage and includes first-hand accounts from the surviving veterans of the unit. Its existence was only made public thirty-five years after the Second World War ended, shortly after Bletchley Park's secrets were exposed. Patrick Reilly, Assistant to Head of MI6 Stewart Menzies, was to say of the RSS 'a team of brilliance unparalleled anywhere in the intelligence machine'.

1

Scrubs

… intercept, locate and close down illicit wireless stations operated either by enemy agents in Great Britain or by other persons not being licensed to do so under Defence Regulations, 1939.

Lt-Col. John P. G. Worlledge's initial brief to establish the RSS

It was an unusually warm September in 1940 for the South of England. In the dark moonlit night of 6 September, a lone Heinkel He 111 plane crossed the calm Channel from its Luftwaffe aerodrome in Rennes. It was carrying a precious cargo, a German agent. As the Heinkel plateaued at 5,000 metres above the Northamptonshire countryside, the parachutist deployed. He was to have a terrible landing close to the village of Denton, becoming concussed in the process. He crawled into a nearby ditch and was discovered by one of the local farmworkers the next day. The owner of the farm, Cliff Beechener, duly escorted the German agent (coded as agent 3719) at the end of a shotgun to the local police station. He had been carrying £200 in cash, a pistol, and, more importantly, a radio transmitter.

This first *Abwehr* agent dropped into Britain was the Swedish national Gösta Caroli, later to be code-named SUMMER. He was arrested and taken to the infamous British Interrogation centre 'Camp 020' at Latchmere House in South London and recruited by MI5 into the Double-Cross System. Instead of being executed, he was tasked with broadcasting false information back to his *Abwehr* handlers in Germany via his radio set. These transmissions were being monitored in secret by an amateur radio operator verifying what his MI5 handlers had told him to broadcast. The radio operator was part of a new intelligence gathering service that was to be an integral part of the pioneering Bletchley Park codebreaking centre. It was known as the Radio Security Service (RSS). By 1941, the Bletchley Park codebreakers had deciphered the complex *Abwehr* hand cipher and could read all of the *Abwehr* agent's wireless transmissions back to Germany.

Between the two world wars, British intelligence was concerned about the threat from illicit wireless communications. It had been exposed when a German agent and ardent Welsh Nationalist Arthur Graham Owens, code-named SNOW, had been caught sending mail to an *Abwehr* cover address in Germany. Without knowing it, his communications with Germany were being monitored by MI5's letter interception unit. He had been in contact with the *Abwehr* while on business in Germany before the war and was trusted by the service, having worked for them since 1936. After interrogation by MI5, Owens admitted to the presence of a German intelligence service miniaturised radio set called an *Agent-Funkgerät*, which was located in a left luggage locker at Victoria Railway Station in London. The set was picked up by Special Branch officers and MI5 passed it across to specialist engineers to examine. It was given back to Owens to allow him to transmit back to his German handlers. SNOW was to become our first double agent of the war, but MI5 quickly came to the conclusion that he could not be trusted and he was interned at Wandsworth Prison.

Owens managed to secure his release from Wandsworth as he had volunteered to work for MI5 and broadcast falsified intelligence back to his handlers using his radio set. Instead of using Owens, however, MI5 had installed a prison warder called John Burton who took over Owens' role with a homemade wireless set tuned to the same broadcast frequency as the German *Agent-Funkgerät*. Owens had been told that his transmissions were being picked up by an *Abwehr* facility just outside Hamburg, but radio operators from the General Post Office (GPO) and the RSS had identified that his transmissions were being received just off the Norwegian coast and then being relayed on to Hamburg.

It had re-established the *Abwehr* link and Owens went on several trips to Antwerp to meet his German handlers, returning with codebooks and wireless instructions that would provide the RSS and the GC&CS codebreakers at Bletchley Park with a significant step forward in breaking the *Abwehr* hand cipher. This in turn would yield a known plaintext sequence, or 'crib', which would help in the eventual exploitation of the Enigma cipher machine.

German spies had been sent to Britain to pass back intelligence to the German Intelligence Services, to undertake sabotage operations against key strategic locations, or to just spread false information to demoralise the civilian population. It was realised at the time that an independent and specialist organisation would have to be created to intercept illicit transmissions by spies from other nation states operating within Britain.

Discussions like these had been talked of as far back as 1915, when the Secretary of the Wireless Society of London (the forerunner of the Radio Society of Great Britain, or RSGB) Rene Klein wrote to the *Times* newspaper with a suggestion that members of the society should be recruited to monitor the airwaves for illicit wireless transmission. The idea was not taken up. A few years later, in 1928, the Standing Inter Departmental Sub Committee of the CID on

Censorship recommended the War Office should use radio amateurs for such a role, to work alongside the already established SIGINT units within the Military and Foreign Office, which monitored transmissions overseas for the GC&CS.

Although the recommendation was produced, there was no decision and it was not until 1933 that the GPO was given responsibility for the development of the organisation, including its manning and technical support. The development of the unit took years to evolve and the GPO agreed by December 1937 to establish three fixed intercept and direction finding (DF) stations. Even then, the first station was not operational until a year later. The early stages of the RSS as an organisation is heavily interwoven and defined by its relationship with the Post Office.

A meeting at the War Office on 13 December 1938 involving the Foreign Office, War Office, Military Intelligence, and the GPO led to the formal creation of an illicit wireless interception organisation. The meeting was chaired by Col. K. J. Martin from MI1, and during it, he referred to a directive as far back as 1933, which was issued by the Committee of Imperial Defence. It would state that the War Office should be responsible for the direction and finance of an organisation for the detection of illicit wireless transmissions. They would need to rely on the Post Office for their skilled wireless operators.

Lt-Col. Adrian Simpson was to be a key figurehead in these vital pre-war years. With his background from the Royal Engineers, he had a vast amount of technical wireless engineering knowledge accrued from his service in the First World War. He had been asked for his advice by MI5 in the summer of 1938 on how illicit wireless traffic could be intercepted in Britain. His damning report was to conclude at the time that British interception efforts against enemy agents was insufficient.

Simpson was tasked to develop plans to detect illicit wireless signals. His initial suggestion was to recruit a network of around sixty specially trained and experienced Morse operators around the country connected into three DF stations linked by landline.

The original manpower was to come from the Army and consisted of serving soldiers carried on War Office establishments, but with no special rates of pay. At this time, the science behind wireless telegraphy (W/T) communications was evolving at a phenomenal rate. The chances of a skilled enemy agent being detected and located were becoming more remote. Simpson recognised that current wireless interception and DF stations around the other services and agencies were at capacity, so they could not be asked to support any additional work. He also recognised that technology had progressed to the extent that an agent working on short reflected waves to a receiving station at a considerable distance away (such as South Africa or Mexico) could be retransmitting information to Germany.

The organisation was referred to as the Illicit Wireless Intercept Organisation (IWIO) to which a number of radio amateurs or VI were assigned to. The name gave too much away as to its function, so the name evolved into the more generic Radio Security Service (RSS). At this stage, overall control of the fledgling RSS was under MI1(g) until November 1939 and by MI8(c) after then. It was to be administered by Section VIII of SIS and had a number of consumers of its product—Section V of SIS, 'B' Division of MI5, and the internal Intelligence Section (RIS) of the RSS itself.

Col. John Pendry Worlledge was a veteran wireless specialist with the Royal Corps of Signals, who had commanded the No. 2 Wireless Company in Palestine up until 1927. He was given overall command of this fledgling organisation, with twenty-four men from the ranks of Military Intelligence and the Royal Signals. His initial brief was to 'intercept, locate and close down illicit wireless stations operated either by enemy agents in Great Britain or by other persons not being licensed to do so under Defence Regulations, 1939'.[1]

The operators were to be virtually all existing radio amateurs who would have held transmitting licences before the war. Recruitment began in earnest from June 1939, starting with Maj. Sclater and Cole-Adams and Maj. Ernest Walter Gill as his chief traffic analyst. Just before this, a number of radio amateurs had volunteered to join the RAF's Civilian Wireless Reserve (RAFCWR) or the similar Royal Navy Wireless Volunteer Reserve (RNWVR).

The RSS was first located in 'C' Wing of Wormwood Scrubs Prison in west London, where MI5 had relocated due to the heavy bombing of central London in the early stages of the Second World War. The prison, affectionately referred to by its inmates as 'Scrubs' was linked by teleprinter to Bletchley Park. Here a key figure in the conception of the RSS, Ralph Sheldon Mansfield, was to lay down the bedrock of the organisation. Mansfield was previously the owner and managing director of Hatch Mansfield wine merchants and had inherited the title of Lord Sandhurst in 1933. He was an enthusiastic and well-known radio ham, having served with the Royal Engineers' Signal Service in France during the First World War.

As war broke out, Mansfield identified a pressing need to expand the fledgling organisation and he consulted Ken Alford (G2DX) who suggested radio amateurs would be keen to help and advised him to discuss the matter with Arthur Watts, the then-president of the Radio Society of Great Britain (RSGB), which still exists to this day. With his links around the country, he was to begin recruiting RSGB members who could form the backbone of the radio monitors required for the new organisation. Watts was also a veteran of the First World War, and had lost a leg at Gallipoli; he later becoming a wireless traffic analyst in Room 40. Watts suggested to Jimmy Sandhurst that they should enrol the entire RSGB Council into the fledgling RSS, which they duly did. As cover, the new organisation was given the Military Intelligence designation MI8c.

Those operators that had not already been called up or being part of the Armed Forces in the Royal Naval Wireless Auxiliary Reserve (RNWAR) formed in 1932 or the RAF Civilian Wireless Reserve (CWR) formed in 1938 would be hand selected by the RSGB for their role as wireless interceptors. Many radio amateurs involved with the RSGB had been mobilised for active service. It was estimated that around

60 per cent of members were working in technical fields within the RAF, 14 per cent in the Royal Navy, and a further 12 per cent of members working with the Army, specifically in the Royal Corps of Signals. The GPO provided a collection of mobile units to hunt down any illicit transmissions through DF.

Another significant senior officer involved in the early days of the IWIO, bringing significant First World War wireless experience with him into the fledgling organisation, was Lt-Col. J. S. Yule. Prior to the First World War, he had become famous for proposing the Royal Flying Corps motto, '*Per Ardua ad Astra*' ('Through Adversity the Air'), which is still used to this day by the RAF. He had a role in preparing financial and staffing records for the IWIO. He was to also lay down the groundwork for establishing an overseas mission for the organisation.

In the early months of the war, it was anticipated enemy aircraft would be guided by enemy agents operating medium-wave (100–2,000-metre wavelength) beacons strategically placed to bomb targets. Subsequently, forty-eight medium-wave DF stations were planned to be situated in vicinity of towns with large industrial and dock areas, backed up with mobile 'beacon vans' with medium-wave DF receivers. They were to be manned by regional GPO staff and linked to a local control centre. Only one of these systems, in London, was completed, the remainder, with the exception of Edinburgh, being dropped before any work had been done.

The GPO internal organisation consisted of an executive engineer responsible to an assistant staff engineer (Radio Branch) on matters affecting equipment and staff and to the military representative for operational work. He was assisted by a small headquarters staff of one chief inspector and one clerical officer until May 1940, when an assistant engineer was appointed. Shortly afterwards, the GPO RSS HQ was further augmented by an assistant staff engineer who was responsible for the general efficiency of the GPO organisation and who acted as the liaison officer between the RSS and GPO. Later, two further assistant engineers were appointed to deal with technical efficiency—they would travel frequently to supervise the calibration of the DF stations and mobile units. Up until December 1940, it was intended that the RSS be staffed almost entirely by Post Office personnel with a small staff of senior military officers to act as liaison between the GPO and the military.

At the end of 1939, arrangements had been made between the GPO, RSS, and MI5 for the reporting on suspicious activities affecting radio security and those that would need to be brought forward for MI5 investigations. These cases were referred to as 'P' cases. By 31 December 1939, thirty separate 'P' cases were reported via the GPO to the RSS and MI5.

By 1940, a GPO inspector was put at the disposal of MI5 to assist with the investigations of illegal possession of radio equipment. The inspector cooperated with the police on such MI5 investigations, examining suspect radio equipment and individuals caught in the act of using them for illicit broadcasts. The authority for action on illicit wireless transmitters came through 'Statutory Rule and Order 1940, No. 828 (Access to Premises and Suppression of Illicit Transmission and Authority to carry Wireless Apparatus in Road Vehicles)'. Among other prosecutions, the GPO inspector was to give technical evidence at the trial of three enemy agents who were executed in December 1940.

It was from 1941 that the RSS started to rapidly transform and improve itself. The best operators from the GPO and VI regions were enlisted into the Royal Signals and provisioned with much better radio equipment, including the HRO receivers from the USA. At this stage, a number of significant interception sites and DF stations were being built around the country. It was necessary to have these scattered in various regions to ensure the reception of monitored frequencies that exhibit a 'skip' effect—the signals being bounced off the atmosphere and heard more clearly at a distance than close to the actual transmitter. The value the British intelligence community placed on the RSS at this early stage of the war was also symptomatic of the key intelligence on the *Abwehr* organisational structures, but also would assist the British in preventing *Abwehr* efforts to establish a network in the country.

Some of the cipher traffic, picked up by the RSS interceptors, began to be studied by the likes of Maj. Ernest Walter Gill and Lt Hugh Trevor-Roper. They had some success in their decryption methods but were treading on thin ice as this was the territory of Bletchley Park.

Hugh Trevor-Roper noted on the initiative to break the *Abwehr* cipher:

In those blacked out evenings, in the flat which we shared in Ealing, we worked on it and, in the end, succeeded in breaking the cipher: which I hasten to add, was not of the highest class. When we read the messages, we found we had stumbled on a great treasure, the radio transmissions of the German Secret Service, or *Abwehr* in particular, its stations in Madrid and Hamburg, the former conversing with its substations in Spain and Spanish Morocco, the latter with its agents on the Baltic and North Sea coasts, some of whom were preparing to land, by boat or parachute, in Britain. There was also a station at Wiesbaden, which seemed to concentrate on training spies for such adventures, and whose laborious initiation of its pupils gave us some valuable hints.[2]

Their work was to cause significant friction between the departments in the early 1940s, until it was agreed in the appointment of Oliver Strachey to bridge the gap and build an effective liaison relationship, which was to last until the end of the Second World War.

We were naturally excited about this coup, and so, when we reported it to our Commanding Officer, Colonel Worlledge he ordered me to write a document about it, which I gladly did, and which he then rather naively I fear circulated to his normal customers with a covering note stating that this document, by Lieutenant Trevor-Roper, seemed to deserve distribution.[3]

When the document reached MI6 in London, 'there was an explosion'. Recently arrived from the Indian Police Service in Calcutta, Maj. Felix Cowgill, the new head of the MI6 Counterespionage section (Section V), sought a formal court-martial for Trevor-Roper. Col. Worlledge was to receive a severe reprimand from his superiors in MI8 who had been instructed to by the seniors at MI6: 'We were gravely reprimanded for having deciphered the documents and formally forbidden to do so again, since that was the province of GC&CS'.[4]

Trevor-Roper was put in front of the GC&CS Director from Bletchley Park Alastair Denniston at Wormwood Scrubs, alongside Oliver Strachey, one of their senior cryptographers, and notably given a dressing down. Although chastised, Trevor-Roper clearly had taken the blame for a lack of inter-branch communications: 'We did not take any of this very seriously. After all, as we understood, GC&CS had refused to handle the stuff, and I was merely obeying the orders of my commanding officer'.[5]

This was not the only issue that emerged during this period. In December 1940, an RSS intelligence summary on German intelligence operations in Morocco was distributed to customers on the orders of Col. Worlledge. On hearing of the publication, Maj. Felix Cowgill sought a prosecution for the authors, which was quickly rebuffed. A consequence was that the RSS was excluded from the distribution of ISOS material from Bletchley for nearly two weeks, until MI8 intervened.

Relations were to improve shortly after. At this time, MI6 was urgently trying to gain success for itself. At the beginning of the war, it had suffered a humiliation due to what became known as the Venlo Incident at the German–Dutch border. Two of its senior officers based at The Hague, Capt. Sigismund Payne Best and Maj. Richard Stevens, overseeing MI6 operations in Western Europe, were lured to a covert meeting with German dissidents near the Dutch town of Venlo on 9 November 1939. It was a ruse by the Germans; Best and Stevens were abducted by the German *Sicherheitsdienst* (SD). They were later imprisoned in the Gestapo Prinz-Albrecht-Strasse headquarters in Berlin.

Over time, they were to reveal much of MI6's espionage operations in Europe, some of the details being leaked into the German media. Stevens was even carrying a list of MI6 agents in Europe on him at the time. One of its knock-on effects was the Germans used this incident—and the evidence of the collusion of Dutch Military Intelligence with the British—to invade the Netherlands in May 1940.

Trevor-Roper regarded Venlo as a blessing for RSS work.

It swept away a rotten system of venal spies which, had it been maintained, would have been controlled by the Germans just as their spies were controlled by us … in these circumstances the penetration of the secrets of the *Abwehr* offered a double benefit: immediately, compensation for a dreadful failure, and, ultimately a far more trustworthy source of information about German espionage.[6]

The Double-Cross System that MI5 developed was to shape the work of the RSS throughout the war.

One of the early RSS visionaries at Wormwood Scrubs was Maj. Ernest Walter Brudenell Gill, whom Trevor-Roper regarded as 'the real genius of the affair'. They complemented each other well, with Trevor-Ropers' analytical skills he had developed as a historian, alongside his fluent German, and Gill, who had real abilities in cryptographic work. He was later to be unceremoniously ditched by MI6 when they took over, but it was his ideas that created the RSS structure and working practices. He had been educated at Bristol grammar school and then Christ Church College in Oxford, where he had acquired a first in physics. A modest man, Gill had served as a wireless intelligence officer within the Royal Engineers during the First World War, and on occasion, he had shown blatant disregard for convention. He notoriously rigged up support aerials for his interception work on the top of the Great Pyramid of Giza. It caused some controversy with his senior commanders but had proven successful in the interception of German Zeppelin transmissions on operations over England.

By the end of the First World War, he had become one of the British Army's leading experts in wireless interception and earned himself an OBE. In 1934, Gill published a book of his experiences, entitled *War, Wireless & Wangles*. He had a naturally inquisitive mind, and as an Oxford physicist and electromagnetic spectrum specialist, his skills and experience were much sought after to unpick the German intelligence service broadcasts during the Second World War. Enrolled within the Royal Signals aged fifty-six, Gill was appointed head of the Discrimination Section of the RSS, essentially the chief traffic analyst for the service. In March 1942, Gill left the RSS, and after a short tour at the Signals Training Centre in Catterick, he joined what would become the Army Operational Research Group (AORG).

He was to help pioneer new approaches to radar jamming techniques and countermeasures. Gill even had suggested some eighteen months prior to joining the AORG that the use of metallic foil strips known as 'Window' by bombers would help cause clutter on German radar systems, helping them to evade German defences. At this stage of the war, radar was still a closely guarded secret, and Gill himself was not aware of it: 'I was then outside the charmed circle of those who were allowed to know about this very secret device and could only guess what it was from effects I had noticed on my shortwave broadcast receiver when aircraft went over my house'.

It was suspected that the Germans would be transmitting in the short-wave bands, broadcasting in the frequency range of 3–12 MHz. To intercept the 'ground-wave' components on these signals would require a significant geographic spread of interceptors at a local level. At this stage of the war, it was also suspected that German bombers were being directed on to their targets by signal transmissions from inside Britain.

In September 1939, Lord Hankey (the then Minister without Portfolio) had received a note that the chiefs of staff were getting increasingly concerned about the leakage of sensitive information on military and shipping movements in Britain. It was suspected that wireless was being used for these purposes. The prime minister had tasked Hankey to ascertain how this information was being transmitted and what could be done to stop it. The IWIO under the control of the War Office and manned and equipped by the GPO comprised six fixed and ten mobile wireless stations. Pre-war, this had been used principally to allow the Post Office to detect radio amateurs infringing the rules on licences to transmit on the airwaves. The mobile vans were normally used to assist listeners in the detection and suppression of radio interference from domestic and industrial machinery.

On the evening of 31 August 1939, the BBC broadcast an announcement on the nine o'clock news bulletin that all full and artificial aerial amateur transmitting licences were to be withdrawn from use. Over the next few days, many of the British radio amateurs were visited by Post Office officials to impound any radio transmitter equipment. They did not take away any receivers. A few days later, on Sunday 3 September 1939, Britain declared war with Germany.

In September 1939, Lord Hankey, in his role on the War Cabinet, was very concerned about the leakage of information of flights from an aerodrome taking part in raids on the Wilhelmshaven and Kiel Canals. It was suspected that wireless radios were being used by German spies to transmit messages back to Germany. At the time of RAF bomber squadrons taking off on a mission, the word '*Achtung*' was been transmitted, arousing suspicion that a message had been sent in proximity of the aerodrome, giving warning to German anti-aircraft batteries. An owner of a transmitter set near the aerodrome was subsequently arrested and the transmissions ceased, although it later transpired there was no link between the radio ham and the German raids. Regardless of this, Hankey was to state 'there are very large gaps through which leakage is liable to occur'. Hankey had identified a 'serious shortage both of personnel and equipment', not least of which was the fact that only one of the ten mobile wireless stations were operational by September 1939.

One clear and identifiable gap was the Republic of Ireland as there was no censorship in place between the UK and Eire. It was thought that intelligence could be gleaned by travelling agents, telegrams and uncensored letters, radio transmissions, and telephone conversations. However, the controller of Postal and Telegraphic Censorship stated that to achieve general censorship control between the UK and Eire, he would require an additional 8,000 staff at Liverpool. While there were clear gaps where leakage of sensitive information could occur, Hankey was most concerned about illicit wireless transmissions due to the rapid tactical nature of short-wave radio broadcasts. His review concluded that whatever organisation was created, it should have a single controller with the relevant authority and resources to run it.

In the initial few months of the war, the radio interceptors involved with the RSS would send in their interception logs to PO Box 385, Howick Place, London, which was in fact Wormwood Scrubs Prison. The RAF CWR and RN Wireless Reserve were mobilised as war threatened. The first draft of the CWR reached France in September 1939 and helped form the RAF's 'Wireless Intelligence Screen', which was to build a close relationship between the 'Y' Service SIGINT teams and the radio amateurs around the country.

The service maintained a number of mobile units dotted around the country. These were typically equipped with a 10-hp Ford Shooting Brake van and manned by GPO operators. After a number of months of use, the Ford vans were decreed obsolescent by the RSS and a fleet of Humber Snipe vehicles with wooden bodies were ordered. These were built on a standard Army design and could be acquired within six weeks of being ordered. A total of fifty-seven vans were established by the GPO in twenty-one different towns within the first weeks of the war. The RSS was to order 100 'Snifters' from the GPO at the end of 1939. Snifters were pocket DF receivers designed by the radio branch at Dollis Hill and were provided with headphones and an output indicator. They were designed for the final location of a transmitter at a local level. The RSS also ordered eighty 'Ferret' receivers, which were designed for interference location.

Each of the vehicles was manned by four personnel, two of which were designated as drivers. The vans were typically fitted out with HRO DF receivers (covering 100–2,000-metre wavelengths), Hallicrafter HT7 receivers (5–10-metre wavelength, fitted with loop aerials) and two Snifters. In February 1940, the RSS requested the GPO investigate the possibility of using cathode ray DF in these mobile units. The following table shows RSS Mobile DF units in August 1940:

Centre	Type of Car or Van
London (RSS Headquarters)	2 10-hp Ford utility cars and 2 Morris RI vans
Edinburgh	1 10-hp Ford utility car and 1 Morris RI van
Leeds	1 10-hp Ford utility car and 1 Morris RI van
Bristol	1 10-hp Ford utility car and 1 Morris RI van

When it later became evident that enemy aircraft were not likely to be guided by medium-wave beacons in this country, the scheme was modified, retaining just twenty-two of the beacon vans and setting up six medium-wave Adcock DF stations located near Thurso, Belfast, Darlington, Manchester, Southampton, and Lydd. By December 1940, the beacon vans were closed down, but the value for close and more localised DF of illicit transmitters led to the establishment of ten teams of mobile DF cars, which comprised forty-eight equipped cars. The project was begun in January 1940 and completed in December 1940, and it included the selection, recruitment, and training of staff. Many of the Mobile Unit (MU) personnel were enrolled into the Home Guard, and they often worked closely with the Home Guard units for security around their bases. As members of the Home Guard, the Mobile Unit staff from 1943 had to adhere to a number of new Defence (Home Guard) Regulations: penalties for breach of discipline (mostly non-attendance); maximum period of forty-eight-hour compulsory training or duty in four weeks; Home Guards may be required to serve continuously and to live away from home during any periods in which units are mustered; and right to resign within fourteen days' notice is withdrawn.

The GPO staff who were based at Barnet were formed up as an independent Home Guard unit, the No. 19 Platoon 'F' Company, 22nd City of London (5th GPO) Battalion Home Guard. This was to comprise No. 1 Section at Barnet RSS Headquarters and Intercept Station and No. 2 Section at the Barnet Mobile Unit base. The unit was to find acclaim in getting first place at the Waterhouse Cup Small Arms competition. The RSS and GPO who were enrolled in the Home Guard were made to take into consideration 'their readiness to accept all the implications of membership of the Home Guard'. As an incentive, special leave was authorised for GPO/RSS personnel to attend any Home Guard training. Much of this liaison was overseen by Col. Frederick Reid, who was the Post Office Commander in the Home Guard.

During some of the first Mobile Unit operations around Felixstowe, Boston, and Cambridge, the RSS was to deploy a military officer alongside the GPO inspector in charge of operations. Four Mobile Unit groups (each group comprising two D/F cars) were deployed on continuous watch in February 1941, patrolling the Essex, Suffolk, and Lincolnshire countryside as a result of reports of parachutes being found. There appeared to be a degree of friction, 'mainly arising out of the fact that the military officer was more fully informed of the object of the operation than the Post Office Inspector and tended to take full charge of the operation, including personal instructions to the Post Office staff in their duties'.[7]

As a result, Lt-Col. Maltby discussed some reports that he had received on the matter of 'alleged obstructive and non-cooperative attitude of Post Office Mobile Unit staff on the Cambridge operation'. He indicated his decision to modify the process of sending a military officer on every Mobile Unit operation and to only deploy an officer when special circumstances dictated it.

Mobile Units and the fixed D/F stations staff often conducted exercises in locating illicit wireless transmissions locally, using Army Wireless Sets No. 1 (operating typically on 5 mc/s or at 14 mc/s frequencies) or transmitters that had been impounded at the start of the war from ex-amateurs. Practice occurred on at least three days a week at each base, and one general wider-scale practice once a month. This was not to interfere with any official interception duties carried out by the Mobile Unit. There were even periodic gas drills throughout the RSS intercept, DF, and Mobile Unit locations, including driving practice during the day and night by the Mobile Unit drivers kitted out with gasmasks.

There were discussions between the RSS and British troops in Northern Ireland regarding proposals to employ Post Office staff operating RSS Mobile Unit bases at Belfast to assist Army Intelligence in the event of the invasion of Ireland. Teams would have been tasked to keep watch for enemy VHF wireless transmissions. Many of the DF operators who worked at the Gilnahirk site were employed routinely in the teams that deployed with the DF vehicles.

Mobile Unit crews were asked to assist British Command Corps in the event of a wider invasion of the British mainland. Crews were to be deployed with 5–10-metre receivers and portable recorders loaned out to the Command Corps to watch for suspect VHF transmissions. Crews stipulated for this work had to be enrolled as Home Guard personnel. It was proposed that special arrangements be made to pay the men, be given Army pay books, and all payments and rationing to be overseen by the Army. Their pay allowances were to be given directly to their next of kin 'as they may become cut off from normal contact with the Post Office'. The scheme that was proposed was similar to that of the Mobile Units operating alongside British troops in Northern Ireland. It would have been more complicated in the Province as Home Guards in Eire were designated as special constables and not associated with the Army in any way. The following table shows RSS/GPO Mobile Unit bases.

Base	Inspectors	SW1	USW	Members of Home Guards (H)
Wormwood Scrubs	1	25	0	26
Gilnahirk	1	8	0	9
Darlington	1	10	0	11
Southampton	1	16	0	4
Bristol	1	16	0	17
Manchester	1	14	0	15
Leeds	1	12	2	15
Edinburgh	1	16	0	17
Birmingham	1	14	0	15
Barnet	1	25	0	26

Mobile Unit staff were routinely notified that the speed limit of the 22-hp Ford Shooting Brake vans was just 30 mph and there were steps taken by the RSS senior officers to include the installation of blue lights to exceed this speed limit 'only when necessary. Any challenge by the Police must be reported immediately so that the matter can be taken up with the Police authorities'. It was often a case of asking for forgiveness rather than permission.

Arising out of a case in which a GPO driver of an RSS vehicle was stopped and later summoned by police for exceeding the speed limit in a built-up area, instructions were issued to all GPO/RSS staff involved with the Mobile Units that they must not give out any details of their employer, either MI5 or RSS, during the course of any police interview. They were to clearly state that they belonged to the engineer in chief, W2 Branch, and had to relay the official box address if the police were to further question them.

During the winter months of early 1941, the GPO and RSS discussed the provision of keeping MU crews warm when keeping long watches in the vehicles in cold weather. Methods of heating from the car engine were ruled out because the engine would have overheated if run standing idle for long periods. They made a suggestion of obtaining Sidcot flying suits—enquiries were made to the Air Ministry on the availability of the suits. The makers had quoted a price of £20 per flying suit. Fifty-four sets of suits and boots were subsequently ordered and distributed among ten Mobile Unit bases, one pair to be issued per group of two equipped cars.

and ammunition held	No. competent in use of firearms	Possibility of obtaining revolvers from HG	Uniforms
	3	Nil	Nil
les, 18 revolvers, and several red rounds of ammunition	All member trained in firearms	Nil	Armlets only: Royal Ulster Special Constabulary
present but local HG trying range	Nil	Very little possibility	Nil
at present as base only just ed	Nil	Very little possibility	Nil
olvers (trying to increase to nd 60 rounds	Nil	Nil	10
olvers	Nil	Nil	Nil
olvers, 72 rounds, no rifles	Nil	Nil	Uniforms being issued
olvers, 40 rounds	Nil	Nil	Uniforms being issued shortly
les and 60 rounds, 8 bleys and 96 rounds	Nil	Nil	All supplied
	Yes all	Nil	All supplied

After the takeover of the RSS in 1941, MI6 had little interest in sustaining the vehicle pool. MI5 complained that MI6 were not doing enough to provide support for them. The vans were used pre-war by the GPO to track pirate unlicensed radio transmitters. They were to work typically to a 5-mile radius for localised DF. By October 1941, the MUs comprised around 125 RSS staff based out of four locations: Barnet, Leatherhead, Gilnahirk, and Darlington.

The RSS Mobile units were responsible for the following:

(i) Investigating suspect transmitters after DF of the signal on the instruction of the Discrimination Group. (The Mobile teams were deployed from three bases in England—Barnet, Bristol and Gateshead with their DF Vans (Snifters) and short-range DF units (Ferrets).

(ii) Maintaining listening watches on suspect buildings by setting up stations with ¼ mile or so of the suspected site. Special equipment was used (designed by GPO or by the Engineering Group) which would mechanically mark signals of interest highlighting frequency and time of transmission.

(iii) Providing Mobile Units for use on the continent.[8]

Although few operations were mounted by these mobile teams in the early part of the war, they were deployed on a number of occasions to investigate illicit wireless activity. In March 1943, it was reported to RSIC that a recent MU operation had been mounted in Britain to try and locate an unlicensed transmitter operating in Warrington. The fact was the transmitter was not being operated by a suspect German agent but rather by one of the VI's employed directly by the RSS, which had not detracted from the fact that the MU had proved its worth. The RSS was to rapidly transform itself, and when it transitioned under the command of MI6, the organisation was to increasingly become militarised. The following table shows militarisation of the RSS from the summer of 1939 to Christmas 1940.

		Authorised War Office Establishment			
Dates	Comments	Officers	Other Ranks	Civilians	Total
July 1939	1 Lt-Col. and 1 civilian	1		1	2
September 1939	Provisional additional establishment of 1 Maj. and 2 Capt.	3		1	4
12 December 1939		25	17	12	54
6 April 1940	2 CQMs added	25	19	12	56
16 May 1940	3 Dispatch riders	25	22	12	59
27 June 1940	1 Capt. Added (for telephone interception at Wood Norton)	26	22	12	60

22 August 1940	1 Capt., 1 CSM, 1 CQMs, 2 Sgts, 1 civilian clerk added	27	26	13	66
29 September 1940	3 orderlies and 1 Cpl, 6 other ranks, and 1 cook added	27	37	13	77
18 December 1940	1 Capt., 1 Lt, 3 L/Sgts added	29	40	13	82

Note: Above includes ten regional officers, each with a CQMS and shorthand typist.

The RSS was to create a national network around the clusters of radio amateurs. They were to send their intercepted transmission log sheets through to Wormwood Scrubs prison to the seemingly anonymous address of Box 485, Howick Place, London SW1. The amateurs in this early organisation failed to pick up the transmissions of any German agents as they had all been turned by MI5 and the Luftwaffe planes were being guided on to their targets by navigational beam from the continent. They did pick up weak Morse signals from occupied Europe, but their call signs were wrong, consisting of only three letters and sent in five letter groups. The amateurs were collecting the wireless transmissions of German intelligence.

Over the course of the early part of the war, the prison was increasingly being hit by Luftwaffe bombs, and the increasing numbers of air raids was making life difficult within the service to maintain its work. MI5 was to move completely outside London, taking up residence at Blenheim Palace in Oxfordshire. The RSS was also to move to a new headquarters location at Arkley village, just outside Barnet. MI5 would post Mr R. L. Hughes as the permanent liaison officer into the RSS to coordinate the activities with the home service.

The success from the establishment of regional RSS groups of VIs brought a realisation that a full-time listening post needed to be established in Britain. The location was identified as Hanslope Park, a country house in Buckinghamshire that, in 1939, had been sold on to Lord Hesketh. In 1941, it had been requisitioned around the same time as Bletchley Park by the Ministry of Defence. The lease for Hanslope Park was taken out in late 1939 by Harold Eastwood of the Foreign Office, before he took over the charge of the King's Messenger Service. The RSS did not start to take over the site until August 1941, and over the next four months, their interception work was done in the corn bins of 'The Granary'. After this, the teams were moved into the lodge about half a mile away, while the new central receiver station was being built. When this was completed in May 1942, the RSS teams took up their positions with sixty-six new state-of-the-art HRO receivers.

Capt. Reggie Wigg (G6JF) was in charge of the advance party deployed to scope out the suitability of Hanslope as an intercept station. Wigg spent a couple of weeks there, based out of his private caravan to see what reception was like before the decision was made to utilise the site. Hanslope was to become operational during 1941 and equipped with the most advanced receivers of their time, the American commercial HRO receiver, which would cost in the region of two to three months' VI pay. Generally speaking, the VI teams did not use the HRO as they could not afford such decadence.

When the RSS was put under the control of old Etonian Lt-Col. Ted Maltby, he was charged with establishing a full-time intercept station at Hanslope Park. Among his contemporaries, Maltby was not well liked. Hugh Trevor-Roper, who headed up the RIS, hated Maltby, and he was to write a number of vitriolic poems about him, which often referred to his leather boots and affiliation to the Whaddon Chase hunt.

Administrative staff began to arrive at Hanslope in August 1941, but it was not fully operational until May 1942 under the command of Capt. Prickett. It was to become affectionately known, by those that worked there, as 'The Farmyard'. He was later to be replaced by Reginald Wigg as its CO. Its first operators were to be William Chittleburgh and Wilfred Limb, whose first role was to clean the corn bins near the house to create space for a number of trestle tables for six HRO receivers. Limb was a licenced radio amateur before the war and had enlisted into the RSS as an operator. He was responsible for testing out the radio signals at Hanslope before the site became operational. At the end of 1941, Lord Sandhurst was to depart the organisation and take up residence with SIS at Whaddon Hall. On occasion, he was to bolster the staff at Whaddon with trained ex-VIs from Hanslope.

Over the course of the next few months, the temporary nature of operations in the corn bins was to continue until the station known as 'The Lodge' was completed in 1942 at Bullington End, on the site that would eventually house 115 radio specialists.

When the VI teams spotted a wanted frequency in operation, it would be passed to Hanslope to monitor it on a twenty-four-hour basis. Of the twenty-three German agents sent to Britain during 1941, the RSS was responsible for directly finding five of them and correctly identifying two others. They had proved their value to service commanders.

One of the Hanslope operators was Pat Hawker (G3VA):

I came up here to Hanslope in November 1941 as one of the early operators in the game after having done it as an amateur for 18 months. We were doing 8 hours listening every day but we were also supposed to be soldiers, but we never felt like soldiers. We were in uniform but we had no training and it used to lead to all sorts of problems. Even years after I found myself saluting with the wrong hand, putting gaiters on the wrong legs.... We were in a tiny station with six receivers. 'The Granary' the station was known as.[9]

An instrumental figure in the early years of engineering at Hanslope was Dud Charman (G6CJ), who received a BEM after the war for the work he pioneered at the station:

> I came up to Hanslope and set up the laboratory ... and designed amplifiers and aerial distribution boards so they could run a large number of receivers and put them onto any of the aerials in the place.[10]

Charman was part of a dedicated and specialist group of engineers, which included Jimmy Matthews (G6LL) and Robin Adie (G8LT), all under the direction of the world's foremost DF engineer Maj. Dick Keen. Keen had previously worked at Marconi and was the author of most of the major texts on the subject of radio DF.

Charman's work caught the eye of a Canadian scientist, Professor Roberts, who had been brought over from McGill University in Montreal to assist with some of the secret wireless work going on in Britain:

> I was told that nobody from Canada knew where he was and that no one knew he was in England. He hadn't even got a ration card. It was so secret. I didn't know what he was here for of course but he was quite fascinated by the work I was doing because of course it was quite unique. I don't think anyone else in the world could have produced those amplifiers in the time and the quality that I knew how to do. It was just my fortune to be able to do it ... later, after the war, I discovered why he was really here. It turned out he was one of the World's cipher machine experts and he'd been brought over to help them with working out how the Enigma system was run.[11]

Radio intercept material would also come to Hanslope Park from France, sent from the Cadix centre in the Vichy region of southern France, run by Col. Gustav Bertrand, tapping into French phone lines linking back to Berlin. It was a rich source of intelligence and provided nearly 3,000 messages between March 1941 and November 1942, when the clandestine operations were discovered by German Intelligence DF vans.

Towards the end of the war, the RSS Administration Group was based at the Headquarters in Hanslope Park. They had responsibility for records, enlistment or recruiting, pay, official postings, travel papers, feeding, accommodation, and even sanitation.

Also at Hanslope was the more significant Engineering Group, which was responsible for the following:

(a) Engineering proper, e.g. acquainting themselves with the technical requirements of RSS, designing, erecting, and maintaining the necessary equipment. This work included:

Provision of special antenna systems, *viz*. Rhombic, V- and omnidirectional aerials.

Special aerial switching systems whereby any set could make use of the most suitable aerial for the task allotted to it.

Frequency measuring facilities.

Wide band amplifiers enabling 10 or more sets to be used on each aerial simultaneously.

Testing proposed intercept station sites.

Providing double-banked positions and signals to line facilities.

(b) Direction Finding. This would include:

Technical control of the DF network.

Taking of numerous check bearings.

Application of statistical methods and averaging to bearings obtained and provision to discrimination of the final results.

This work was of great importance and a new technique had been worked out in this department by Major Keen, O i/c, who was frequently called in as advisor on DF methods by the Military and Naval Y organisations.

(c) Provision of communication apparatus for Foreign Units and radio intercommunication for Mobile units.

A Marconi radio engineer from Great Baddow and expert in direction finding signals, Major Dick Keen assisted Hanslope RSS staff in establishing their DF network. He helped build the concentrator unit that would enable radio operators to communicate directly with their supervisors via microphone and Morse keys—allowing them to relay instructions to the DF stations.

In early 1943, Hanslope was to accidentally intercept transmissions from some of the local British black propaganda radio broadcasts from sites like Gawcott and Potsgrove, being run by the Political Warfare Executive (PWE). Lt-Col. Ted Maltby was to inquire about the sources of these suspicious transmissions with the BBC and was politely referred to the SIS wireless technical director. He was from then on informed of all the future broadcast scheduling from PWE.

Hanslope used both rhombic and 'V-beam' antennas spread over 200 acres of land to collect and transmit radio signals, and they found it difficult to get their outputs into a wide bank of numerous receivers. It was Dud Charman who solved the problem by designing and constructing wide band distribution amplifiers, which would help obviate for any antenna tuning. The aerials and radio masts at the site extending a mile in each direction. The erection of these huge masts was the responsibility of an Australian Army soldier called Ernie 'Digger' Buick, who was in charge of a small but merry band of aerial erectors. He had a wider responsibility at Nash, Calverton, Weald, and Hanslope, and they were often seen on an old trustworthy Queen Mary trailer, which was the only vehicle around capable of carrying the 30-foot-long telegraph poles that were used to rig the aerials.

Robin Addie (G8LT) amiably described Buick:

The Australian was in charge of the team that did the erections. They did the splicing, the rigging and the putting up of all these masts. He was a remarkable man although his language, parliamentary and otherwise was fairly extensive! He had under his command a gang of chaps who, although non-combatants, made up for their wishes not to do one thing by piling into putting these masts up and they had to be done in a pretty short time. And 'Digger' used to get them all together and they did all the splicing into the stays and then in the morning they would set off, winter or summer, rain or shine ... how they put up with his language I don't know![13]

It was Robin Addie's section that was to become a vital link to engineering advice and support to covert operations in occupied Europe. His role as officer in charge, RSS Engineering Section, was to receive German wireless transmitter and receiver sets for examination and to assist with the Allied intelligence efforts of understanding their techniques and procedures. An example of this was when the section at Hanslope received the W/T set of Joseph Edouard Corneilie Gesquières, a Belgian arrested on 5 September 1944 who was operating as a stay-behind agent. Addie was to produce reports to the RSS controller on the specification of each of these W/T sets, down to the level of circuitry diagrams.

Following the Allied invasion of France in June 1944, the RSS would give implicit instructions to the Field Security Police teams to make sure any W/T sets they were to come across, particularly those belonging to agents, to be handed on to the commanding officer of the Special Communications Unit 9 (SCU9).

At the height of the war, Hanslope had become such an integral part of the signal's intelligence machinery on which the RSS had been built that Brigadier Gambier-Parry hosted visits from General Eisenhower, Field Marshal Montgomery, and General Alexander.

The RSS was run throughout the war ultimately by Brigadier Richard Gambier-Parry (referred to in this context as Controller of Special Communications, or CSC). He had responsibilities in this role for overseeing SIS agent communications, the RSS, and the Political Warfare Executive (PWE) black propaganda broadcasting effort.

Gambier-Parry had been recruited by Admiral Sir Hugh Sinclair, Director of MI6 (or 'C') in 1938. He had been schooled at Eton College, but understood and had a real affinity for the RSS, as he had been a licenced wireless operator from 1920 onwards. He had been brought up in a rich household, his family owning a large portion of Oxfordshire, and was well connected, often fox hunting with Stewart Menzies, the future head of MI6. Gambier-Parry was recruited by the BBC as a press officer in 1926, where he stayed for five years learning the trade and being exposed to the value of radio as a broadcast medium. In 1931, he left to join Philco, at that stage the largest radio manufacturer in the world, to become the UK general sales manager.

During his appointment with SIS, the contacts and skills he had acquired at Philco were to serve him well. He would help forge the newly formed PWE, which controlled all propaganda missions against the Axis powers.

Leadership from Gambier-Parry and others was to be critical to these early stages of the RSS, to forge its identity. With the infighting going on in the early part of the Second World War between the hierarchy at MI5, MI6, and the GPO, a balance needed to be struck on how the RSS was to be tasked and used effectively against a difficult German Intelligence Services target. It would need a committee.

2

Committee

The story of the Radio Security Service is one of sacrifice, dedication and improvisation of the typically British variety.

Nigel West in *GCHQ: The Secret Wireless War 1939–1945*

The original decision around the control of RSS was that it should sit with MI5 'so as to avoid divided control and to obtain closer cooperation in the interests of efficiency'. Rather humorously, the decision would be circumspect, 'we would be glad to be rid of this commitment in order to concentrate more thoroughly on Y work and Lord Hankey has set the seal of his approval on the transfer … it should be made clear that we do not accept any responsibility for the consequences'.

During the autumn of 1940, RSS monitoring of illicit wireless activity within Britain was extended to cover the communications of the *Abwehr* and associated axis enemy intelligence services wherever they operated in the world. By October 1940, MI8 put forward a proposal that MI5 should take over administrative control of the RSS, which was resisted until January 1941 when the decision was made to get SIS to take over the RSS. This was not made a reality until May 1941.

It was in May 1941 that formal control of the RSS was removed from the War Office into the MI8(c) organisation under the command of SIS. It was Felix Cowgill, originally an Indian police officer from Calcutta, who oversaw the transfer in ownership. Felix was not his real name, and he used to sign off memos and letters with the letter 'V' to designate his section. It was informally referred to as Special Communications Unit 3 (SCU3), with its overseas section called Special Communications Unit 4 (SCU4).

There was a realisation by 1941 that the organisation of the RSS was not fit for purpose. There was a clear dependency on the part-time services of the GPO for the supply of equipment, construction of stations and maintenance, and the supply of sufficiently trained and skilled personnel. Organisationally, the GPO was completely unsuitable for war.

Originally established to monitor illicit enemy agent radio broadcasts within Britain, which was not being covered by the military 'Y' service collection sites. It was filling a niche, but in the first few months of its operations, it was also able to identify German agents operating as far afield as Norway and Iceland. Its official role was to 'discover and locate any enemy agents using wireless in this country'.

The RSS functions were as follows:

1. The discovery and identification of all clandestine transmissions of all types in all areas, entailing general search of all frequencies for all types of signals.
2. The monitoring of all clandestine networks discovered to be active.
3. The location of clandestine transmitters by fixed and mobile DF units in the UK, the Colonies and protectorates and territories occupied by the British and Allied armies.
4. The monitoring of all authorised British channels of communications as the agent of the Inter-Service Signals Security Committee.
5. The discovery of free frequencies for use by British and Allied secret communications networks.
6. The control and supervision of the clandestine and secret W/T networks of the Allies in Great Britain.

Discussions took place in the dusty corridors of Whitehall as to how this fledgling organisation should be governed. In correspondence with the Security Service, Lt-Col. Adrian Simpson brought forward the suggestion of a 'Technical Advisor Committee'. Choosing the right people for the committee was to be critical to how it would run. Simpson states: 'The composition of the Committee should not comprise more than three or four technical members and from many years practical experience of such committees and their work, I consider that the members should be chosen not only for their technical knowledge but also for their temperamental ability to work together!' Simpson suggested a number of names for the committee:

1. Dr James Robinson (ex-Director of Wireless Research to the Air Ministry): 'Dr Robinson has an extensive grasp of the whole subject under consideration and is in my opinion the leading authority on all questions of selectivity and technical coding'.
2. Capt. Round 'who has made a life study of DF and interception work and is one of the most brilliant experimentalists in this country'.
3. Mr K. Tremellen 'who is without question the greatest practical authority alive on the subject of short-wave communication'.

Between early 1941 and the middle of 1942, there was a lot of friction between SIS and MI5 over the control and running of the RSS. The joint MI5/SIS Wireless Committee established in 1941 had failed to resolve the dispute, and subsequently, the committee was dissolved in December 1941 to be replaced by two new committees. The high-level, more senior Radio Security Committee was established to oversee RSS policy and strategy; established in March 1943, it was a standing committee to the Security Executive. It was to be directly responsible for coordinating the SIS and MI5 interests within the RSS and to provide effective oversight of radio security within Britain. Its parallel and more working level committee would become so successful for the RSS coordination that the Radio Security Committee would only meet twice before the end of the war.

Customers of the RSS intercept reports would have markedly different views of the priorities of the RSS intercept, so the working level committee had to be created to prioritise the intercepts. From the beginning of 1943, this committee started to sit and became known as the Radio Security Intelligence Conference (RSIC).

The *Abwehr* stations were allocated W/T cover names, which were used in the clear in the preamble and post-amble of messages passed from one station to another. These cover names were indexed to build up a significant library of nearly 1,500 by the end of the war.

The chairman of the Radio Security Committee was also the resident chairman for the Security Executive. The RSC had numerous senior representatives from the intelligence services. These included Sir David Petrie and Capt. G. M. Liddell from MI5, Brig. Sir Stuart Menzies and Col. V. P. T Vivian from MI6, Brig. Richard Gambier-Parry representing the RSS, and Sir Herbert Creedy for the Security Executive. An *ex officio* member of the committee would be Mr Dick Goldsmith White in his role as chairman of the subservient RSIC.

The functions of the RSC were as follows:

(a) To coordinate the mutual interests of SIS and the Security Service in the technical, cryptographic and intelligence problems arising out of Radio Security Intelligence.
(b) To consider and approve the claims of all Departments, both at home and overseas, on Radio Security Intelligence.
(c) To approve the broad disposition of Radio Security Intelligence resources both at home and overseas.
(d) To consider, and give directions upon, any recommendation which may be referred to it concerning the material intercepted by RSS or its means of interception.
(e) To approve any alterations which may from time to time be necessary in the constitution, terms of reference etc of the Radio Security Intelligence Conference.
(f) To consider and make recommendations on any other matters relevant to Radio Security.[1]

The secretary of the committee was Mr W. Armstrong.

The RSIC was chaired by Mr Dick Goldsmith White from 'B' Division MI5. He had been educated at Bishop's Stortford College holding the school athletics record for running the mile. After the war, he was instrumental in modernising MI5, most notably on their counterintelligence work. He had gained a reputation at the service as one of the greatest counterintelligence officers they have ever had, but his ideas had gone against some of MI5's traditions and structures and he was recruited to be the chief of MI6. It was widely thought that if he had stayed at MI5, he would have steered the service through the difficult 1960s and 1970s.

The RSIC would meet fortnightly and had representation from RSS, GC&CS, MI5, Section V of SIS, Section Vw, and the relevant armed services intelligence departments. Part of the committee's function was to set the interception priorities and discuss ISOS-ISK production and use at Bletchley. RSIC was to meet fortnightly and had the following terms of reference:

1. To settle the priorities for the interception of the various Groups
2. To discuss and, if necessary, make recommendations upon any problem, whether of a technical, cryptographic or intelligence nature, arising out of ordinary business concerning material intercepted by RSS with a view to possible improvements in its development and use.
3. To consider and make recommendations upon any matter concerning the material intercepted by RSS which may be referred to the Committee by hither authorities.[2]

The RSIC was in reality the heartbeat of the RSS throughout the Second World War. As Col. Vivian from SIS stated at the time, the committee was 'as a result of continuous and intimate study of the whole field of ISOS, will be the body best qualified to put forward suggestions from time to time as to the future disposal of RSS sources … intelligence and intelligence needs should guide the allocation of the technical tools'. The following is an example of the RSIC monthly priority list for coverage:

Radio Security Intelligence Conference	
Priority List	
ISK	
Spanish Groups	(a) 2/1, 2/2, 2/3, 2/120, 2/132, 2/151, 2/184, 2/350, 2/380, 2/1211, 2/1212, 14/39
	(b) 2/124, 2/126, 2/129, 2/141
Italian Groups	2/56, 2/110, 2/1101, 2/1111, 2/1113, 2/117
Balkan Groups	2/10, 2/13, 2/20, 2/26, 2/38, 2/69, 2/501, 2/506, 2/511, 2/517, 2/521, 2/522, 2/253, 2/524, 2/530, 2/536, 2/538, 2/539, 2/543, 2/5157, 2/5186, 2/5223

Turkish Groups	(a) 14/28, 14/38
	(b) 14/100, 14/102, 14/103, 14/105, 14/106, 14/107, 14/120, 14/121, 14/122, 14/123, 14/160, 14/172
Norway	2/240, 2/241, 2/242, 2/244, 2/245, 2/249
France, etc.	14/6, 2/49, 2/389
ISOS	
Spain, Portugal, and Spanish and Portuguese Africa	1/37, 1/55, 1/81, 1/92, 1/95, 2/122, 2/123, 2/125, 2/136, 2/144, 2/148, 2/150, 2/163, 2/169, 2/175, 2/178, 2/180, 2/191, 2/1200, 2/1201, 2/1207, 2/1214, 17/39
Norway	2/243
Balkans	AEGEAN network, BULGARIAN network, JUGOSLAVIAN network. 13/35, 2/5265
France	2/351, 2/380, 2/480, Group 17 (non-practice services)
Operational Services	X/212, X/213 ('EASTER' traffic), 8/53 (Italian Naval traffic), Group 16
Etc.	All Group 13 services, X/7000
'Priority 1'	
2/5265: 2/1, 2/2, 2/3, 2/56: Spanish	
ISKs: X/212: 14/58: 2/147: 13/52: 13/55	
RIS 27/10/43	

Chairman Dick Goldsmith White was to remark:

The RSIC was brought into being for the purpose of coordinating the somewhat illogical organisation of radio intercept work. Owing to the fact that the Radio Security Section was administered by Section VIII of SIS and that consumers of its product were Section V of SIS, B Division of MI5, and the Intelligence Section of the RSS itself, the points of view of these three departments were apt to be divergent and it was therefore necessary to agree between them an order of traffic priorities. Besides this it was felt that some formal and regular meetings were required for the purpose of pooling expertise on the subject of the RSS product, and the RSIC came to be in addition to a 'fair-play' committee, a forum for discussion and for planning. For example, at the time of the operation HUSKY, plans were drawn up under the auspices of the RSIC for traffic priorities in connection with the campaign and movement of equipment etc. There can be no doubt that the RSIC proved a very useful safety valve, preventing friction between the technical administrators of the RSS and the several consumer interests. The fact that MI5 furnished the Chairman (Mr White and subsequently Lt. Colonel Robertson) somewhat restored their sense of loss over the fact that the RSS, which began the war under MI5's technical direction, was subsequently handed over to SIS. Moreover, the slight rivalry which had developed between the RIS interpretations of the product and those of Section V were able to be ironed out.[3]

As the RSS evolved, it was structured into a number of groups—two of these were known as the Administration and Engineering Groups, which were headquartered at Hanslope Park. But the bulk of the organisation was headquartered at Arkley View, with the Signals and Discrimination Groups, Mobile Units Section, and Foreign Units all based out of Barnet.

The Administration Group was responsible for record keeping, enlistment or recruiting, pay, official postings, travel reports, feeding, sanitation, and accommodation.

The Engineering Group had three main areas of responsibility:

(i)   Engineering support—designing, erecting and maintaining the RSS equipment. This would have included the provision of special antenna systems (rhombic, V- and omnidirectional aerials), aerial switching systems where any set could utilise the most relevant aerial for the task allotted to it, frequency measuring systems. They would also maintain the wide band amplifiers (which would enable 10 or more sets to be used on each aerial simultaneously). They would oversee the testing at proposed intercept sites.

(ii) Direction Finding—technical control of the nationwide DF network. They would have developed statistical methods for the calculation of bearings, providing the results to the Discrimination groups. (Major Keen had developed new DF techniques and was frequently called upon to advise the Military Y services).

(iii) Provision of communications systems for the Foreign Units and radio intercommunication for the Mobile Units.[4]

The Signals Group was responsible for the following:

(i)   Selection, testing, training, discipline and welfare of operators. The Group would have administrative control of the stations. They also supplied trained operators to SCU4, the overseas unit of the RSS.

(ii) The organisation of the Voluntary Interceptors (VI), and their nine regional officers who provided oversight of the nine regions.

(iii) Controlled the teleprinter room and its staff, along with the telephone operators.[5]

The RSS also had Mobile and Foreign Units, which made up a significant component of their work during the Second World War. Their responsibilities are covered later.

The Discrimination Group was the operational hub of the RSS, directing the tasks of the interceptors, collaborating with the RIS, GC&CS, etc. The RIS was virtually integrated with this group. The group had a number of core responsibilities for the RSS:

1. General Search: would receive search logs from VI teams (read on desks which specialised in frequency bands of 2 megacycles width). They would identify and separate relevant from unwanted traffic passing material to the appropriate group officers.
2. Research: investigation of new key suspects, utilising a Special Research Station (with eight to twelve dedicated positions) manned by handpicked specialist radio operators.
3. Groups: signals analysis was broken down into key groups each under the responsibility of a group officer who reconstructed the signals plans and communications networks being used. They could rely on DF or other sources to discover locations of the signals, checking coverage with the Allocation and Collation teams. The group officer would consult daily with RIS reading all decrypts appropriate to his work.

The groups were:

Group I and II	*Abwehr*
Group VIII	Italian IS
Group XII	Russian clandestine
Group XIII	*Sicherheitsdienst*
Group XIV	'Nauen' Group or German Secret Diplomatic network. Assistance in interception from Foreign Office station at Sandridge
Group IX	Palestine traffic
Group XX	Yugoslav traffic, quasi-diplomatic
Group XXI	French DGER now SDECE
Miscellaneous	Many odd circuits, some being of great importance: (i) Northern Water Meteorological Service (ii) X73 Tokyo–Budapest (iii) Spain to Russia, Spanish Blue Division, etc.

4. Maps and Library: a small one- to two-man section maintaining a highly valued reference library of observed traffic signals and procedures including Allied traffic (from MI6 and SOE agents for example). It was to be the most complete reference resource on radio signals in the world. A chart of all RSS commitments supplied by the group officers was also maintained within this section. This relatively small section dealt with lapses of W/T security by the enemy, and it was to serve the RIS, T/A officers and log readers. It had been established from the summer of 1941 where the teams would methodically record the initials periodically exchanged between enemy operators during W/T transmissions. It soon became apparent that a complete picture of the W/T networks could be quickly built up by using these initials.
5. Collation: messages for GC&CS passed through the Collation Section. Enemy clandestine networks would use low-powered transmitters and would

frequently change both call signs and frequency. All of these versions were collated and a master copy maintained by the section. Information such as the complete heading of the group and service number, call signs, time of intercept (TOI), frequency, location of terminals, etc., would all be shared with Bletchley. The section would also keep records of the amount of traffic handled and made assessments of the interception quality provided by individual stations. On average, around 15,000 messages per week were being passed to GC&CS.

6. Allocation: under the direction of OIC Allocation Capt. Rhodes tasks from the General Search, group officers, or Discrimination teams would be prioritised for allocation to the stations for specific and detailed analysis. However, many of the overseas stations and VI teams only monitored static block allocations of frequencies. Allocation would issue signal plans or schedules for coverage of specific groups or suspect lists. Changes to these plans were discussed in the Discrimination Section and conveyed by amendments issued daily at 5 p.m. via cable to the stations and via telegrams to overseas units. The Allocation Section also had a dedicated DF control station manned twenty-four hours a day. Bearings on signals would be passed immediately to a plotting room at Hanslope—the results were issued on maps subsequently distributed to allocation who would send them to the relevant stations.

7. Duty Officer: this position was manned twenty-four hours a day. Capt. Rutland was the Duty Officer, supported by four NCOs and was the main RSS contact with the outside world, e.g. BBC, military commands, etc. It would conduct routine enquiries to check the identities of signals transmitted by SIS, SOE, and military services where existing records were inadequate. The office would handle requests from the BBC for DF bearings on foreign broadcast stations and also provide direct support to a deployed Mobile Unit.

8. Discrimination: would provide day to day direction of RSS operations, and oversee planning and policy. The OIC discrimination role was a key liaison function within the RSS to provide assistance to RSS foreign units, the RSS liaison officers deployed (USA, India, and Australia), and via TP link to the French. They would also provide direct day-to-day liaison with GC&CS and attend weekly or fortnightly visits to Bletchley. They would also provide direct liaison with the RIS.

9. RIS (Radio Intelligence Section): was the recipient of decrypts from GC&CS and other source material on specific target radio networks RSS was covering. They would receive, maintain, and publish target knowledge on the enemy intelligence services being intercepted by the RSS.

The quarrelling between MI5, MI6, and DMI on the role and future of the RSS came to a head in February 1941, when correspondence was feverishly being passed between Sir David Petrie, DMI; Lord Swinton; and Col. Worlledge, Controller of the RSS. In a letter dated 12 February 1941, Worlledge was to clarify his position:

As you have been for some long-time well aware I consider that the present organisation of RSS is unsound. I am responsible for the work done but I have no control over the personnel who carry that work out, other than the small military staff. We are dependent upon a part time service from the Post Office for the supply of all equipment, construction of stations and maintenance, and supply of personnel. The personnel are subject to their peace time terms of employment and the rules and regulations, both Post Office and Trades Union, which are based upon normal peace conditions. The Post Office organisation, being based upon peace conditions, is utterly unsuitable for war. The result is a state of incompetence and inefficiency which would not be tolerated for one moment in any fighting service. So long as the present organisation continues it will be impossible for RSS ever to become properly efficient as an active war organisation ... in my opinion, RSS should be organised as one unit, preferably a purely military unit though I would not exclude the possibility of a mixed military and civilian organisation.

The essential point is that it should be one definite unit. There is a very acute shortage of wireless operators in the country. Any re-organisation of RSS should assure the retention of all the efficient operators and senior staff of the Post Office. The work is very highly specialised, a large proportion of the present Post Office staff have been employed on this work for nearly 18 months and it would be intolerable to lose their acquired experience and training. Authority should be retained by the Commanding Officer to select for transfer or seconding personnel from the Post Office now employed with RSS. Exact figures are not yet available but at a rough guess it seems likely that we could select possibly as many as 200 operators from the present staff of approximately 300 as suitable for continuance in the work. The establishment of operators which is considered necessary is approximately 450. It would probably be necessary therefore to recruit a further 200–250 efficient operators if they can be found.

There is only one source which can supply operators who already possess the necessary qualifications and experience in this work, namely, those civilians, ex-amateurs principally, who are now and have been for many months employed as Voluntary Interceptors by RSS and who at the present time number about 1100. The vast majority of these are in reserved occupations or are over military age and in good jobs. A previous attempt to enlist these people in the Post Office for RSS work failed owing to the small wages offered by the Post Office. In my opinion it would be necessary to offer £7 a week if we are to entice sufficient numbers of VI's to give up their present employment and join the unit. This would imply a similar payment to such Post Office operators as we would accept. I am aware that this would cause repercussions in the 'Y' Services and also among MI6's men employed on wireless work, but I can see no alternative if it is desired to make RSS efficient. It must be remembered that the work is even more highly specialised and difficult than that of the 'Y' Services.[6]

Sir David Petrie recommends that RSS 'be equipped, staffed and run purely as an Intelligence instrument' by MI6. From a brief conversation with Colonel Gambier Parry yesterday I am left with some doubt as to whether MI6 does actually possess the necessary powers or administrative organisation to the extent which Sir David Petrie appears to believe.

That a very much closer liaison between MI6 and RSS would be of great benefit to both is undeniable but this could be arranged in the present circumstances. The work of RSS concerns MI5 and MI6 and has little to do with purely Military Intelligence, nevertheless it may be anticipated that in the event of invasion a considerable number of illicit wireless transmitters will be dropped in the country, manned by soldiers in uniform. Again in the event of invasion, it seems probable that the resources of RSS could be of direct military value. It would therefore appear that the DMI would be directly concerned in this event with the efficiency of RSS.

I am extremely anxious to make RSS an efficient unit, but I can see no hopes of being able to do this under the present organisation. If MI6 can offer a solution to the difficulty I would welcome the transfer.[7]

One of the responses back on this subject in the middle of May 1941, from Col. D. A. Butler on the General Staff, authorised the transfer to MI6, with the caveat that the intelligence work done on the RSS traffic would cease. Butler wanted the organisation of IWI to remain under the control of MI8(b) for just six months. The section was to be responsible for 'coordinating the foreign organisation with the RSS at home. MI6 have appointed Colonel Worlledge as Liaison Officer to MI8 for this work'.

RSS Annual Estimate	
(Year 1 April 1942–31 March 1943)	
Home Establishment:	£
Salaries and Wages	175,000
Subsistence Allowance at Standard Rate	24,000
Military Pay	45,000
Works and Buildings	10,000
Northern Intercept station	15,000
Special Apparatus	10,000
Transport	5,000
Travelling Expenses	5,000
General Expenses (including telephones)	8,000
VI Expenses	15,000
Stores (Forward Buying of Technical Equipment)	10,000
PO Lines	40,000
Expenses of Mobile Unit Operations	8,000
Total	370,000

In November 1940, with the war in Europe taking hold, MI8(a) was reorganised to focus on operational radio exploitation and given responsibility for the 'Y' Service, basing itself in 2 Caxton Street, London. Interception had originally been coordinated by MI1(b) and subsequently transferred across to MI8 at the beginning of the war. MI1(b) lost its cryptologic work to the newly formed team at Bletchley under GC&CS, but the organisation would maintain the following main tasks: wireless intercept and its coordination; dissemination of decoded traffic; and supply of suitably trained personnel and intercept equipment.

From February 1940, the 'Y' Service introduced an official training formation referred to as the Special Operator Training Battalion (SOTB) based at the barracks in the quiet market town of Trowbridge. Its intent was to produce 100 W/T operators every month from their sixteen-week-long training programme, which was later extended to twenty weeks. After Luftwaffe bombing, the training was moved to the Isle of Man.

Their intensive training covered the teaching of Morse (to thirty words per minute level), maintaining their radio sets, and doing rudimentary DF alongside the usual military training. They would also learn the 'Q-codes', which is a group of three-letter international standardised signals to convey instructions or conditions to the receiver station. QRM, for example, means interference, and QSA is the signal strength.

There were three grades of Morse speeds: B3—eight words per minute; B2—twenty-five words per minute; and B1—thirty words per minute. Each grade would incur an increase in pay for one of the newly qualified Special Wireless Operators (SWOPS), who had graduated from the SOTB.

The 'Y' Service recruited a lot of Auxiliary Territorial Service (ATS) women for the course, but in the initial SOTB courses, there was concern about the throughput of new operators. The ATS element of the War Office 'Y' Group (WOYG) became so dominant during the war that they were responsible for 75 per cent of the wartime intercept.

The opening of a second front for the Allies was going to be a major challenge for the RSS and the other interception services. In the weeks before D-Day and the implementation of Operation Overlord, the RSIC had much to discuss to prepare the RSS for a significant increase in its workload. At a meeting on 25 May 1944 in MI5 Headquarters, the RSIC agreed that both the RSS and the GC&CS 'should be empowered to give priority to the W/T services of stay-behind agents … as these services become operationally "hot"'. The RSIC also debated the potential merit in targeting enemy W/T stations and tasking the Allied air forces with bombing them. The RSIC decreed that these German stations should not be made the targets for bombing raids because:

1. The first few days of invasion operations would not be the period during which leakages from stay-behind agents would matter most.

2. Operational by-products of ISK and ISOS are very important, and the diminution in their supply might be extremely damaging.

3. On the whole, controlled agents seem to be in better repute with the Germans than the others, and there are consequently great advantages in the continuance of these 'managed' leakages.

4. *Abwehr* sources are far from being the OKW's sole source of operational intelligence. They do not even rank among its major sources. It would therefore seriously cripple the enemy's Military Intelligence system if the *Abwehr* were silenced for a period.

One of the main conclusions from the debate was that stay-behind agents would not be expected to start transmitting intelligence reports for a significant time after the first landing operations in Normandy. Even after this prolonged hiatus, it would take further time for the agent's reliability to be assessed by their controllers.

The May 1944 RSIC meeting was significant as it would give Lt-Col. Maltby the opportunity to brief other senior officers of the plans to deploy a SCU mobile unit overseas with the 21st Army Group. Maltby described the team's composition, equipment, and communications reach back to Britain. Alongside this, a specialist American signals team was to be deployed with the 1st US Army, which was to get expert training from the teams at Hanslope Park.

A couple of months before this meeting, the RSIC was to debate and assess the W/T security apparatus for the Allies who were stationed in Britain. There was concern that possible leakages may influence the prevailing secrecy on Operation Overlord and the opening of a second front in Europe. Maj. Sclater lead the discussion on the transmissions from the Czech, Norwegian, Belgian, Polish, and Dutch units who were all using British issued W/T sets, cipher systems, and call sign procedures. Sclater's assessment on these units were their W/T security protocols were good and on par with the British teams. The investigations had not been undertaken by the RSS or military 'Y' service interceptors but by ordinary British Army Signals Units who had not been specifically trained on this type of target.

In July 1944, the RSIC meeting at MI5 brought the rapid expansion of the RSS into focus for the senior officers. GC&CS representative Denys Page, who was to go on and become a classics scholar at both Oxford and Cambridge universities after the war, made a pitch on the dire state of resources. Page took the committee back in time to emphasise the point. In November 1943, the RSS was intercepting in the region of 8,000–10,000 messages per fortnight and the RSIC had agreed to drop Groups V and XV. By February 1944, the service was intercepting up to 13,000 messages per fortnight and the RSIC subsequently agreed to stop work on the whole Warsaw W/T network in Poland. A month later, the intercept total had risen to nearly 14,000 messages per fortnight, which caused the RSIC to agree that the RSS drop the Sofia ISOS network and collection against the Brandenburg Division.

Page pressured the RSIC to consider 'whether the policy of clipping interception to fit the capacity of RSS should not be replaced by the policy of expanding RSS to enable it to intercept the existent and required traffic … coverage is now, from the cryptographic point of view, at the irreducible minimum'.

Resources for skilled W/T operators were at breaking point, and it was vital in this critical stage of the war to maintain coverage: '… the present degree of coverage … is essential to insure (so far as it can be insured) the continuance of the present supply of decodes. Small cessations of coverage of operationally unimportant W/T links might result in the collapse of the decipherment of much *Abwehr* traffic'.

Maltby warned the RSIC that the general manpower shortage in the RSS would curtail any positive moves to expand the RSS. He wanted the RSIC to put a case forward to direct the Ministry of Labour to allot to the RSS the required extra staff. There was no external pool of trained W/T operators in Britain. Any new staff would have to be untested new recruits that would not increase the interception capacity of the RSS for at least nine months, by which time the war might well be over. Allied air efforts in Europe were now targeting German landline communications to push the operators back onto the radio networks, subsequently increasing the need for further RSS operations. The case was to be pushed up to the point of escalation in the RSC for review.

The RSS was suggesting bolstering the resources by at least 150 operators, which would in reality help man some twenty-five receiver banks. After the meeting, Lt-Col. Maltby was to say: '… if another, say, 25 banks are to be provided, an extra intercept-station will have to be built'.

Lt-Col. Maltby and Maj. Jameson Till would also represent RSS views on another high-level committee during the Second World War. This was set up to assist the SOE in establishing the Polish Military Wireless Research (PMWR) unit in Stanmore. The Poles had become capable and productive Allies in the fight against German cipher systems, and there was a genuine effort to assist the Poles in clandestine activity in occupied Europe. In 1943, the 'Works Sub-Committee' of the PMWR unit convened in May 1943 and authorised the manufacture of the black box AP.4 wireless transmitter sets (covering a frequency range 2–8 Mc/s or 3.5–9.5 Mc/s). The SOE placed an order of 500 sets, and the Polish 6th Bureau placed a smaller order of just 200 sets. The RSS controller said at the time:

[The] relative importance of this work against other W/T priorities—and to find occasion either to support or otherwise the big demand on material supplies that these orders are going to entail … also to satisfy himself as to the exact purpose and destination of all this equipment.[8]

Both the SOE and the RSS were to appoint a joint Anglo-Polish Board of Directors representing all parties to govern the policy of the unit at Stanmore. Alongside

Maltby and Jameson Till, the board was to comprise the following additional staff: Grp Capt. Benner, RAF (SOE), Chairman; Sir Robert Watson Watt (TRE); Col. Sulisławski, Polish Deputy Chief of Staff; Col. Heliodor Cepa, Chief of PMWR unit; Lt-Col. Gano, Chief of Polish 2nd Bureau; Cdr Wilfred Dunderdale, SIS Liaison to Polish; Lt-Col. Wilkinson (SOE); and Lt-Col. Protasewicz, Chief of Polish 6th Bureau.

The board often met at Norgeby House on Baker Street, or sometimes at the Ruben Hotel in London. It was responsible for management of the factory, which was opened at Stanmore on 25 March 1943 in time for the preparations of the invasion of France the next year. The board also oversaw purchasing, development, and research for wireless technologies, production, and planning.

The unit at Stanmore was run by Polish Col. Heliodor Cepa, who was lauded for the work the factory was doing to support the SOE. Brig. Colin Gubbins from the SOE was to say of the Poles wireless set:

> They are extremely compact and most suitable for the purpose for which I require them.... I have the highest opinion of your sets and fully realise the difficulties involved in their production. Please accept my sincere thanks for coming forward so splendidly to my assistance.

Cepa was vehemently pro-British and assisted greatly in establishing an effective working relationship with British Intelligence. This was often in opposition to other parts of the Polish General Staff, which did not want such an open relationship with the British. This faction was headed up by Col. Sulisławski who wanted to ostracise Cepa and take control of all the Polish W/T communications operations, but the SOE was to approach the problem from the Polish 6th Bureau angle and support Cepa in what he was trying to achieve with the Stanmore initiative. Cepa was constrained on increasing wireless intercept operations due to a lack of skilled personnel, lack of funding, and suitable components to build the wireless sets. Cepa was to fight an uphill battle with his own, non-supportive General Staff.

The Whitehall committees had brought structure and governance to the wireless interception priorities of the RSS. It had been achieved through some delicate interagency negotiations on the ownership and governance of the service. The result was clear direction and prioritisation of requirements for all the RSS stations. It would help steer not just the full-time operators working at stations like Hanslope or St Erth, but also the hundreds of VIs scattered around the country who would play a vital part in the expansive coverage of the German intelligence services in occupied Europe.

3

Volunteers

I now realise the importance of the job I was doing as a civilian VI in the RSS...I am proud to have been a small part of the team which provided the Bletchley Park decoders with the messages they needed to be able to decipher them.

Raymond Fautley, Home South region VI

Lt-Col. Adrian Simpson was adamant that a small number of intercept stations around Britain would not be sufficient to monitor the German Intelligence Services. His original proposal for the creation of a comprehensive listening organisation would be given to Ralph Mansfield, 4th Baron Sandhurst, who had been an enthusiastic amateur radio ham for many years and had service within the wireless service of the Royal Signals during the First World War.

In a memo to the director of the Security Service written in October 1938, Simpson articulated the value of recruiting experienced radio specialists for this work:

The average GPO, Naval or Signals operator is not suited to this work. It will be self-evident that unless the work of the interception and DF stations is carried out thoroughly and conscientiously much of its potential value will be lost. The work is far from mechanical and to do it properly requires, on the part of the operating staff, a very high degree of keenness, initiative, coolness and power of concentration. To find men combining these qualities with the necessary technical knowledge to handle the apparatus efficiently is far from easy. Even after they have been found it requires several months training before they become proficient at their work.[1]

The use of civilian spare-time interceptors would be fraught with an array of practical problems. With the threat of invasion by the Germans, the British authorities impounded the radio transmitters. Many radio amateurs were often reported to the police for suspicious activity and arrested as potential spies.

Simpson relayed the valuable reflections of the work against the Germans in the First World War:

> In the last war experience taught us that first class operators know what is going on almost by instinct, and on many occasions the operator who received it was able to give valuable suggestions as to the nature of the message, if not as to the actual contents.

Simpson knew that to find a cadre of wireless specialists was going to be hard but that they would need to be rewarded for their specialist skills:

> I strongly recommend ear-marking such men, once they have been found, paying them a higher rate of wage than the ordinary operator and placing them on the permanent staff.
>
> It will be quite an easy task to form such an auxiliary corps and in this way we shall be able to maintain an organised watch in districts which in certain circumstances could not be properly covered by the official organisation. Naturally the members of the auxiliary observer corps would have to be very carefully selected, not only as to their antecedents but also as to their willingness to serve and their technical knowledge and ability. A corps of this nature would cost practically nothing at all and we should have the benefit of some of the ablest technical brains in the country. The type of man I have in mind would consider it an honour to serve and his keenness would be beyond measure.[2]

Simpson would need to be selective in the type of men and women they would need for this work:

> As far as possible men should be chosen who are ex-fighting service, Mercantile Marine, or GPO operators with a good knowledge of Morse, or who have made radio their hobby in peace time. Of the latter, the men who have belonged to purely listening societies may possibly be of more value than the average member of the RSGB who, as a rule, is prone to have been more interested in using his own transmitting set than in listening to others.[3]

The initial discussions on the recruitment of volunteer radio hams throughout the country was to fall on Arthur Watts, who had been injured as a RN officer in the Dardanelles campaign and subsequently joined Naval Intelligence as soon as he could walk again. He worked as the president of the Radio Society of Great Britain (RSGB):

I was asked to go down and see Lord Sandhurst … we want to get chaps listening out for enemy signals, and we want heaps of amateurs doing this work.… I felt it was a golden opportunity to be able to show that the amateurs were an asset to the country. And so of course everybody had to be vetted. I was closely aligned with the council, Doug Chalmers, Eddie Gaye and others and from then I went all over the country seeing the people we knew and that is how we started the thing off.[4]

RSS enlistment would occur at Arkley View, whereby the new wireless operators or support staff would be given an Army Book 64 (AB64), Parts I and II. Part I would contain details of the recruit's name, date of birth, rank, service number, next of kin information, and any vaccinations the individual may have had. Any military RSS recruits were not given AB64 Part II as their pay would have come directly from the Foreign Office rather than the Army. If any of these recruits were to be posted at an overseas RSS station, this would have caused problems. These staff would have been given an AB64 Part II and given Army pay at the appropriate scale to rank.

Often, RSS personnel were recruited into the Royal Corps of Signals with a service number in a special block. They were assigned a unique number, which started with 260 followed by four other numbers taken in sequence order of their enlistment. It did not conform to any usual military numbering system so they could easily be spotted. Their pay books were marked with the initials NPAF (Not Paid from Army Funds). RSS personnel were paid significantly more than other Royal Signals personnel with the same rank.

Sandhurst would keep his fledgling VI community together with a fortnightly newsletter called *The Hunt* whereby the Germans acted as the 'Foxes' and his RSS stations as 'rabbits'. He mockingly referred to himself in the publication as 'T.W.Earp' or 'Dogsbody.'

If you can find a fox on your RX
And copy him whatever be his fist,
If you can dig him out of the schedule BERTIE,
And get his traffic daily, nothing missed,
If you can find his QSU's and answers,
Or supply Group 13's missing link;
If you can copy SHL's fast bug-key
And send the log in neatly done in ink,
If you can dodge the blinking German Army,
Or copy AOR through thick and thin
And you can copy VIOLET's QRX's,
You're a better bloke than me so
BUNG IT IN!

Lord Sandhurst's VI poem explaining the procedure for new VIs

Each interceptor was given the responsibility for a part of the short-wave radio band to monitor faint signals that stood out as been out of the ordinary. They were looking for sporadic signals often hidden among a wealth of strong signals from military or commercial radio traffic. Maintaining watch on the same frequency band got the VI operators experience on what was routinely operating in that band and so would give them the ability to spot irregular signals. The VIs were to unearth something far more important than a few lone spies operating on British soil. They were to uncover the vast German intelligence service radio network with fixed stations in Berlin, Wiesbaden, Stuttgart, Hamburg, and Vienna. The network reached into the far corners of Europe, as well as occupied countries and neutral countries around the world, including Argentina—it even reached ships.

These networks would stand out as being clandestine due to the operating procedures being used. Call signs, for example, were not linked and frequently changed on the network. Outlying stations on the network would often reply on any one of a number of frequencies without the use of a centralised network frequency. The VIs were adept at spotting these transmissions, probably because many of the German operators were ex-radio amateurs themselves. The transposition cipher systems they were using were often very different on the air than the military substitution ciphers being used by the German Army. The VI who was willing to commit forty-eight hours a month to the RSS was exempt from duties such as fire watching and the Home Guard. Many operators would do more than 160 hours a month.

Many of the VI operators were issued with the military uniform and badges of the Royal Observer Corps (ROC) as a cover from around September–October 1941, along with the standard enlistment forms for the corps. The arrangement to use the ROC for cover had been brokered by Gambier-Parry or Lt-Col. Maltby in mid-1941. Some VIs received the ROC uniform as soon as it was available to the observers themselves. These uniforms had to be returned to the ROC when the VI retired from the RSS, but there was no official link to the ROC for the individual. The ROC cover was extended to include those RSS operators who were working at the fixed stations around Britain. There was some inconsistency within the RSS as not everyone was issued with the ROC uniform. Some were issued the uniform of the Home Guard, or the Royal Corps of Signals and some VIs did not have any official military uniform as cover at all.

Every VI had to sign the Official Secrets Act before commencing work for the RSS. Potential VIs were investigated and vetted very thoroughly. Sometimes the local police unit was used to make the initial approach, as was the case for VI Hugh Lawley who was approached to see if he would be interested in doing some work for His Majesty's government:

I was a bit apprehensive but nevertheless I thought it must be important so I agreed ... the Official Secrets Act was read over to me, then I was to receive what I would call my first briefing. About a week later, I received a confidential communication from a mysterious box number in Hertfordshire. And this communication requested I carry out certain periods of watchkeeping on the radio frequency spectrum and specifically pay attention to any repetitive signals that were being transmitted from any source whatsoever.[5]

Each VI would be given a registration number as a unique RSS identifier. For example, VI/HS/407 would indicate the RSS operator was a VI in the Home South region and assigned a number of 407.

Bob King states:

So the Radio Society of Great Britain was approached and they responded enthusiastically and contacted as many amateurs as they could and got them to listen. The idea was that they listen to see if there were any nearby transmitters, which could be distinguished by things called key clicks, Morse code not speech. Before long they were about 1000 people all over the British Isles listening to German agents.[6]

Even husband and wife teams were recruited as VIs. Before the war, Helena and Leslie Crawley worked for Henley and Sons of High Holborn and were both keen radio hams (G2DDY and G3DT respectively). When war was declared, they were contacted by John Clarricoats (G6CL), the then-secretary of the Radio Society of Great Britain. He said he had a special job for a married couple and they were encouraged to get married quickly, which they did on 14 October 1939 by Special Licence. Leslie was in a reserved occupation as a civil engineer and was duly posted to Orkney by the Admiralty to build naval air stations in December 1939. They were housed at a cottage in Castlehill on the mainland island of Orkney from March 1940 to August 1943 on the shore of Loch of Boardhouse. The cottage had no electricity or running water, so the radio receiver relied on accumulators for electricity. When these needed charging, one of them would take them to the Royal Corps of Signals unit in Stromness.

Helena was able to come with Leslie because she had a high-level security clearance and the fact they needed a pair of interceptors on Orkney. The RSS had had concerns about Orkney as far back as the summer of 1940, when a post office inspector had deployed up there from RSS HQ to investigate allegations of information leakage via short-wave radio transmissions, and reports of radio jamming operations. Investigations over a number of weeks yielded nothing.

The DR12 security passes given to VIs gave them the right to enter any premises where they suspected the enemy were sending messages. Helena was told that the messages she monitored were from Allied agents in occupied Europe, but she was actually listening to the *Abwehr* network in Oslo. This network was not easily available to other VI groups in more southern parts of the country, so Orkney provided a valuable access point into the *Abwehr* northern networks. Only senior officers, and then only if they had to know, knew this. Although Helena never knew who the W/T operators were or what they were sending, she was able to recognise them by their rhythm, which was useful when they had to change frequency. The battery powered set was possibly an SCU Mk III as designed by Bob Hornby and built at Whaddon. When needed, she made contact with the service through Capt. J. Wallace based at 67 Port Street, Stirling.

One of the stations Leslie built was HMS Tern (RNAS Twatt). Working on the air stations, he got to know Cdr Rotherham quite well. Whenever radio traffic was quiet Cdr Rotherham would invite them to dine in the wardroom. Cdr Rotherham was shrouded in fame on the station as he was the navigator on the patrol to see if the *Bismarck* had left its moorings and had sent the radio message, which resulted in HMS *Hood* and *Prince of Wales* being sent to sea to intercept her.

The Crawley's left Orkney in August 1943 when Leslie was posted to the Admiralty office in Bath, Somerset, to help with the planning for the expected invasion of Japan. In 2010, Helena received some recognition of her secret work with a certificate signed by Prime Minister David Cameron and the Bletchley badge from GCHQ.

Bill Peek was one of the first radio hams in London with the call sign G2ZZ. He was born in December 1908, the first of a large Poplar family in the East End. He had been interested in radio and electronics at an early age and left school aged fourteen. In 1940, one of his radio friends, Bill Matthews (G2CD), got him an introduction into VI work, and he was formally enlisted into the RSS in November 1941. Matthews was the area coordinator for the local VI group, which was designated G5, covering East London and its outlying areas to the East. Each of these groups was issued with instructions as to how the group would operate in the event of an enemy invasion. There was an edict issued by the RSS Controller on 19 March 1941 that, in the event of an invasion, all VIs 'should immediately burn all papers which could in any way connect then with RSS or the War Office, or any activity in the war—particularly should their Passes be burnt'.

In early September 1943, Bill was deployed to Montreathmont Moor, just outside Forfar in the far north of Scotland, returning in late November, and he was part of the group that assisted with establishing the DF station there. He was also billeted on occasion at Arkley View in Barnet. By the end of the war and Bill's subsequent discharge, he had attained the rank of sergeant. His discharge note was to be glowing in praise: '... this NCO has been employed as Chief Technical Clerk in a Training School. He has shown himself to be capable and industrious and has always carved out his duties in an excellent manner. He is thoroughly trustworthy, and very well able to handle men'.

When Peek was discharged, he was accompanied by a letter from the SCU3 Training School Officer in Charge Capt. Kelsall Royal Signals. These were scripted to help the VI operators get work when they were demobilised and left the RSS. Peek's was to read:

> Sgt Peek has served with me since March 1942 to date in the capacity of senior NCO Chief Technical Clerk. He has proved himself to be a most efficient and reliable worker and organiser of well above average ability and in whom the utmost confidence could be placed. I have no hesitation whatsoever in recommending him for any position of trust and am confident that with his marked ability to handle men he would give the utmost satisfaction.[7]

Many of the VI groups maintained their own in-house magazines in which they would publish details of their successes, instructions, and news of relevance to radio monitoring by the group. Lt-Col. Hornby orchestrated an intercept test between the VI and 'Y' Service operators and it was established the VI operators were vastly superior to the 'Y' Services.

As short-wave radio transmissions propagate, it was necessary to establish a nationwide network of collectors to pick up any prospective illicit signals. The concept was to recruit and deploy the VI operators around the country every 10–15 miles to have the best opportunity to intercept illicit German wireless transmissions from wherever in the country they may be broadcast. The whole country was divided by the RSS into nine distinct regions. An RSS Army officer, typically a captain in the Royal Signals, was in overall command of each of these regions. His duties included:

(i) He will be responsible for the selection of civilian observers, having regard to their character, reliability and qualifications.

(ii) He will see that all listeners, whether members of the Force or civilians, are supplied with special forms for logging intercepts, showing call signs, frequency, nature of signals.

(iii) He will arrange for the transmission of one copy direct to the HQ of the RSS with the least possible delay, anything of a suspicious nature being forwarded by telephone, in code if necessary, or by teleprinter if available.

(iv) Any deductions or suggestions which the Officer i/c District is able to make will be forwarded in the form of a report in duplicate for instructions as to what action (if any) is to be taken.

(v) He will arrange for the calibration of all receiving sets in his district.

(vi) He will endeavour to arrange for the receipt of reports from trustworthy dealers regarding any unusual enquiries or sales of parts of transmitting apparatus, or other information of a suspicious nature.

(vii) He should endeavour to obtain from local electricity supply companies reports of any unusual consumption of current.

(viii) He will be furnished with a complete list, containing names and addresses, of all individuals in his district who have held transmitting licences in peace time, as well as a list of any exemptions from the closing down order.

If a suspicious wireless transmission was found, the VI would have the authority, working in conjunction with the police, to provide information that would lead to the property being raided. This was done under the authority provisioned by No. 88A(1) of the Defence Regulations (Search Warrant), or if the case was deemed urgent under No. 88A(2) Superintendent's Authority. In both of these cases, the suspected offence would have been against No. 8 of the regulations dealing with possession and use of illicit wireless transmitting equipment.

The work was hard and a significant challenge even for an experienced radio amateur. The BBC transmitted its programmes at a broadcast strength of 100 millivolts per metre, whereas most of the weakest German intelligence service transmitters would have a meagre strength a million times below that BBC value. The VI would spend a lot of his time discriminating through known Allied signals to go after the target *Abwehr* traffic. They became adept at spotting frequency changes or unusual operating procedures that typified German Intelligence Service transmissions. For a VI to get to understand the operating methods of a particular *Abwehr* network, the RSS recognised they would need to produce at a minimum eight log sheets a month, but most typically produced ten; forty-eight was considered the benchmark to be excluded from other duties such as fire watch patrols or the Home Guard.

The country was divided into nine regional areas and some of these covered vast areas of the country. The VIs had to be skilled and dedicated, so recruitment into the local regions was both difficult and long. The sensitivities around the work made the vetting process important and this often took a lot of time. For example, by Christmas 1939, the Home South region had only enrolled seven VIs. When the RSS was at its most active, it had around 2,000 VIs operating in the following nine regions, which corresponded with the GPO Regional Centres:

Home South: Highlands House, Clinton Road, Leatherhead, under Capt. Alan Sabine (later at Arkley View/PO Box 25).

Home North: 83 Regent Street, Cambridge, under Capt. Hall, then Capt. Rolfe.

South West: 27 Dixs Field, Exeter, under D. N. Norton.

North East: (no available information).

North West: 6 Jordan Street, Preston, under Capt. A. E. Scarratt.

Wales: Cardiff under Capt. Edmund Vale and D. Lowe.

Scotland: 67 Port Street, Stirling, under Capt. Wallace.

Northern Ireland: Telephone House, Cromac Street (and later in the Second World War, Heathcote), Belfast, under Capt. Joe Banham.

Midlands (referred to colloquially as 'M' Region): 3 Bank Chambers, Town Hall Square, Leicester, under Capt. Aubrey Johnson, then Capt. A. E. Scarratt.

Each region had its own Regional Office (RO) with permanent staff, including a small staff of typists. Home North, for example, covered an area north of the River Thames to well north of Oxford, which included several hundred VIs. Sandhurst had recruited twenty regional officers to oversee the British RSS network. These ROs were further subdivided into smaller areas or groups overseen by group leaders. Three months after the RSS started, its fifty VIs at that stage helped identify 600 *Abwehr* radio operators in occupied Europe.

Ray Fautley was based out of the Home South region, which had its headquarters team in Leatherhead in Surrey. He first started as a VI with the RSS in the summer of 1941 using a six-valve short-wave receiver, which he had built during the early part of that year. It had a built-in beat frequency oscillator (BFO), which would enable the Morse code signals to be audible as tones. During 1942, Ray was given permission to take home, on loan, one of the RAF R1155 receivers that were being manufactured by Marconi's WT Company and would provide much finer signal selectivity than his previous receiver. Many of the VIs recruited into the RSS would have their wireless receivers maintained and supplied by the GPO.

Although a VI based in the Home South region, he never visited the RSS office in Leatherhead during the Second World War, but he was issued with a ROC uniform, which he would wear occasionally on weekends. He always wore uniform when the regional VI operators would get together with his officer in charge, Maj. Bellringer, and his second in command, Capt. Johnson.

These meetings occurred about every six weeks at a local pub for their 'pep' talks. The pub was in Sutton, a short bus ride from where Ray lived in North Cheam. The meetings were held in a small room in the pub to keep a low-security profile. The talks would cover what the volunteers were being asked to do and the importance of the work and its secrecy. Bellringer would emphasise the importance of keeping listening and concentrating even when there appeared to be no audible Morse code signals. Ray had been asked to cover the frequency range of 7–7.5 Mc/s.

These were the only times that he would meet with his VI colleagues. At some of these meetings, another VI (Nell Corry, G2YL, from Tamworth in Surrey) would give the rest of the VI team some Morse code practice up to twenty-five words per minute.

Raymond Fautley was proud to be a VI:

I now realise the importance of the job I was doing as a civilian VI in the RSS during WWII. I am proud to have been a small part of the team which provided the Bletchley Park decoders with the messages they needed to be able to decipher them. At the time it was just a job that I felt was in some way helping the war effort after working for Marconi's W.T Company during the daytime. Wearing the ROC uniform helped me to keep the secret of what I was really doing.[8]

The number of VIs in each region varied considerably (typically between 200 and 400) and so would the distance travelled by the RO. Many of the VIs rarely saw their RO, and normally when they did, it was in connection with recruitment. 'G' call signs were used for English VIs, GW for Wales, GM for Scotland, and GI for Ireland.

Arkley would receive notice of a new VI and most likely Capt. Bellringer would select which RO to contact the new recruit. Arkley would have kept full records of the VIs as the invitation for them to become full time would have come from there. These full-time enlistments were managed and overseen by Arkley View. VIs were spaced throughout the country in the main centres of population, working either singly or in groups for as many hours a day as their civilian vocations allowed them. They were asked to collate intercept logs, daily wherever possible, but at a minimum of three times per week. The VI was to return from a day's work and in the evening commit to typically three to four hours' radio, monitoring a predetermined wavelength band.

The log sheets that were the mainstay of the VI work were supplied to the VIs from the RO. Every day, the VI was responsible for sending their log sheets through to Barnet. They were posted in double envelopes (one inside the other), stamped, and then sent to Box 25, Barnet, Herts. In December 1939, the Home South regional VI network produced nearly 2,000 log sheets, which increased to 3,000 by March 1940. By this stage, the RSS had built up such a wealth of knowledge on the German *Abwehr* wireless networks that they produced a handbook of German Morse techniques that got issued to all the VIs around the country.

Once received by Arkley View, they were processed and acknowledgement slips returned to the individual interceptor. They were stamped with strict RSS guidance as to what to do with the frequency range or call sign covered: 'MORE TRAFFIC PLEASE'; 'OBSERVE'; 'UNWANTED HUN'; 'WATCH PLEASE'; 'NOTED THANKS'; 'VERY GOOD'; 'OK COVERED THANKS'; and 'STILL WANTED'.

Short-wave receivers were considered by the War Office to be safe to use by radio amateurs, but at the beginning of the war, they placed heavy restrictions on the use of transmitters. The VIs would often use home-built receiver sets. In some circumstances, the RSS did supply on loan various American receivers such as the Hallicrafters 'Sky Champion' and more unusually the higher specification National HRO set, which was the standard receiver fit for many of the receiver banks at the full-time listening stations at Hanslope Park, Forfar, or St Erth.

A HRO receiver would have in the region of £329 in 1942 with four ham band coils, which would have required an additional power supply (costing around £29) and general coverage coils at £18. At 1942 exchange rates, a HRO would have been around fourteen weeks' wages for a typical amateur, so they were more reliant on home-built receivers.

Enlistment of a VI followed a distinct protocol. For reasons of security and discipline, personnel who were employed by the RSS were enlisted as serving soldiers. A special form of enlistment was used, whereby the soldier was bound only to serve in the RSS. Should his engagement in the RSS be terminated, he would become automatically entitled to a free discharge from the Army and return to civilian life. In common with all other essential public services in wartime, members of the RSS were subject to definite discipline. Serving soldiers were, of course, subject to the King's Regulations, Army Council Instructions, and to orders from the controller of the RSS and other duly appointed officers, although it is pointed out that the whole organisation was run very differently from traditional notions of Army discipline.

Each VI was graded (from 'A' to 'C') according to his skills at Morse, which was established through testing. All operators would also have to have a 'sound knowledge of handling modern communications receivers and must pass a simple oral examination on the set'.

Grade 'A' operators would need to have a Morse keying speed of at least twenty-three words per minute, as well as an ability to read weak signals through jamming and a general aptitude for wireless interception work. They would qualify for a £7 per week rate of pay.

Grade 'B' operators had to attain a Morse speed of twenty words per minute and have a good general aptitude for interception work, qualifying them for a £6 a week salary.

Grade 'C' operators needed to reach eighteen words per minute or less where the applicant shows definite promise and aptitude for wireless interception work. They would receive £5 a week.

Accuracy in recording a message that had been sent in Morse was of fundamental importance, most especially for the code breakers at Bletchley. Everyone has their own distinct style of writing, some more readable than others. When the transmitted messages are in five-letter groups, it was best practice to print the letters in upper case. When these messages had to be taken down at pace, mistakes were often frequently identified further up the chain. To reduce any mistakes, the RSS brought in an innovative technique called 'blocking'. This was to bring clarity and uniformity to the messages, making them easier to read. All those who entered the intercept training at Arkley could already read Morse at a reasonably high speed; the training was intended to improve this speed and blocking was brought in to provide a clear method of transcribing.

Blocking involved transcribing letters in the messages with the least number of strokes possible. Take, for example, the letter 'E', which in Morse is the shortest symbol, a single 'dit' that at speed is come and gone by writing it as a '3' backwards. Letters 'M' and 'N' are done by keeping the pencil on the paper and going up and down accordingly with it. Letter 'B' is up and two loops, all done in a smooth motion. This principle of minimising pencil strokes for each letter of the alphabet to increase transcription speeds was difficult to master. During the training at Arkley, the incentive was to mark any letter not in blocking format as a mistake. This was drilled into the wireless operators and many of them used it instinctively for the rest of their lives.

Not all VIs or amateurs in Britain during the war could be applauded for their activity. In the first few weeks of hostilities, all amateurs had had their wireless transmitters confiscated, but some had kept them. One such amateur, Nicholas Norman, was investigated by the GPO and MI5, and evidence was presented at the Ipswich Borough Police Court. Norman was to plead guilty of using a banned transmitter and was fined £25. All of his radio equipment was impounded by the local Post Office Engineering Department for the duration of the war. Norman fought the conviction and via his solicitor lobbied for his equipment's return: 'MI5 state that the Police think they are being baited by Nicholas Norman and recommend that the apparatus impounded'.

Security was a paramount concern for the work of each VI. It was a testament to the patriotism of each interceptor that their secretive interception duties for the RSS never got out. It was only exposed in the British media once, when an article entitled 'Spies Tap Nazi Code' appeared in the *Daily Mirror* on Friday 14 February 1941. The text would read:

> Britain's radio spies are at work every night. During the day they work in factories, shops and offices. Colleagues wonder why they never go to cinemas or dances. But questions are parried with a smile—and silence. Their job isn't one to be talked about. Home from work, a quick meal, and the hush-hush men unlock the door of a room usually at the top of the house. There, until the small hours, they sit, head-phones on ears, taking down the Morse code messages which fill the air. To the layman these would be just a meaningless jumble of letters. But in the hands of code experts they might produce a message of vital importance to our Intelligence Service. No pay is given to the men who tap the air for these messages. They are drawn from the radio enthusiasts who operated their own short-wave transmitters before the war. A letter of thanks from headquarters telling us that we have been able to supply some useful information is all the reward we ask. Naturally we have no idea of the codes used by German agents. But it is a great thrill to feel you might be getting down a message which decoded, might prove of supreme importance.[9]

The article was at least an embarrassment to the RSS. The newspaper was jumped upon very quickly and the article removed from later issues of the newspaper. It was not the only time that the RSS was to be exposed in the British newspapers. In early 1943, *The Daily Herald* reported a story in Northern Ireland under a headline 'IRA Man in Radio Hunt'. The story contained reference to 'experts with direction finding apparatus' who were monitoring the Belfast area in case an escaped IRA Chief of Staff should broadcast as if from Germany. The *Nottingham Guardian* newspaper contained a note about German paratroopers landing on British soil with pocket wireless transmitters. The paper suggested an official government statement should be made of the existence of any government organisation, which could counter these nefarious wireless activities:

8th September 1944   Controller RSS
TO ALL V.I.s

It is appreciated that with the stand-down of the Home Guard and the reduction of demands on other Civil Defence workers, there is a tendency for some V.I.s to ease up on their work, with is [*sic*.] regretted. You must be aware that all Civil Defence workers are concerned with duties affecting this country only, whereas the work V.I.s covers the whole of Europe and will continue so long as fighting lasts and possibly after that. Please carry on the good work and support our lads at the front.

SCU No. 3 Stirling   Signed J. Wallace Capt.
2nd November 1944

The VI organisation sitting within the RSS was to change the face of British intelligence during the Second World War. These were dedicated men and women, often experienced wireless operators who were invaluable in the new realm of radio technology evolving at pace. The RSS need the VIs and their devotion to duty. The dedication and sacrifice that the VI operators gave was immeasurable. This can be emphasised by some insight into a couple of men who were VI operators but were badly disabled.

One of them, Mr H. J. Long, who lived in North Oxford, was crippled with poliomyelitis and confined to a wheelchair. He used a Hallicrafter receiver set and was a full-time VI. His logs were routinely sent to the RSS HQ at Arkley and his work was highly valued.

In the summer of 1940, a VI living in 'humble circumstances' in the north-west region discovered and intercepted traffic from a new group of German agents operating in New York and communicating back to Germany. The RSS was to write to the VI congratulating him and despatched his RO, who reported 'you may not realise that, owing to too close an acquaintance with a land mine in the last war, this VI is completely bed-ridden and has not the strength even to roll a bandage. You can imagine the kick it gives him to feel he can still get one on the Hun'.

Shortly after his RO visited, a senior officer from RSS HQ was despatched to meet the VI. The operator lay permanently on his back, slightly to the right with a window behind him and his W/T set on the table at his right-hand side. He had fitted long extensions on his W/T set knobs and an array of mirrors enabled him to see what was happening on the set dials. Above his head, he had a frame with his RSS logbooks mounted so he could write his daily entries. In the autumn of 1941, he was to copy a message of vital importance consisting of 4,429 letters and was the only operator in the country to get the complete message, and at the end, he was so fatigued that he could scarcely grip his pencil.

For this outstanding work, the king approved the award of the BEM (Civilian Division) for public service. In recognition of this, he was to get the following letter from the prime minister:

> 10 Downing Street
> 20 December 1941   Whitehall
> My Dear Sir
>   I was stirred to hear of your splendid war work. You have no allowed physical disability to prevent you playing a fine part in the fight against Nazi Germany. May I send you all good wishes and my warmest congratulations upon your success.
>   Yours faithfully,
>   [signed] Winston Churchill

The success of integrating VIs alongside full-time RSS wireless operators at sites like Hanslope and Forfar was at the core of the mission. The VIs more than proved their value to the signals intelligence effort of the RSS. On a typical day during the Second World War, around 300 logs would have been received at Arkley View from the British network of VIs (some of these logs would contain over fifty sheets of collected signals). As the RSS was to evolve in the first two years of the war, the service would need to rely on a nationwide network of stations for both intercept and DF. They were dealing with a target spread across continental Europe and would need both sufficient professional manpower and fixed sites to maximise the potential for coverage of the enemy networks.

Stations

We fought in no battles and won no medals ... to capture the vital enemy
signals and we kept our work secret for half a century.

Ray Wright, wireless operator at Gilnahirk RSS Station

The whole organisation is run in accordance with modern ideas which are very
different from traditional notions of Army discipline.

Letter from the RSS to Merchant Navy Radio Operator Mr Mitchell

A large fairly nondescript country house on the right-hand side of the road leading to Stirling Corner in Barnet was to become the hub for the RSS during the early years of the Second World War. The organisation had marked out its success at Wormwood Scrubs but it had been quickly realised then that it needed its own headquarters, with a dedicated analysis and monitoring function. On 3 October 1940, the unit moved to Arkley View, 2 miles north of Barnet, a house and grounds that had already been requisitioned by the GPO as an intercept station. The move was expedited when the German Luftwaffe had targeted the area of London, which contained Wormwood Scrubs Prison. In September 1940, a bomb hit an outbuilding housing the MI5 Registry.

Log sheets from the stations or VI operators were sent to a covert address, referred to as 'Box 25', which was a cover name for the RSS HQ at Arkley View near Barnet, North London, before a full-time listening station was established at Hanslope Park from June 1941 under the leadership of Capt. Prickett. Arkley would become the operational HQ of the RSS, directing the intercept and DF priorities and being the representative voice on a number of committees with GC&CS, MI5, and MI6. Hanslope would become the administrative HQ, and the hub for all RSS engineering, DF, and other secret engineering work that often involved the likes of Alan Turing from Bletchley.

It was at Arkley that teams called the Collation and Discrimination Departments would sift through the logs, extracting all the information they could out of the interceptors' log sheets to discern patterns and frequencies of interest. Any decoding that was needed would be sent through to Bletchley Park. Arkley would become the experts in *Abwehr* traffic, and from 1941, it was placed under the control of Section V of SIS.

The hierarchy of the fledgling RSS began to take shape. The following were the organisations senior leadership team: Lt-Col. John Pendry Worlledge, CO RSS; Maj. Lacey, 2iC RSS; and Maj. Lord Sandhurst, Commander of VIs.

Arkley HQ was initially led by Worlledge, but after he resigned on an issue of policy in the summer of 1941, he was replaced for only a brief period by Lt-Col. Frederick Stratton, former professor of astrophysics at Cambridge. Stratton was subsequently moved aside by Brig. Gambier-Parry in the latter half of 1941 to make way for the younger Lt-Col. Kenneth Morton Evans (G5KJ) who was to create his office headquarters on the first floor of Arkley View, remaining there until the end of the war. He was given the salubrious title of deputy controller RSS. At the outbreak of war, Morton Evans was a company commander with the 4th Battalion, The Welsh Regiment (TA). His course of the war was to fatefully change after consuming a Pembrokeshire sausage, which infected him with Trichinosis. He was duly placed on sick leave until the spring of 1940, when returning from a medical board. On a train home, Morton Evans met Capt. Edmund Vale, the then RSS Regional Officer for Wales, who encouraged him to use his rehabilitation time at home effectively by listening into potential enemy signals and reporting them through to the RSS.

Another key figure was Maj. Hugh Trevor-Roper, and his Section Vw, which was to become a critical component to the RSS, and he was a stalwart of Arkley. He wanted to retain his team in Barnet as it was the contact with the teams collecting the first-hand information from listening on short-wave wireless that was vital to the onward analysis. Among friends, he was also glad to be away from the confines of Cowgill's influence in St Albans.

Trevor-Roper was well ahead of the game when it came to the interpretation of what was contained in the *Abwehr* messages. Trevor-Roper also brought with him Gilbert Ryle (the Waynflete professor of philosophy at Oxford); Stuart Hampshire (fellow and warden at Wadham College, Oxford), and Charles Stuart (a history don at Christchurch College, Oxford).

Trevor-Roper used to ride with the Bicester Hunt along with both Maltby and Gambier-Parry. The participants of the hunt would often be served drinks outside The Crown pub in Shenley Brook End, a village just to the west of Bletchley. It was a pub with a degree of celebrity, as it was where Alan Turing stayed until 1944.

As the RSS expanded during the early stages of the war, its hub at Arkley View needed to evolve with the organisation. There was discussion in early 1941 to evacuate the RSS Headquarters, D/F control, and Barnet intercept site from Barnet to the vicinity of Warwick in case of Luftwaffe targeting. Offices and living accommodation could have been erected in less than three weeks at the proposed site, but the idea was later abandoned, even though they had already moved extensive quantities of stores to Leamington station in preparation.

The service was to take on much more staff to do its collation work. One of those was Bob King, who worked at the site from January 1942, at the time being underage for general service. He worked in the General Search Department, and his work was to identify suspicious stations broadcasting over the airwaves in Britain from the log sheets sent through from the dispersed VI collectors.

As Arkley expanded, the number of huts had to be increased at the back of the View, which would house the General Search and Discrimination Groups and also any teleprinter services teams. Close by, to the right of Arkley Lane, was where the orderly room and administrative sections were housed at Oaklands, another large house just across the road on Arkley Lane. Oaklands also contained the orderly room and despatch riders who would take important intercepted messages to Bletchley Park. Staff from the main site at Arkley View would often use Oaklands for club meetings and to try to instil some military ethos into the RSS operators wearing uniform.

Arkley was closely connected with Ravenscroft Park in Barnet, where a lot of the RSS wireless operators were tested in their Morse code skills, overseen by a testing officer from the GPO and run by CQMS Soames, who was later to transfer across to The Lawns. In the grounds of Ravenscroft was an intercept station, manned by twenty operators from the GPO Engineering Department, which collected Central European diplomatic traffic. Ravenscroft was also used for billeting of these GPO engineers and RSS staff. The officers' and sergeants' messes were located a stone's throw from Arkley View, directly opposite at Scotswood. There were other large houses in vicinity of Arkley View, including Rowley Lodge, Meadowbank, and The Lawns, which were used for billeting RSS staff, messing, and also acted as training venues for new recruits.

The main functions at Arkley were intercept and scrutiny of all logs for signals of interest; RSS operator groups, which retained the target knowledge for each *Abwehr* or other intelligence services radio network; induction of new RSS recruits; control of DF stations and RSS Mobile Units; traffic analysis and deductions—RIS under Hugh Trevor-Roper; radio training; and oversight of RSS Liaison and representation on XX Committee (Col. Morton Evans).

Of most significance was the team referred to as Discrimination, which was responsible for the intercept and scrutiny of the signals logs from VI and permanent RSS interceptors. It also had subsidiary sections such as the Collation and Allocation teams, along with the teams that coordinated the teleprinters and landline maintenance throughout the RSS estate across the country.

The times of broadcast and the call signs used in the transmissions would help the search teams to pattern match from previous logs, allowing them to pinpoint both halves of a two-way exchange, often operating on different broadcast frequencies. The German short-wave transmissions were always in the frequency range between 3–12 MHz. All this would help shape the knowledge behind the thirteen or so German intelligence networks that the signals emanated from.

The basis of the RSS network was the GPO telephone conference system, which permitted an intercept from any station to be played to a number of DF station operators simultaneously so they could get a bearing of the signal being transmitted. The DF operator would have had the interception signal playing in one of his earphones and the sound from his own receiver in the other. When the two signals matched, he knew he was locked on to the correct target.

An important part of the operator's work was the initial recognition and subsequent elimination of radio transmissions from our own Allied forces, and any from foreign Axis forces that the military 'Y' service collectors would have responsibility for.

One of the key functions of Arkley was the daily log processing and administration around the RSS Groups. It needed a veritable army of skilled administrators. One of these was Ruth Luxford, who had enlisted into the WRNS in December 1943. She was given a number to ring when she enrolled, and it happened to be a direct dial through to the RSS at Arkley View.

She secured an interview with Lt-Col. Bellringer:

> I was given a written and typing test on the spot and was then told that if I proved suitable I would receive notice by post. I received a letter from Capt. J.A. Allerton, Royal Signals, P.O. Box 25, to say it was agreed that I should start employment on January 3rd 1944 and enclosed was a pass to admit me through the security gate.... I was escorted to Lt. Col. Morton Evans and had to sign a few forms of entry which included the Official Secrets Act. From an upstairs office in Arkley View I was then taken to Major John Howard, Group 2 R.S.S. Discrimination S.C.U.3. After a very friendly welcome chat he suggested that I spend a short time with each group in the room to get the gist of work I would be doing. Three essential things were required of me; typing, to be able to print quickly, and to have a good memory.[1]

Despite the lure of a ten-day holiday every three months, Ruth persevered with the mundane and tiring administrative work. She highlighted some of the methods the RSS employed at Arkley:

> The work was tedious and monotonous, checking and re-checking numerous sheets straight from the teleprinters—always with hard working, friendly folk

willing to help to make the task more interesting. Top Secret signs stamped on every paper around and scramble phones gave one a real feeling of doing war work although of course not being able to talk about it to anyone, not even one's family. The months went by and the routine was consistent.

The lunch breaks in the canteen were often very cheerful, especially if Ron Delahunt was encouraged to play Boogie Woogie on the piano. Sgt. Al Webster ran classes some evenings for ballroom dancing—these proved very popular and were great fun. We had a bomb drop behind our site but luckily no one was hurt—plenty of glass and the office covered in plaster.[2]

Work began on the building of a Northern Ireland RSS intercept site at Gilnahirk in the Castlereagh Hills after a survey undertaken in November 1939. It was operational by May 1940, manned by GPO civilian staff. The main building itself contained twelve double-banked positions, and by 1942, the site consisted of five separate buildings. The site was to include a medium-wave DF station, a short-wave DF station, a wireless intercept station, and nine mobile vans for detecting illicit transmissions in the province. The Pantechnicon vehicles were designed specifically as mobile wireless detection vans and were routinely deployed along the border with Ireland.

In total, the Second World War Gilnahirk RSS site would have a total manpower of fifty-eight GPO civilian personnel who would man the fifty-two radio sets twenty-four hours a day over the course of three watches.

Ray Wright was one of the Royal Signals personnel based at the Gilnahirk site in Northern Ireland. He initially had the ambition of joining the Merchant Navy as a radio operator while studying at Cardiff Wireless College during the war. The principal at the college was to persuade him to take a different approach and improve his Morse skills for a role he might be interested in. He had not been keen on serving at sea, with stories his family had been told of his cousin working as an engineering officer with the Merchant Navy, and his father encouraged him to look into the offer. He went through the lengthy vetting process to get the appropriate security clearance and was subsequently invited to Arkley View. Wright spent the three months at the RSS headquarters improving his Morse skills before taking on a short clerical duty in the Arkley traffic section. He was soon selected for a post at Gilnahirk:

I left Arkley in April 1945 and said goodbye to all my colleagues in the hut … and made my way to London to take the train to Scotland, eventually finding my way to Stranraer. I went by ship from Stranraer to Larne in Northern Ireland and as the war was still in progress we had a Royal Navy escort … nevertheless I arrived and took a train from Larne to Belfast where I was to be picked up by a truck and taken to Knock.

The truck eventually arrived and I reported into the camp administration office which was an old country house in Barnett's Road with the name of

Crofton Hall. The grounds had a high wire fence around the perimeter and a number of Nissen huts were located near the house.... I was given a day to settle in and then taken to where the work was done, the intercept station at Gilnahirk.

The station was manned 24 hours a day and staffed by three shifts. As far as I can recall the shifts were from 7am to 3pm, 3pm to 11pm, and the night shift was 11pm to 7am. A separate Nissen hut at Crofton Hall provided a quiet place to sleep for those coming off night duty if your own hut had members who were off duty and up and about.

The station, comprising of a long low shed-like structure set in open country. Inside there were banks of radio receivers along each wall in the receiving room. A supervisor's desk was placed in the centre at one end. On my first day on shift I was informed that my main job was to maintain the land line link ... my main job was to send and receive messages via the on-line Morse link while others did the more challenging jobs of meeting 'skeds' i.e. intercepting enemy traffic.[3]

There were the old RSS hands some of whom had been involved in the communications business all their lives, either professional telegraphists or as radio amateurs. Their contribution to the war effort and their peers at other stations must have been enormous. Some had been former VIs who had been drafted into the RSS and into uniform. A few lived locally and went home after shift. Others who came from elsewhere lived on camp and they were a very fine bunch of men for whom I had the greatest respect. They were mainly middle aged, some even older, and they came from a variety of different backgrounds. I would describe these worthy gentlemen as civilians who had been put in uniform for either convenience or for administration purposes. They were not soldiers in the full sense of the word.[4]

Capt. Joe Banham was the officer in charge of the RSS operation in Gilnahirk from the beginning to the end of the Second World War. Gilnahirk was referred to colloquially as 'Station No. 4'. Prior to 1 October 1942, the wireless station at Gilnahirk was under the control and direction of the RSS. Alongside the creation of a fixed intercept site, a scheme to recruit VIs in Northern Ireland began. The Gilnahirk station's DF system relied on the Marconi Adcock installation, which comprised of four 10-metre-tall antenna all linked together into an underground tank.

As with VI operations on the mainland, the physical RSS log sheets were sent to Barnet. But logs carrying vital intelligence were sent electronically using GPO teleprinter lines, which were manned by three dedicated GPO teleprinter operators.

It was the Discrimination Section at Arkley that spent its time mapping out the German Intelligence service radio networks. The General Search Section was headed up by Capt. Tant (referred to affectionately as 'Auntie'). This team was vital to the Arkley operation. They were able to ascertain the movement of operators and the position of transmitters very quickly. Through detailed analysis of operating procedures, call sign usage, the preambles to broadcast messages, and any locational information ascertained through DF made it possible to divide the Axis intelligence radio networks into distinct groups.

The group would allocate four to five sections of the radio spectrum, and a group of discriminators (under a group leader) would study the logs from both the full-time interceptors and VIs. Suspect unidentified signals were logged in a call book with information regarding call sign, time of intercept, frequency, and any transmission procedures used. This allowed for cross-comparison on networks and stations operating at the same time, and the information would be sent to the relevant group in a nearly Arkley hut.

A separate traffic analysis team under Hugh Trevor-Roper referred to formally as the Radio Intelligence Section (RIS) resided in the upper storey of the Arkley View headquarters building. It was regarded as the most secret of all the RSS teams. It was this team that received the decrypted and translated messages for studying and picking apart the German Intelligence networks. It was the RIS that guided the priorities for interception and helped advise the group leaders as to what to focus the various group's interception efforts on in the short-term.

The Analysis Section at Arkley identified and classified various Axis radio networks into a number of distinct groups, each of which had dedicated staff working against and were allocated code names (in capitals):

Group 1 (HARRY) and 6: number of *Abwehr* networks controlled from Hamburg transmitter. Networks were usually long-distance radio links with clandestine agents operating overseas, as far afield as South America, the USA, Angola, and Mozambique. The group was run by Chief Petty Officer Denis (the only RN member of staff at Arkley).

Group 2 (BERTIE), 4, and 18: *Abwehr* station (code-named SCHLOSS) near Berlin, which was controlled by the RSHA (*Reichssicherheitshauptamt*). This was arguably the most significant of all the groups monitored by the RSS. The network had linkages and sub-centres across Europe, as far afield as Poland, Norway, and Spain, which routed daily information back to Berlin. The sub-centres controlled their own networks with the regional RSHA offices in major towns and cities.

Group 3 (WILLIE): covered the *Sicherheitsdienst* (SD) network based out of Wiesbaden, which was linked to outstations in North Africa and occupied France. Analysis of the Wiesbaden traffic in the summer of 1940 gave many clues to the German offensive of May 1940 (although unnoticed at the time) showing the value of tapping into German intelligence agent networks to get strategic intelligence on German intent.

Group 5 (PATRICK): a Prague-based network operating around Central Europe with additional links to sub-stations in Italy.

Group 6: a small indeterminate network linked to the Group 1 set up.

Group 7 (VIOLET): Vienna-based German network with links to the Balkans, Turkey, and, later in the war, the Aegean and Greece.

Group 8 (IVOR): covered the traffic from the Italian secret intelligence networks mostly operating out of North Africa and Spain.

Group 11 and 19: Jewish communications.

Group 12: covered Russian resistance groups.

Group 13: Himmler's *Sicherheitsdienst* (SD) network of high importance to the RSS. It was originally an *Abwehr* network operating out of Hamburg (similar to Group 1), but after its takeover by the RSHA in 1944, the centre transferred to Berlin.

Group 14: Berlin-based diplomatic network, using the German Post Office point-to-point wireless stations. The networks main transmitter was at Nauen.

Communications between all units, stations, and the GC&CS were via telephone and teleprinter. The Communications Section at Barnet was connected by W/T to the overseas stations, with cable to the interception site at Gibraltar. Cable was also used to relay traffic to Cairo and Rome.

The Discrimination Group had a number of core functions.

RIS (Trevor-Ropers group) produced a multitude of network diagrams.

(*Amt Mil* being the military division of the German *Abwehr*; when Canaris was arrested, the *Abwehr* ceased to function as an effective intelligence organisation, and from 1944 to 1945, *Amt Mil* continued to operate as it had done.)

Group 13 was the W/T communications network for the Amt VI of the *Reichssicherheitshauptamt* (RSHA), which was the central office of SIPO and SD. The RSHA primed itself on carrying out Himmler's strategy as Minister for the Interior and *Reichsführer* SS for the police and espionage/counterespionage work. Group 13 traffic steadily increased over the course of the war. In the middle of 1941, the RSS had just three Group 13 services covered, which rapidly increased to thirty-three. The RSS regarded the most important sign of this expansion to be the building of a large W/T station in Prague, which was to work alongside the station at Wannsee.

The *Abwehr* was reliant on its W/T networks and became indispensable to its operational work worldwide. They produced high-value reporting in the form of W/T telegrams to the OKW and its subordinate command structures. To the contrary, the German SD service stations outside Germany did not have a significant uptake in using W/T communications during the early years of the war, as they trusted the method less than the *Abwehr*. The SD teams seem to be more conscious of the potential threat from interception than their *Abwehr* counterparts. They did, however, rely on it to transmit urgent reports during crisis periods or when other means of communications failed.

By 1943, the SD was making plans for stay-behind agents in occupied Europe, equipped and deploying with W/T transmitters. Often, planning would be reliant on just a few of these scattered individual agents.

The RSS developed great inroads into the PARIS network, identified as Service 13/36, which helped expose the preparations of an invasion network in France. As the RSS interceptors were to establish, it was difficult to find stay-behind network wireless traffic with their intermittent nature. As the Mediterranean Theatre evolved and the Allies advanced through Italy, the SD and *Abwehr* networks became overrun before they were established and the RSS requirement was to get access to any captured agents or equipment so they could understand the operating procedures being used.

The site at Arkley View consisted of the main house and, at the back, a number of one-storey huts around 100 feet long. Being temporary, they could be easily extended as they often were. Each of these huts housed different sections of the RSS Discrimination Group, such as the Duty Office, General Search, Groups, and the Collation and Allocation teams. The mainstay of all this work was the painstaking scrutiny of logs from the full-time interceptors at places like Forfar and Hanslope and the VIs scattered around the country. At the height of the war, Arkley would receive and process 1,000 logs every day from interceptors. These logs were examined to identify any new German Intelligence networks or operators and also to keep monitoring those previously known and recorded. The logs would be identified through the time of transmission, frequency, type of radio procedure used, a call sign, or information in the preamble of the message. Call signs were often changed on a daily basis. Not far from Arkley were The Granary and Arkley Lodge, which had DF control centres linked through by landline to other RSS sites.

This information was collated and shared between the various teams in numerous huts. In one hut, a wall had been dedicated to mapping out the German Intelligence Service radio networks using pieces of string and card. It was covered with a curtain to prevent any visitors to the site identifying what the operators in the hut were doing.

One of the biggest RSS stations during the Second World War was Forfar, which became operational in 1943 to complement the interception work at Hanslope and Arkley, at a prohibitive cost of £90,000. It was known within RSS circles as the 'No. 5 Intercept Station'. Lt-Col. Maltby was to announce the new station functional at the RSIC on 9 September 1943, although 'it would not be in full production for some time'. Forfar was going to be vital for the RSS mission as it had excellent reception of German wireless transmissions. Hanslope was often at the mercy of environmental conditions, which affected the interception of German transmissions. This fading and drifting was such a problem that the RSS built the interception site in the far north of Scotland. The site was originally selected by Capt. Walter Robertson from the Royal Signals, who had been working at the listening station at Thurso and was also a keen member of the Forfar District Amateur Radio Society. He reconnoitred the local area with his receiver set up over a number of nights and found the ideal location. Robertson was to become second in command at the station, under the leadership of Maj. McHarg.

No. 5 Intercept station was located at Montreathmont, adjacent to a wooded area a mile west from the Kinnell crossroads on the Arbroath to Brechin road. It consisted of a two-storey main building with flat roof, which housed the wireless operators on the ground floor and the DF operators on the upper floor. The long flat roof was adorned with the DF aerials, but most of the aerial arrays were situated on an adjacent building. In between the main building and the road were a number of Nissen huts, which were used to accommodate the station's staff. Many of the Arkley HQ engineering staff were involved in setting up these remote RSS stations. One of them was Robin Addie (G8LT), who helped build Forfar:

When we came to do the station at Forfar, which was a very big one, we had no public supply at all. We had to provide all out own power and we had to build a separate power station and we put in three beautiful Rustin-Hornsby slow speed diesel alternators and those used to run very merrily indeed in charge of a very well qualified engineer. He had two available for running and one under maintenance and as far as I know we never went without power even though the public supply wasn't available at Forfar.[5]

The wireless operator worked an arduous shift pattern to maintain a permanent watch on German Intelligence services radio networks. There were three shifts between 8 a.m. and 4 p.m.; 4 p.m. to midnight; and midnight to 8 a.m. The teams would routinely listen into known frequencies, which were referred to as 'Schedule Operations', and also more speculative sweeps across a frequency range, which were known as 'General Searches'.

Some of the Forfar recruits had been identified by staff at the Caledonian Wireless College in Edinburgh, who would select specific students who had the requisite skills for RSS work. Others were deployed up from Arkley.

On 8 January 1943, tragedy was to hit the Thurso DF station when one of the operators was to be electrocuted and later died. It was to cause a widespread safety review across all the intercept, mobile unit, and DF sites. Advice cards were produced and issued to all the stations on the best practice for the treatment of electric shocks.

Bob King worked as part of the Arkley View Discrimination Section, one of the most important sub-units of the RSS. He was an experienced radio amateur before the outbreak of war and was an ideal candidate for the RSS work:

My interest in radio started with crystal sets in 1936 and I graduated to two-valve shortwave wireless sets constructed from an old battery KB Pup medium wave set. Listening to broadcasting stations, including a Spanish civil war one which closed as the enemy approached, I realised that there were many Morse signals which I longed to understand. So I taught myself to read Morse Code and reached a good speed by listening to press stations apart from radio amateurs.

I used to get break-through on my simple radio sets from Harry Wadley, G8LV, who ran a wireless, watch and gun shop nearby on the Market Square in Bicester. In 1941, knowing my ability to read Morse, he must have given my name to Box 25, because a Captain Hall called to check me over and asked if I was willing to use my knowledge for a job he had in mind. Soon the police superintendent came over from the police station opposite to my house (he had known me and the family for years) to check that I had no criminal record I suppose. However, I must have passed because the Captain returned a few days later with forms for me to sign, dire warnings about secrecy and a pad of sheets plus envelopes, stamps and a few instructions to listen on a certain band of frequencies putting down all the Morse signals I could read. The receiver I used was an Eddystone All World Two, a two-valve set not all that easy to operate. I made a pre-selector (radio frequency amplifier) to work in front of the Eddystone which added considerably to the difficulty of operating it but also improved the performance. Later I bought an American Sky Buddy superhet receiver which, again using the pre-selector, gave excellent results and throughout 1941 I spent any available time listening and getting a large pack of acknowledgements from the Regional Office in Cambridge.

Came 1942, within six months of call-up expectations, when a letter arrived from Box 25 suggesting that I may like to consider taking up full-time work with the Radio Security Service or otherwise they would have to let me go to be called up in the normal way. My idea at that time was of course to shoot down Me 109s from a Spitfire, or as otherwise. After much soul searching and advice I accepted the Box 25 offer especially as I had grave doubts about my passing the medical for air crew, as spectacle wearing was not usual.

In January I found myself trudging up, in deep snow, the driveway to Arkley View after the first experience of travelling alone by train and bus in my life. Little did I know that Arkley was to be my home for the next five years.

Captain Bellringer interviewed me and told me I was too young to be enlisted. I thought that this must be another cock-up when he added, 'But we can put your age up six months. You will not be the first to do so.' Nevertheless at that time I always did as I was told and was sent to a private billet with Gerald Openshaw, a man of the world, in the luxury of a Humber staff car. From then on VIP treatment ceased and Signalman King got used to a khaki uniform instead of his ATC Flight Sergeant's one left behind in Bicester. After Morse speed and procedure knowledge testing at Ravenscroft Park in Barnet I was despatched back the 'View' to be given a seat between Captain Tant and Sergeant Edwards, a man with a limp, a bent back, a chain smoker, bad temper and yet in Royal Corps of Signals uniform. I hesitate to think what civilians thought of the sight of him hobbling along the road.

I was presented with a pile of VI logs and told to identify the stations recorded thereon. Apparently I passed because I continued to do this work with variations for the rest of the war. Nearly all my colleagues were radio amateurs from all walks of life and so my true education began in earnest in a way school could not provide.[6]

Eric Chambers was at Arkley when Bob King joined in January 1942 and was regarded as an old hand by the new recruits. Chambers was a keen cyclist, and Bob recalled:

I thought I was no sluggard but he used to steam past me on his racing bike most mornings going into work from Barnet. I was always impressed by his form of complete stillness of body with just his legs working. It's a funny thing one remembers.[7]

The operators would really appreciate the enemy wireless operators who would repeat the transmission, as they often had to due to fading of the signal. If the sender repeated the transmission, it allowed the RSS interceptors to double check their original take.

Any non-machine-coded traffic collected at Arkley was originally exploited by a team at Bletchley Park headed up by Leslie Lambert (G2ST) who also doubled up as the BBC storyteller A. J. Alan. He was to be succeeded early on in the war by Oliver Strachey, which would generate the Intelligence Summary Oliver Strachey (ISOS) Ultra product. Strachey was succeeded by Denys Page (who was professor of Greek at Oxford University, and later master of Jesus College, Cambridge). Morton Evans fostered a good working relationship with Bletchley and would regularly meet up with Denys and Trevor Roper over a bottle of Russian vodka.

The GC&CS Department at Bletchley Park, which would deal with the machine cipher material from the RSS, was headed up by Dilly Knox, which generated the Intelligence Summary Knox (ISK) Ultra product. This department was taken over later in the war by Peter Twinn. Twinn was a regular attendee, along with Denys Page, at the intercept priorities committee meetings with MI6 and MI5.

By the spring of 1943, the RSIC pioneered a project to create a Central Card Index in London for the use of ISOS recipients, under the proposal from Maj. Melland, the War Office representative on the committee. The idea was to economise on the time and manpower to carding and classifying the ISOS material in his section. As the RSIC chairman concluded, the proposal would only work if Section V were to move to London:

... since the Section V Index is by far the most important one in existence, the Central Index would have to be built upon it, and the resources of the other interested departments if necessary added to it.[8]

The Joint Index, as it was to become known, was in reality an index of people and not of subjects; it would have had to be supplemented by the ISOS Subject Index maintained by MI5 and four of the MI5 staff engaged on the index. It was to be accessible to any recipient of ISOS or ISK via personal visit or, if required due to operational urgency, via scrambler telephone. The index would be overseen by the present head of the Section V Index.

RSS War projected budget estimates 1945–1946	
	£
Salaries and Wages	530,000
Subsistence	40,000
Works and Buildings	32,500
Purchase of Stores and Technical Equipment	55,000
Transport	1,500
Travelling	10,000
General Expenses	12,500
VI Expenses	15,000
Total	696,500

Just as in the First World War, the DF of a radio signal was to be vitally important to understanding the importance of a transmission to discriminate the user. Originally, the RSS had to rely on the GPO DF stations at St Erth in Cornwall, Gilnahirk in Northern Ireland, Sandridge near St Albans, and Thurso in the far north of Scotland. From 1941 onwards, the RSS was to develop its own independent access to a nationwide efficient DF network to locate and triangulate suspect radio signals. Knowing where these signals were being transmitted from would be of value to ascertain whether it was the *Abwehr*, *Gestapo*, or *Sicherheitsdienst* (SD), as they would use different radio and cipher systems. During the course of the Second World War, Bletchley Park was to decipher 268,000 RSS messages they had collected. The RSS were responsible for the identification and subsequent capture of five of the twenty-three German *Abwehr* agents who had been sent to Britain in 1941. Lt-Col. Maltby describes:

… this business of getting the D/F operator onto the signal had to be done very very quickly indeed, because obviously these stations who are pretending not to exist are on the air for a short a time as possible. And I think we were able to do it in 15-20 seconds, so the whole thing had to be very highly organised and very highly drilled.[9]

The following table shows Naval SIGINT organisation in the UK from May to June 1944. It is copied from *History of SIGINT in WWII* (p. 793).

Y Stations	Sets	D/F Stations	VHF Coastal stations
Cupar	10	Cupar	Sheringham
Portrush	1	Portrush	Trimingham
Shetlands	2	Shetlands	Winterton
Scarborough	120	Anstruther	Southwold
Chicksands	10	Bower	Felixstowe
Flowerdown	32 German Naval, 17 Japanese Naval, and 6 Spanish/Portuguese Naval	Scarborough, Kilminning, Oban, Norwich, and Ford End	Aldeburgh, Scarborough (Withernsea), Fayreness, and Abbotscliff
Sutton Valence	1	Pembroke	Ventnor Portland
Pembroke	1	Land's End	Lyme Regis
Naval Section		Sutton Valence	Torquay
GC&Cs	7	Perran, Lydd, Crawley, Chilbottan, and Goonhaven	Looe and Coverack

DF would usually produce an ellipse of high probability. An interesting signal would be put on a line to all DF stations, and the DF operators would match the signal on their equipment and DF it. This DF and the work of the General Search/Discrimination teams at Barnet would successfully produce the layout of many of the German Intelligence Services radio networks, without any input from Bletchley Park.

The central DF plotting room conference control at Barnet was designed and built by an ex-GPO engineer, Gerry Openshaw (G2BTO), who had enlisted into SCU3 in January 1942. The RSS DF network consisted of Adcock DF units situated at St Erth, Leedstown (Penzance), Bridgwater (Somerset), Wymondham (Norfolk), Gilnahirk (Belfast), Forfar (Angus), and two at Thurso. These were all connected into the GPO landline network, at the centre of which was the special telephone switchboard and plotting unit team at Arkley View. This was situated in the room to the left of the front entrance. The ATS girls there plotted the results on a large map of Europe. Communications with the outstations on the communal landline was by both speech and Morse code via an audio oscillator.

In late 1940, a demonstration of a new DF system (referred to as the 'Spaced Loop Direction Finder') was to take place at Ditton Park for representatives from the RSS, GPO, Air Ministry, and the Admiralty. The system had been developed by scientists at the National Physical Laboratory. The technology was clearly of utility to the RSS/GPO DF network.

The RSS requirement was to have a DF system that could be relied upon to give good bearings at distances up to 500 miles. The wavelength to be covered would be in the range of 2,000 metres to 10 metres. The RSS stipulated that the system should be suitable for the receiver and operator to be housed in an underground tank to avoid interference. Gerald Openshaw was instrumental in bringing in this new system to the RSS with his two colleagues, Capt. Louis Varney (G5RV) and Horace Bannister (G8OM). They also helped take over the servicing and maintenance of the auto-telephone system and teleprinters at Arkley and other local private houses like Ravenscroft.

They were to go on to order seven Spaced Loop DF systems, which were to be installed at sites near each of the existing RSS Adcock DF stations. They intended to replace the Adcock site at Lydd with a new site in Darlington, along with a new East Anglian site away from the current Adcock site facility in Sandridge.

The DF station at Weaverthorpe in Yorkshire trialled the new underground tank Spaced Loop system. These tanks, buried in the ground, screened out any radio interference. This tank was connected to four external aerials linked to rotatable coils (called a goniometer) down inside the tank. After numerous trials, the system was found to be unsuitable and the Weaverthorpe station was closed down after about six months of tests.

The radio operators during their search and survey work would often rely on two receivers to acquire both ends of the transmission, which would be operating on different frequencies. The DF network would consist of Adcock DF units scattered around the country in places such as Leedstown near Penzance, the two sites at St Erth, Wymondham in Norfolk, Bridgwater in Somerset, Forfar in Angus, two sites based at Thurso in the far north of Scotland, and the Belfast site at Gilnahirk. They also had the experimental station at Hanslope Park. In total, these nine DF stations that the RSS relied on were connected into the GPO landline network at the core of which was the telephone switchboard at Arkley View. The GPO engineers that had been recruited at the start of the war by the RSS were used to check and calibrate the DF units, which had been installed by the GPO Engineering Department under the direction of Percy Parker, the GPO engineer-in-chief based in London.

There was only one above-ground DF hut at Hanslope, which was located nearer to Haversham than Hanslope. There were five underground DF tanks located all around Britain. These were located at Wymondham, Harpsdale in Northern Scotland, Leedstown, St Just, and St Erth.

Wymondham was a typical DF station. It comprised of eight staff—a sergeant in charge and seven other ranks. The team would do three eight-hour shifts, but with only one operator at a time actually housed inside the metal tank. During the day, there was other people around with routine maintenance work to be done, such as running the auxiliary power generators in case the mains failed and checking the calibration of the DF equipment. The night shift was from 11 p.m. to 7 a.m. During the long night shift, the operator was on his own entirely.

There were two RSS DF stations near the village of Stockland Bristol outside Bridgewater in Somerset. Both the Caithness and Wymondham tanks were removed recently. The tank at Stockland, Bristol, looks to be still in place in the ground.

It was Maj. Dick Keen who ran RSS engineering, and he was to become an important figure in the history of the RSS. Keen had been formerly employed with Marconi in Great Baddow. He was in ultimate control of the DF network, and was the most significant authority of the DF aspect of radio intercept in the world at that time. He was literally to write the book on the subject and his work is still quoted in patents to this day. Keen had two key assistants in Capt. Louis Varney (G5RV) and Cpl Frank Bott.

The targeted German signals were put on the line to all DF stations on the network and the DF teams would match the signal onto their receivers and DF them. The DF bearings that were produced from this process, plus the General Search or Discrimination, alongside the analysis of radio operating procedures, would generate a great deal of knowledge on the active radio networks. Over time, combining this network knowledge with the decryption work at Bletchley gave a richer picture.

There was a notable link between the RSS and the Foreign Office station at Sandridge. There was not only an intercept station at Sandridge but also a DF station in an adjoining field operated by the RSS as part of their DF network. The material being passed over this network was wireless teleprinter traffic, which the RSS logged as ISTUN (TUNNY) traffic.

RSS Paris: Kommando Ring			
12 June 1944			
Service	Sent	Intercepted	Approximate relation of interception to transmission
Kdo. 180L			
2/3243 Orkan–Taifun	63	63	100 per cent
Taifun–Orkan	57	49	88 per cent
2/3230 Orkan–Monsun	43	51	100 per cent
Monsun–Orkan	45	47	100 per cent
Kdo. 120 Rhoen			
2/33/22 Paris–Rhoen	83	52	63 per cent
Rhoen–Paris	104	87	85 per cent
Kdo. 130 Harz			
2/4044 Harz–Jura	32	33	100 per cent
Jura–Harz	22	19	95 per cent
2/3300 Harz–Taunus	52	24	49 per cent
+Taunus–Harz	(72	29	40 per cent)
2/3266 +Harz–Schwarzwald	(60	11	18 per cent)
+Schwarzwald–Harz	(59	21	36 per cent)
(+: approx. no. of transmissions and intercepts for whole month given for both ends of 2/3266, and up to 28/6 for out station of 2/3300)			

In summary, 692 messages were transmitted and 486 intercepted (70 per cent).

By May 1941, there was genuine concern about a German invasion of Britain. MI6 was making plans in the summer of 1941 to form military mobile units working alongside GHQ whereby the RSS would supply vans and equipment for radio interception. It is certain they would have been integrated into any resistance network that would have been established. Ironically, the Germans would have probably known the locations of all the RSS operators, as the RSGB openly published the RSGB Callbook—a directory of call signs, names, and addresses. Undoubtedly, the known radio hams would have been the first to be rounded up.

The senior officers of both MI8 and MI6 were keen to utilise the skills and experience of the RSS wireless operators in case such an event was to occur. They started to coordinate efforts with General Headquarters (GHQ) to supply the necessary vans and equipment from the present RSS resources.

The GPO personnel embedded within the RSS were deemed to be unsuitable to the role of supporting GHQ in active operations. They recommended that the work should be done by military personnel who could use the RSS vans if required.

The RSS had a significant invasion instruction to guide the service in case of German invasion. The VIs were to 'find out from your employer if he will release you in the event of an invasion, so that as long as you are in unoccupied territory you can put in full-time watch.... HQ will arrange to collect logs from convenient centres, and we can possibly arrange to centralise receiving points'.

Arkley quickly became the operational hub of the RSS Discrimination effort. To fuel this, some 23,000 log sheets were being received at the site every month, which totalled 10,000 individual sheets a day by August 1941. Much of this was *Abwehr* hand cipher traffic. Typically, the machine cipher traffic was being collected and processed at the major military 'Y' service intercept sites at Chicksands, Montrose, Cheadle, Waddington, and Beaumanor.

Arkley had revolutionised the approach to industrial-scale signals analysis and collation and had a marked effect on the British intelligence understanding of the German Intelligence Service operations overseas, most notably in Europe. The *Abwehr* were a hard target and it had taken considerable time, effort, and dedication by some of the country's leading wireless experts and cipher specialists to open up their networks. They were a worthy and respected adversary.

5

Adversary

*By early 1942, the trickle of intercepted Abwehr telegrams had become a flood
... their efforts were supplemented by the Radio Security Service (RSS), which
intercepted enemy intelligence signals and by GC&CS which read them.*

Kim Philby
My Silent War, p. 53

The RSS had successfully filled a niche and found a specialist function within the architecture of British Intelligence to collect German Intelligence wireless traffic. It was one of the main sources for the valued, but highly compartmented Ultra intelligence from the ISOS teams at Bletchley Park.

But the RSS was not unique. Our collective enemy was doing the same thing. There were a number of German signals interception organisations tasked with detecting illicit radio transmissions from deployed SOE, BCRA, or OSS agents in occupied territories. The Army High Command had its own signals agency—*Oberkommando des Heeres, General der Nachrichtenaufklärung* (OKH/GdNA). This was known as Inspectorate 7/VI prior to 1944. The Supreme Command of the Armed Forces also had its own signals organisation—the *Oberkommando der Wehrmacht/Chiffrier Abteilung* (OKW/Chi). This unit had the responsibility for the deciphering of coded radio messages.

The direct counterpart to the RSS in the Germany was the *Funkabwehr*. This catchall phrase is used to describe two distinct organisations within German intelligence—the OKW/WFst/WNV/FU III and of the *Funkabwehrdienst* of the *Ordnungspolizei*. It was this organisation that was used to monitor foreign agents' radio transmissions and also to locate the site of these broadcasts through DF. Any collected cipher material was exploited by a section within the unit led by Dr Wilhelm Vauck. They had the ability to identify the cipher systems being employed, break them, and then decode the actual traffic being transmitted.

Much of the insight into this organisation came from the interrogation of German prisoners through an organisation called the Combined Services Detailed Interrogation Centre (CSDIC). POW intelligence has always played a critical part in intelligence gathering in war. The Second World War was no exception. The Military Intelligence section that was responsible for interrogating POWs was MI19. This actually had a number of roles, one of which was to collect and disseminate intelligence from POW. MI19 was divided into two distinct parts: MI9a dealt with enemy POW and oversaw the work of the CSDIC and MI9b, which dealt with British and Allied prisoners and evaders. Before the war started, all three of the military services established a combined services interrogation centre, which was initially located in the Tower of London. On 12 December, 1939 CSDIC moved to Trent Park, near Barnet in Hertfordshire, just a short distance from Arkley View. This tri-service collaboration and joint approach to POW intelligence gathering stayed firm until the end of the war.

Both the German and British organisations had one core mission to discover and locate illicit wireless transmissions in the territory of or occupied by the respective countries. There were some key differences, though, in that the *Funkabwehr* was ostensibly a defensive weapon, whereas the RSS began with and retained a defensive function but it had also developed a successful offensive function.

The RSS was also defined by being a single centralised organisation unlike the *Funkabwehr*, which like many of its sister intelligence organisations in Germany was fractured by the political divide between the *Wehrmacht* and the Nazi Party. Initially, it fell under the subordination of the WNV/FU III but achieved a degree of independence later was ultimately under the control of Himmler's police machinery.

The *Funkabwehr* was distributed across much of German occupied Europe. A significant central function was maintained in Paris with over 300 radio sets or banks, alongside a further station in Brest. There were further stations at Augsberg and Nuremburg, each with 150 banks engaged in general search tasks for clandestine wireless transmissions. Within a period of two minutes, a suspicious signal could be identified and reported by line to a system of DF networks that could obtain an accurate line bearing of the broadcasts. These bearings could have an error of less than half a degree so could be plotted to an area of between 4 and 10 kilometres, which could take in the region of an additional seven minutes to get this accurate fix.

Once this location was identified, a mobile DF unit could be deployed within the area of the transmission to locate the radio sets being used. If a mobile unit was close to the transmitting sets, the whole process could take less than fifteen minutes, although the accuracy and timeliness of the *Funkabwehr* detection teams has been debated since the end of the war and it may have been broadly exaggerated to discourage the Allies from the use of illicit wireless.

The OKW/WFst/WNV/FU III was the main Germany intelligence unit that dealt with signals security, the interception of illicit wireless traffic, and the location of the enemy's broadcasts. The WNV or *Wehrmachts Nachrichten Verbinden* formed the wireless department of the signals directorate of the OKW. The WNV had the following departments: Administration—Z; Line Communications— KFA; Production—GBN; Ciphers—CHI; and Wireless—FU.

The head of the unit was responsible to the OKW chief of staff. The WNV/ FU had the responsibility for W/T communications of the OKW, the distribution of ciphers and of call signs, frequency bands, the provision of equipment, and security.

With its role strategically positioned within the OKW, the WNV had some degree of influence over the signals organisations of the German military 'Y' services, although, in reality, the Navy and Luftwaffe were autonomous. There was close coordination with the Army, however, as the WNV chief was also the chief of the Army Signals Service (HNW—*Heeres Nachrichtenwesen*). The German Army 'Y' Service would provide the bulk of trained WNV/FU III personnel, particularly in operational areas of German occupied countries.

The roles and functions of the WNV/FU III and the Orpo *Funkabwehrdienst* of the *Ordnungspolizei* were, in many cases, the same. They both had the remit to locate and apprehend a clandestine transmitter. During 1943, the Orpo established complete independence of the control of the OKW, resulting in a geographical division of effort between the police and OKW intercept services. WNV/FU III was to take responsibility for Northern France, Italy, Belgium, southern Holland, the Balkans, and sections of the Eastern Front, whereas Orpo had authority in southern France, Norway, Germany, and the rest of Holland and the Eastern Front. Coordination for both units would lay with the Joint Signals Board in Berlin, which was chaired by the WNV chief.

As was the case in Britain with the RSS and the GC&CS, in Germany, cryptography was dealt with by a separate organisation to that of the interceptors. The enciphered material collected by the WNV/FU was passed to the WNV/CHI, which was concerned with the deciphering of political and diplomatic messages and separately the provision of ciphers for the OKW.

In the early stages of the war, as the German occupation of Europe progressed with speed, a number of *Funkabwehr* companies were created, with many personnel drawn from the German Army 'Y' Service and placed under the command of WNV/ FU III. These *Funküberwachungs* companies were the principal resources of the *Funkabwehr*. They covered the following geographic regions:

612 Intercept Company: Poland, Russia. One platoon
                        maintained in France and one in Denmark.

615 Intercept Company:	Norway and Western Europe.
616 Intercept Company:	North France, Belgium, and southern Holland.
1 (GAF) Special Intercept Company:	Northern Balkans and Italy.
2 (GAF) Special Intercept Company:	Southern and Eastern Balkans.

Operational control of these intercept companies was the responsibility of the *Außenstellen* of WNV/FU. They would have acted as the link between the HQ at Berlin and the intercept companies, directing the latter's interception activity. The Air Force Companies (GAF) were formed in 1942 and covered the Balkans. Each of these companies consisted of a small discrimination section (*Auswertung*), an intercept station of ten double-bank positions (*Überwachungsstelle*), a long-range DF platoon (*Fernfeldzug*), and a short-range DF platoon (*Nahfeldzug*). Each short-range DF platoon contained five sections (*Messtrupps*), each of two DF cars. Including administrative staff, an intercept company would typically have in the region of 130 men.

No. 615 Company was a special unit as it had a capability to intercept VHF radio telephony, including ground to air contacts. The company operated in France, Belgium, and Holland, with a small detachment deployed to Norway. The unit used the cover name URSULA.

The *Funkabwehr* had a degree of cryptographic success against British agents' wireless traffic. They were also involved in the tracking of illicit transmission in Germany. In November 1944, they published a report, which stated: '… all reports regarding known or suspected secret transmitters, suspected radio cases and monitoring reports are to be passed without delay to the local *Funkabwehr* office for appreciation and transmission to OKW/AG/WNV/FU'.

The organisation in general operated much like the RSS, although it was less effective as an organisation and technically less well equipped. The *Funkabwehr* had the following features of interest:

(i) Its role was largely defensive (concerned with the rounding up of Allied agents) as contrasted with the RSS which was largely offensive being involved with attacking the enemy intelligence system at the highest level.

(ii) The fissure between the *Wehrmacht* and the Nazi Party kept the *Funkabwehr* dysfunctional, causing duplication and inefficiency.

(iii) *Wehrmacht* security intercept resources originally came from Army 'Y' services. Liaison with the Army 'Y' service was good, and particularly tough tasks like the Russian Partisans were tackled jointly by the *Funkabwehr* and Army 'Y' service.

(iv) Mobile interception was critical to the *Funkabwehr*, including the employment of Naval cutters and *Fieseler Storchs*. Mobile teams had success in France, Holland. and Greece.

(v)   Search intercept and traffic analysis techniques mirrored that of the RSS. They had recruited amateurs but not on the same scale as the VI teams in RSS. The fixed intercept stations were small, with never more than 20 watches.

(vi) The *Funkabwehr* had a functional intercept station under diplomatic cover in Turkey.[1]

At the end of February 1944, Admiral Canaris was dismissed and Himmler, who had instigated the dismissal with Hitler, demanded the *Abwehr* be merged into the SIPO and SD. The proposal was thrown out by the OKW, and for the next three months, the German Intelligence services were in disarray. Temporary leadership of the *Abwehr Amt* was gifted to Canaris' deputy, *Oberst* I. G. Hansen. The *Amt Ausland* was put under the command of *Konteradmiral* Bürkner and the *Amt* functioned under the direction of SD and SIPO. The OKW resistance was overcome in May that year, and the *Abwehr* was made subordinate to the SD and SIPO, being formally agreed on 1 June 1944. The organisational changes were to 'entail certain changes in the policy and method of the *Abwehr*'. It was to be a major headache for the RIS.

By the spring of 1944, the *Abwehr* was beginning to prepare for the opening of an Allied second front. The threat of invasion in Western Europe had led the *Abwehr* to prepare a new system of wireless communications networks encompassing the *Abwehrkommandos* and their subsidiary *Trupps*, covering territory held by the German Army.

The W/T communications networks for the *Amt Mil* operating within Germany depended on a network of seven fixed stations: BELZIG (Berlin); KRUGSDORF (Stettin); WOHLDORF (Hamburg); COLOGNE; WIESBADEN; SIGMARINGEN (Stuttgart); and VIENNA.

There were other W/T stations attached to various KdMs in Germany but these were not equipped for running a communications network. Six of the stations above have had wireless characteristics of the centres of traffic rings. HAMBURG was one of the most significant stations for the RSS and the centre of its Group I network. BELZIG (originally STAHNSDORF) was for Group II; WIESBADEN, Group III; SIGMARINGEN, Group IV; STETTIN, Group VI; and VIENNA, the centre of all RSS Group VII work.

The whole interoperability of this German *Amt Mil* network was described as following a simple geographical pattern:

BELZIG, as the final recipient of all messages for the *Amt Mil* is primarily the terminus of the trunk lines, so each of the other 6 stations is linked with it by a direct W/T service. WIESBADEN, as the seat of the *Funkleiter* West, coordinates the subsidiary networks of SIGMARINGEN and COLOGNE in the western area, and is responsible for a large network of its own. For this purpose it has W/T links with COLOGNE and SIGMARINGEN; at the same time it is joined to HAMBURG and VIENNA, the first being the location of the *Fulei Uebersee* and the second of the *Fulei Sued Ost*. These in their turn control particular areas—HAMBURG is the reply station for agents overseas and in the Scandinavian area. VIENNA controls, directly and indirectly, communications in Italy, the Balkans and Turkey … these fixed stations receives or will probably receive signals of two types; first there are the signals of agents left behind the Allied lines, which are passed to the interested operational command … the *Amt Mil* at Berlin tried to arrange for agents' messages to be passed direct to it from the stations receiving them (i.e. Wiesbaden, Stuttgart and Cologne) and then to circulate the reports itself to the interested commands.… Secondly there are the signals of the subordinate intelligence units, fixed or mobile, which are at work within the area of each fixed station. Thus SIGMARINGEN, though technically directly under the *Amt Mil* as a W/T station is factually subordinated to KdM STUTTGART and is used by the latter for maintaining contact with its outstations across the Rhine in Strasbourg and Altkirch.[2]

Besides these fixed stations in Germany, the *Amt Mil* had several more temporary wireless stations linked with its emergency HQ, alongside individual KdMs like Munich that had set up their own W/T stations, which were typically linked through to the BELZIG fixed station.

The Germans W/T operators were to have one considerable flaw—a careless use of low-grade cryptographic techniques. During radio transmissions, they would frequently re-encode messages sent in a lower-grade code, word for word, into a higher-grade code for retransmission.

In the autumn of 1944, all the intercept companies of the WNV/FU III were organised into a regiment as the *Überwachungs* Regiment, OKW, under the command of Maj. von Bary. This was largely an administrative change rather than anything that broadly affected the command, deployment, or duties of the intercept companies. The executive control of the intercept units in their respective zones was the responsibility of two *Offiziere für Funkabwehr*, in the central HQ in Berlin. They had no direct oversight of the discrimination (or *Auswertung*) sections of the *Außenstellen*, though they would have had close contact with the officers in charge of these (an analogous situation to the RSS, where the officer in charge (OIC) of operations and the OIC Discrimination, although independent, worked in close collaboration).

There was also an organisation in Germany that mirrored the British amateur radio network. In the interwar period, it was referred to as the DFTV, which stood for the *Deutsche Funktechnische Verband*. Essentially, they were an authorised amateur radio society. Around 1928, the German government officially licenced amateur transmitters, only 500 of which were granted. Just before the Nazi regime got its hold on Germany, the DFTV changed its name to the *Deutsche*

Amateure Sendungs-Dienst (DASD). Its secretary was a Jewish man called Kurt Lamm, who was to later be removed from office. He had built up an extensive relationship with radio amateurs in Britain. Lamm was to suggest that the DASD had become an arm for the Nazi regime. It had restricted its membership to 600, but the organisation had plans to recruit many more to act as short-wave listeners and unable to transmit. It has been estimated there were in the region of 7,000–7,500 radio amateurs in DASD at the height of the war.

At the beginning of the war, a number of DASD members were recruited by Maj. Schmolinske of the *Abwehr* into a clandestine organisation known as the *Kriegs Funkverkehr* (KFV) for *Abwehr* work. The KFV function was to check for illicit transmitters, but after a year, the unit was removed from the *Abwehr* and incorporated into the WNV/FU III.

Many German radio amateurs had been asked by the DASD to intercept suspect transmissions in Germany. Amateurs were also employed for other purposes by the OKW and some of them were issued with special war transmitting licences by the WNV/FU.

These German amateurs were allowed to operate throughout the war, and the RSS had kept an eye on them from April 1942. The DASD was organised into twenty-two districts (*Landesverbände*), each under the control of a district leader. A number of networks and stations were in almost continuous operation on fixed frequencies. Over the course of the war, an RSS study of the DASD network identified fifteen known pre-war German amateurs and provided a list of forty-eight others who were deemed to be certainly involved with the organisation. The assessment from the RSS on the DASD was that there was not a more elaborate organisation that existed in Germany than a few selected members of the DASD, who had been asked by the WNV/FU III to monitor suspect amateur transmissions. Members of the DASD were often drafted into the services to bolster the skilled pool of W/T operators.

A squadron of *Fieseler Storch* aircraft fitted out with close range DF and photographic equipment were placed under the command of the WNV/FU III in 1942. The unit was a squadron in strength and flights were deployed to different operational areas. These aircraft were often described by the local Maquis resistance groups in occupied France as '*Mouches*' (flies) in the more rural areas, when their actions became more open around July–August 1944. Individual units, known as *Kommandos*, were deployed across Europe under the control of the *Außenstellen*. The intent was to use these aircraft in conjunction with short-range ground DF units. Many units were deployed to the Eastern Front and to the Balkans. Any triangulated DF positions taken from partisan transmissions would be followed by a bombing run from the Luftwaffe.

The deployment of these units was constrained by petrol and equipment shortages alongside Allied air superiority across most of occupied Europe. The aircraft achieved little in supporting wider intercept efforts on the ground and were often less effective than the vehicle mounted mobile DF units. The DF capability of these aircraft was limited—HF propagation would negate their effectiveness, but they may have worked better on the VHF sets the groups used towards the latter end of the war. It was only along the Eastern Front where they achieved some successes due to the geography of flat featureless plains and large-scale partisan activity.

Like that of the RSS, the work of the *Funkabwehr* was based on General Search of the radio spectrum and subsequent monitoring of all signals, which could not be immediately identified. The aim of the service was to sustain at least a quarter of all the *Funkabwehr* intercept resources on General Search. Their intercept stations were normally on a small scale and averaged from four to ten banks. They were to establish a sizeable station at Jueterbog in the autumn of 1944 with the combined strengths of 1 and 2 Special Intercept Companies.

The radio networks covered by the *Funkabwehr* were distinguished on a geographical basis rather than one of procedure as was the usual custom for the RSS. The transmissions of SOE and of SIS Section VIII were classed together in a single net, despite all differences of procedure.

1. Western or LCA net—links from the UK to France, Belgium, Holland, Norway, and Denmark.
2. MBM net—covered links between the UK and Czechoslovakia.
3. PS net—all links between the UK and Poland.
4. ZZZ net—covered all links between the UK and the Iberian peninsular.
5. South Eastern or Balkan net—links controlled from the Middle East.
6. Algiers net—covering all links controlled from Algiers.
7. Eastern or WNA net—links working to controls in Russia.

The three-letter groups annotated above were how the nets were identified and they were typically their call signs. The interception teams would maintain a card index system, recording network activity, schedules, and procedures used on each link covered.

It was the responsibility of the *Auswertung* of WNV/FU III to produce a monthly report (called a *Verslachliche Nachrichten*), which contained detailed information on the detection and capture of W/T agents, alongside details of cryptographic information and deciphered texts. This publication was, over time, to become a security risk to the organisation as it was disseminated to comparatively low levels of the *Funkabwehr* and other German intelligence service organisations.

Any captured documents that dealt with agent cipher systems seized during operations were passed through to the Referat Vauck, although realistically, when Allied agents were captured in occupied Europe, both the *Außenstellen* and intercept units would work locally on any cipher documents or traffic before they forwarded it through to headquarters. Referat Vauck was only a small specialist unit, numbering only about thirty-five staff.

The German intelligence DF system was centrally controlled by the *Auswertung* HQ in Berlin. It was a dysfunctional set up and rarely did the intercept stations work effectively with the DF network. But in some areas of Europe, W/T operators would work in the same set room as the DF operators, which would foster some good working practices, akin to what the RSS was doing in Britain. DF assignments were sent out from the WNV/FU III via the nominated *Außenstellen* or intercept company headquarters, which would use DF to augment their standing collection requirements.

Mobile units and their deployments were coordinated through the *Außenstellen* and *Funkmess stellen*, which worked closely with Berlin and the local counter espionage units. Even so, all these units had some independent ability to deploy against specific intelligence leads on illicit radio transmissions. Up to three cars would be employed on a target, but typically it would only be one vehicle. The infamous 'guertel' snifter did not become operational until early 1943, a product of the police technical college at Berlin-Spandau. Exact figures of the success rates of these mobile DF units are hard to come by, but there is some circumstantial evidence of their operational capabilities.

During interrogation, a former member of the Zemke close-range DF platoon of the No. 2 Special Intercept Company confirmed that six agents working for the Allies were caught by the unit in Northern Italy. An RIS report indicated that members of the *Funkabwehr*, under interrogation, had conveyed the relative ineffectiveness of their mobile unit work. Around a dozen agents were rounded up by the *Funkabwehr* in Holland and Belgium, mostly in late 1943. This ineffectiveness was in large part due to the organisational failings and technical difficulties. The mobile teams were constrained by a lack of equipment and technical training. The DF equipment was found to be inadequate when dealing with high-frequency ranges, or when used near large stretches of water or electrical installations, such as transformers or sub-stations. The agents using W/T transmitters were also getting more professional in the way they did their transmissions. They would frequently change locations, only do short bursts of transmissions, use local people as lookouts, and have previously reconnoitred escape routes.

The *Funkabwehr* was never primarily concerned with the intelligence aspects of Double-Cross work, although where there was good cooperation with the counter espionage service, officers of the *Außenstellen* would be kept fully in the picture. Generally, the *Funkabwehr* supervised the technical W/T aspects of the Double-Cross cases, and where Referat Vauck cryptographers were available at the *Außenstellen*, these handled the cipher work.

By September 1940, twenty-one German spies had arrived in Britain. Four of these arrived on the coast by dinghy, two by parachute, and some delivered by fishing vessels, but the majority arrived hidden among the vast numbers of legitimate refugees coming out of occupied Europe. These first-wave German-sponsored agents were often poorly trained and equipped and came from a variety of nations, including Denmark (two), Cuba (three), Belgium (one), Germany (five), Switzerland (one), and Norway (two). Because of their poor training and lack of identity and allegiance, they often gave themselves up at the earliest opportunity. Some of the most determined agents that arrived in Britain were so due to blackmail, or the fact their families were being held as hostages in their home nation. It has been estimated that during the Second World War, there were 120 illicit agents deployed into Britain and thirty of them were made into double agents working to British objectives.

They would often have little appreciation of British culture or ways. One agent was apprehended on a rail journey as when he was asked for the 10s and 6d payment for the ticket, he offered £10 and 6s in return. Many of the German identity document forgeries they had were of such poor quality that they were almost always apprehended.

Not all of them could be successfully turned into double agents, and some refused to cooperate. These were moved to either Wandsworth or Pentonville Prisons, where they were swiftly executed. Over seventeen German agents were to meet this fate, either by hanging or firing squad, often dictated by whether they were military personnel or civilian agents.

Another such German double agent was CICERO, the alias of Elyesa Bazna, who was to become one of the most famous spies of the war. He was dutifully employed as the valet to the British Ambassador to Turkey, Sir Hughe Montgomery Knatchbull-Hugessen, from 20 July 1943 to the end of March/early April 1944. It would later transpire that CICERO had been on the payroll for the German *Abwehr* from October 1943 until April 1944.

He was notorious for photographing vitally secret documents in the British Embassy safe, and sold them via the German Military *Attaché* (and head of the German SD in Ankara) Ludwig Carl Moyzisch to the German Ambassador in Ankara. It has been widely speculated that the intelligence was to include plans for Operation Overlord, the invasion of Normandy in June 1944, but this material did not get to German intelligence until after the war. The RSS and Bletchley were aware from intercepted messages that there was an intelligence leak at the embassy and this was confirmed by October 1943.

In a MI5 memo produced years after the war, the service was categorical:

> He was responsible for a serious leakage to the enemy because for a considerable time he kept highly secret papers in his box at home and carried the key on his person, so that it was a simple matter for CICERO to obtain an impression.[3]

It is certainly sceptical that details for Overlord were ever sent to Ankara, although an interrogation report on a Miss Molkenteller—a clerk from Berlin who was a civil servant from 1942–1944 in Amt VI of the RSHA and acted as the translator for very high-grade espionage material in English received from Ankara—had stated that Overlord was referred to in two telegrams or reports obtained by CICERO.

It is without doubt that Bazna did get access to papers that were in Sir Hughe Knatchbull-Hugessen red official diplomatic box. The ambassador used these boxes, in defiance of warnings from the Foreign Office, to keep secret papers in during the night, often including sensitive operational military plans. Official British Government guidance was as follows:

> Papers must either be in a combination lock safe, the setting of which is changed
> at least every three months or returned in a locked box to the Embassy Offices
> by a British member of staff and not kept at home overnight.[4]

Bazna was described affectionately by one of the staff at the British Embassy in Ankara as a 'clever idiot, suave and always trying to put a fast one across somebody'. He had been born in Istanbul to Yugoslav parents and married to a Greek. He was adept at a number of languages, including French, Turkish, and even some Greek. He had been previously employed as a chauffeur for the Yugoslav legation.

It was on 17 January 1944 that the British were to get conclusive proof that specific leakages were attributable to a British source, and directly from the British Embassy in Ankara. For the princely sum of 5,000 Turkish pounds and a 15,000-pound monthly salary, Bazna had agreed to supply a camera film with photographed secret documents from Knatchbull-Hugessen's diplomatic box. The first film the Germans were to receive from Bazna 'showed documents of a most secret political nature'. Moyzisch was even despatched on the first available aircraft with the film directly to Berlin as it was deemed so important.

From then on, Bazna and Moyzisch were to meet regularly at night to exchange camera films and money. Three weeks after he got on the *Abwehr* payroll, Bazna was to raise his price to 10,000 Turkish pounds per film, which was subsequently agreed by Berlin. Bazna was to supply in the region of forty to fifty camera films in total, often containing multiple photographs of the same document. One of his most significant coups was photographs he took of the protocols of the Cairo meeting between Churchill, Eden, Roosevelt, and the Turkish President and Minister for Foreign Affairs. Moyzisch estimated that he had paid him in the region of 600,000 to 700,000 Turkish pounds (roughly between £75,000 and £88,000).

Bazna was to be eventually caught in January 1944 by the use of a forged War Cabinet paper placed in the ambassador's red box at the embassy as bait. The intent was to test the reliability of Knatchbull-Hugessen's diplomatic box and his valet. The forgery was produced by Victor Cavendish-Bentinck, Chairman of the

Joint Intelligence Committee (JIC), in conjunction with a number of stock brokers he had recruited for the task. The 'investigation shows how many opportunities are afforded to enemy agents where heads of missions insist on working in their own residencies. The precautions necessary to make this practice reasonably safe would involve so much inconvenience that they would outweigh the advantage of working at home'.

Hugh Trevor-Roper was to state on the CICERO work:

CICERO photographed secret documents in the Embassy and sold them to the Germans and we knew all about this and we saw our secret documents being sent to Germany from the German Secret Service in Ankara. But we were hamstrung because we couldn't communicate this fact to the Ambassador by the ordinary telegrams because it was precisely these telegrams which CICERO was photographing and sending to Germany. Therefore, if we indicated that we knew about CICERO the Germans would know that we were reading the messages. So the whole CICERO affair had to be done by sending people out in order to convey personal messages because we simply couldn't afford to mention it in any radio communication we sent out. It wasn't that the Germans were deciphering our traffic, we weren't frightened about that, we were pretty sure that they weren't. It was that when they were deciphered at the other end, the Ambassador's valet was taking them out of the safe, photographing them and sending them to Germany.[5]

As a result of this serious breach in embassy protocol, the Foreign Office published a memo in April 1944 to all the British diplomatic missions around the world stating that all the locks on the red boxes should be changed—a case of locking the stable door after the horse has bolted.

In the early hours of 1 October 1943, a lorry driver called Norman Cameron was on route from Ullapool to Fraserburgh, laden with boxes of fresh Herring. About 11 miles west of Fraserburgh Cameron 'Saw an aeroplane circling at what [he] thought was a low altitude, over the vicinity of Boyndlie Moss, Tyrie. It circled three or four times; [he] saw it was showing a red light … the last glimpse [he] got of it was when it disappeared towards the ground … on the south side of the road'.[6]

Cameron had been driving in sync with another lorry, driven by Ian Park. On seeing the aerial affray, Park pulled up in his lorry, with Cameron shortly behind. Cameron found Park standing alongside a young man and asked Cameron if he could speak German:

The man behind him was a parachutist. I saw he was dressed in flying overalls … the man asked something about soldier in a foreign accent … he then said something about police and telephone; he also said he was a Norwegian.[7]

Cameron called the police from Tyrie Post Office and then arrived in the area just before 12.50 a.m. and accompanied them back to the station.

Norwegian national Nicolay Steen Marinius Hansen (code-named HEINI) arrived in Scotland via parachute on the night of 30 September–1 October 1943 into the Den of Boyndlie, Tyrie, about 10 miles from the town of Fraserburgh in Aberdeenshire. Shortly after landing, Hansen used his torch to signal to a passing lorry and he was in due course arrested by the local police. He was accompanied by two W/T sets, the second of which he was told to hide and the first he was to give up to the British authorities. He was also in possession of a number of wireless cipher books. He was to hide material in a tooth, which he confessed to and this was removed by an officer at Camp 020.

All the CSDIC reporting out of Camp 020 on Hansen was distributed to the RIS at Arkley. In October 1941, Hansen had been working on the construction of a new dry dock in his town of Harstad in occupied Norway, and a few weeks later, he had secured a job in the German Naval stores but got dismissed due to being implicated in theft from the stores and was duly imprisoned at the Fuhlsbüttel Prison in Hamburg.

After a few months, he was visited by German Naval Lieutenant Winter and was offered release if he would agree to learn W/T and be deployed to Spitzbergen to work for the Germans, which he accepted to avoid the rest of his twenty-one-month sentence. After a lengthy period undertaking W/T set operations and maintenance, and the use of coding, he was requested not to deploy to Spitzbergen but to England in the late summer of 1943. He had managed to achieve a transmission speed of fifty to sixty groups per minute and forty to fifty groups per minute in receiving.

He was under the control of Doctor Kellner, who had agreed a contract of 25,000 Kroner to be paid on his return to Norway, with a possible bonus for any valuable information. He was trained for three and a half months on enciphering messages before he deployed. He was given two codes to use, one for his English W/T set and the other for his German W/T set. Both the codes were based on the words of a song. He was even given training on secret writing methods and how to hide them in two of his teeth.

Hansen's mission for England was to arrive by plane, bury his German W/T set on arrival, and give himself up to the authorities while in possession of his English W/T set. After this, he was to secure a job as a miner in Glasgow or Aberdeenshire, which would be convenient for gathering intelligence on the movements of convoys. He was required to provide intelligence on the British military, with a special focus on new types of landing craft being used by the Navy in addition to anything on convoys. His cover story was that he had been trained as a spy and had decided to give himself up to the British.

Hansen had been ordered by Kellner to return to Oslo after some nine months in Britain, regardless of whether his W/T operations had been successful or not. He was to return via Lisbon and Spain or into German-occupied territory. After being detained in Scotland, Hansen was eventually moved down into England and was admitted to Camp 020 on 2 October 1943. Some of the initial assessments on Hansen himself were revelatory 'Hansen himself is a dull, unobservant, peasant type, but he is possessed of a great deal of natural low cunning and shrewdness. He has few scruples and seems quite devoid of patriotism'.[8]

The team had concluded that 'granted his liberty without supervision, Hansen would be a dangerous man. I do not believe that he can be used, as I consider that he cannot be trusted. The only alternative is to detain him'.[9] He was to spend the rest of the war in prison.

During the interrogations at Camp 020, the interrogation team from CSDIC noted 'the ingenuity displayed by the Germans in hiding the secret ink materials'. This had been concealed in a hollow tooth. The report concluded that 'the case of a parachute spy never fails to capture the imagination … urgency, ingenuity, sometimes courage are present'. The reports of all his interrogations were to make their way to Hugh Trevor-Roper in the RSS:

Nikolay Hansen—Wireless Callsigns and Instructions

As the whole object of this spy's mission was to disclose to the British authorities at the earliest possible moment the existence of the English type transmitting set and the code attached thereto, no normal control sign showing that the agent is operating with our knowledge had been found necessary. He was instructed, however, to sign the message with his spy name 'HEINI' if, on any occasion, he had found it possible to operate without our control.

CALLSIGNS:

The callsigns to be used for the English set were fixed, together with the frequences and hours of transmission, as set out below:

| Transmitting times: | Tuesday 1735 (Central European Time) | |
| | Friday 1510 (Central European Time) | |

Agent's Callsign:	Frequency 1	7,402 Khz—callsign—KLM, ATR, SWV
	Frequency 2	6,556 Khz—callsign—FBI, ODC, NSG
	Frequency 3	6,353 Khz—callsign—EJP, UHQ, RZW

Main frequency: Frequency 1

| Control Station: | Frequency 1 | 7,530 Khz 0.8° | FIQ, JAV, HEX |
| | Frequency 2 | 6,870 Khz 1.5° | BDG, MPR, LCN |

The out station uses any one of the above 9 callsigns. The control station replies with any one of the following 6 callsigns. With continuous contact change the callsign, if possible.

The control station will listen for ten minutes for messages from the out station at the above mentioned transmitting times, commencing in October 1943. After getting into touch for the first time only call when there is something to report.

Special Signs: qwp—Do not call for so long
                      qlm—Check the message
                      qtk—Transmission is bad

Hansen had a special code sign to indicate to the Germans that he would shortly be getting hold of his German set. In reply to the international call 'qsv' he would normally reply with the letter 'v' in groups of four or five, with his callsign of the day between each group. If, however, he wished to indicate that he would soon be gaining access to the German set, he would vary this procedure, and instead of sending the letter 'v' in groups of four or five he would send it in groups of eight or ten.[10]

A considerable part of the RSS overseas work during the Second World War was centred in the Middle East. Intercept began to expose a network of German intelligence agents operating in Iran, under the control of a native German called Franz Mayr. Mayr occupied a secretariat post with the *Reichsgruppe Industrie* to the German diplomatic mission in Moscow at the outbreak of war. Intercept and disruption operations in cities like Tehran would lead to Allied interrogations of these agents, which was to help further infiltrate the wider network around Mayr. He was to return to Germany to enlist into a Signals Unit in Potsdam, but after receiving orders from the office of the Führer's military adjutant in Berlin, he was transferred across to the *Sicherheitsdienst* (SD) and volunteered for service in the Middle East. It was not until October 1940 that he reached Iran, but still without any official intelligence training nor any requirements for what Germany was asking him to do. When Britain took the country in August 1941, Mayr went into hiding in the outskirts of Tehran until he resurfaced in March 1942 to meet the Japanese minister, who he had befriended. The minister was to leave Mayr with five W/T sets and some money in return for a letter to the German Embassy in Tokyo giving them a situation report and a suggestion that the *Kameradschaftsdienst Marine* greetings broadcasts should be used as a channel for communication with him, enclosing a code to be used for transmissions.

Over the course of the next few months, Mayr developed a significant network of contacts within prominent circles of Iranian society, including well-placed government officials and high-ranking army officers. Principle among them was

Sandhurst's idea of the Radio Security Service's insignia, developed by Dud Charman (one of the chief RSS engineers at Hanslope Park in WWII – the logo first appeared in news leaflets)

(From GCHQ: the Secret Wireless War 1900-1986 by Nigel West Page 163)

It reads. 'Work Conquers All...the Fox Shall Not Escape'
(Fox refers to the Abwehr signals that Voluntary Interceptors chased around the Short-Wave frequencies)

The crest of the Radio Security Service (RSS)
ost receptive rampant on field electromagnetic, key telegraphic stagnant, bar sinister poignant, quarter censored. Surmounted helmet armour civilian duty

(From GCHQ: the Secret Wireless War 1900-1986 by Nigel West Page 124)

Above left: Lord Sandhurst's idea of the RSS's insignia, which was developed by Dud Charman (one of the chief RSS engineers at Hanslope Park in the Second World War); the logo first appeared in his news leaflets. It reads 'Work Conquers All ... the Fox shall not escape'. The 'Fox' refers to the *Abwehr* signals that VIs chased around the short-wave frequencies. (*GCHQ: the Secret Wireless War 1900–1986 by Nigel West, p. 163*)

Above right: The crest of the RSS. (*GCHQ: the Secret Wireless War 1900–1986 by Nigel West, p. 124*)

Below left: Lord Sandhurst of MI5 and the RSS.

Below right: Maj. Ernest Walter Brudenell Gill (rare photograph taken in 1922).

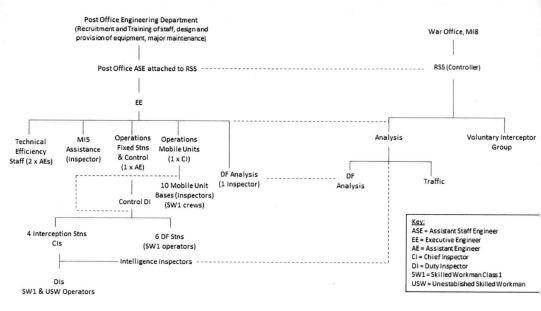

Above: GPO and RSS structures, 1940. (*POST56/144*)

Left: Simpson's organisational plan for the original IWIO. (*WO208/5102*)

A Second World War picture of a GPO DF van.

RSS Radio Operator Wilf Limb at the first receiving position in 'The Granary' at Hanslope Park, August–September 1941. (© *IWM ref HU 68038*)

A HRO receiver. (© *Crown Copyright, by kind permission of Director GCHQ*)

A HRO receiver, inside top. (© *Crown Copyright, by kind permission of Director GCHQ*)

Above: Aerial photograph of Hanslope Park during the Second World War. (*c/o David White*)

Below: A photograph of RSS operators relaxing in a Nissen hut at Hanslope Park; this was to become the sergeants' mess. (*c/o Jeanette and Michael Chamberlain*)

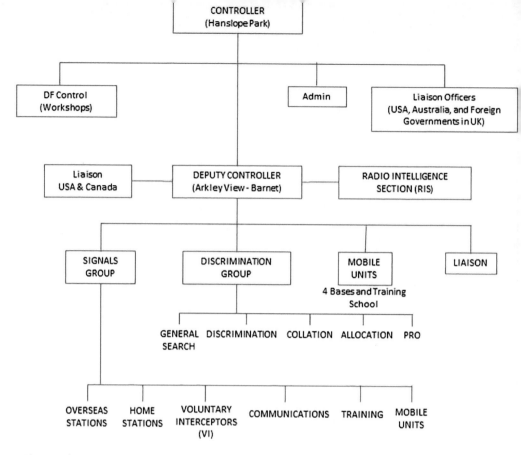

Above: The RSS's organisation structure, 1941 onwards. (*History of SIGINT in WWII*)

Below: Structure of the RSS Signals Group ('D' refers to a double receiver position for radio interception). (*History of SIGINT in WWII*)

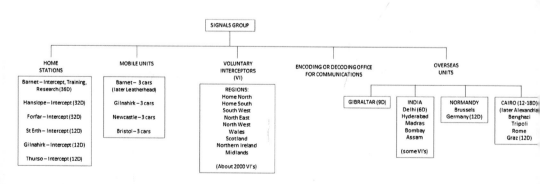

Above left: Polish AP.5 wireless set, produced by PMWR unit at Stanmore under guidance from the RSS. (*©Polish Heritage Society*)

Above right: Castle Hill cottage in Orkney, used by Helena and Leslie Crawley during their RSS VI work. (*c/o Gardner Crawley*)

Below: The certificate of employment for Leslie Crawley, internal pages. (*c/o Gardner Crawley*)

Page 2   D.R. Form 12

CERTIFICATE OF EMPLOYMENT

In Essential Services in War

This is to certify that

LESLIE ROBERT CRAWLEY

is a.....*British*.....subject employed in

essential war services by..*The Admiralty*

Superintending Civil Engineer

of .....*Lyness*

in the capacity of *Temp: Architectural*

and Engineering Asst:

It is requested that he may be afforded all facilities necessary for the discharge of his duties in the above capacity.

Signature .....

Date of Issue.....*16/1/41*

Page 3

General Serial **N⁰ 090739**

Employer's Reference No.............

(Photograph partly over-Employer wi die st

SECURITY 1 5 JAN 19 LYNESS B

Signature of Bearer *L R Crawley*

Postal Address of Bearer *"Castlehill"* *Twatt Manse*

Twatt Kirkwall

ORKNEY.

CAPT.RM

CERTIFICATE
OF EMPLOYMENT
In Essential Services in War

General Serial **N⁰ 090739**

Employer's Reference No...............

STAMP OF ISSUING OFFICE

SECURITY OFFICE
LYNESS BASE

THIS DOCUMENT IS NOT
A PERMIT OR PASS

D.R. Form 12

CONDITIONS

1. This Certificate does not authorize the Bearer to enter any Prohibited or Protected Place or Area, without the permission of the Official in charge thereof. It is a Certificate of Identity and Employment only.

2. This Certificate is an Official Document issued and held subject to the provisions of Section 1 of the Official Secrets Act, 1920, and of the Defence Regulations, 1939. Its unauthorized use, retention, alteration, destruction, or transfer to another person are penal offences.

3. This Certificate must be presented for inspection on the demand of a person on duty who is a member of His Majesty's Forces, a Policeman, or an Employee of the Official in Charge of a Prohibited or Protected Place or Area duly authorized for this purpose.

4. This Certificate must be returned to the issuing office on demand, or on the Bearer ceasing to hold the appointment or occupation on account of which it was issued.

5. This Certificate should be carried in an addressed envelope to facilitate restoration if mislaid. The loss or finding of it should be reported at once to the issuing office or to the Police

(S.4615) 10,000 pads 6/40 Hw.

Above: The certificate of employment for Leslie Crawley, external pages. (*c/o Gardner Crawley*)

Below left: VI Helena Hope Crawley (G2DDY). (*c/o Gardner Crawley*)

Below right: VI team Helena and Leslie Crawley. (*c/o Gardner Crawley*)

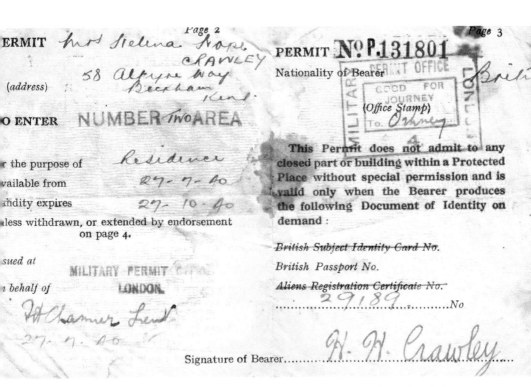

ERMIT *Mrs Helena Hope* *Page 2* CRAWLEY

(address) 58 Alpine Way Beckham Kent.

O ENTER NUMBER TWO AREA

r the purpose of Residence

vailable from 27-7-40

indity expires 27-10-40

less withdrawn, or extended by endorsement on page 4.

sued at MILITARY PERMIT

behalf of LONDON.

H Chanmer Lieut

27-7-40

PERMIT **N.º P.131801**

Nationality of Bearer Briti

MILITARY PERMIT OFFICE

GOOD FOR JOURNEY

(Office Stamp) To Orkney

This Permit does not admit to any closed part or building within a Protected Place without special permission and is valid only when the Bearer produces the following Document of Identity on demand:

British Subject Identity Card No.

British Passport No.

Aliens Registration Certificate No.
..............29189..............No

Signature of Bearer.............*H. W. Crawley*..........

Permit to enter for VI Helena Crawley, internal pages. (*c/o Gardner Crawley*)

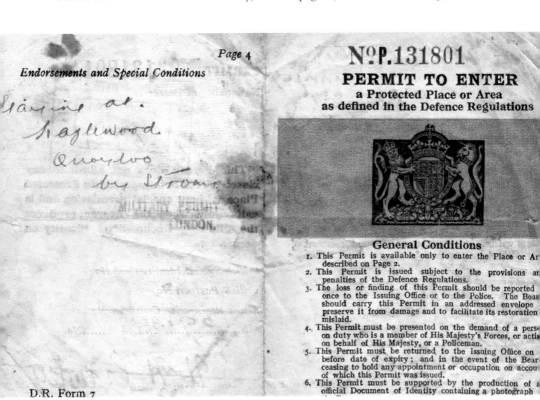

Page 4

Endorsements and Special Conditions

Staying at.
Haylewood
Quoyloo
by Stromness

MILITARY PERMIT
LONDON.

N.º P.131801

PERMIT TO ENTER
a Protected Place or Area
as defined in the Defence Regulations

General Conditions

1. This Permit is available only to enter the Place or Ar described on Page 2.
2. This Permit is issued subject to the provisions a penalties of the Defence Regulations.
3. The loss or finding of this Permit should be reported once to the Issuing Office or to the Police. The Bea should carry this Permit in an addressed envelope preserve it from damage and to facilitate its restoration mislaid.
4. This Permit must be presented on the demand of a pers on duty who is a member of His Majesty's Forces, or acti on behalf of His Majesty, or a Policeman.
5. This Permit must be returned to the Issuing Office on before date of expiry; and in the event of the Bea ceasing to hold any appointment or occupation on accou of which this Permit was issued.
6. This Permit must be supported by the production of official Document of Identity containing a photograph

D.R. Form 7

Permit to enter for VI Helena Crawley, external pages. (*c/o Gardner Crawley*)

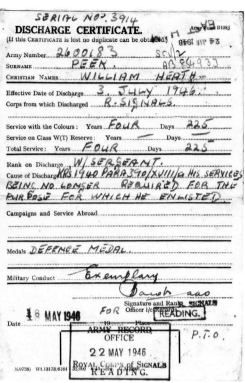

Above left: VI Sgt Bill Peek (G2ZZ). (*c/o Bill Peek*)

Above right: Sgt Bill Peek's discharge certificate from 1946. (*c/o Bill Peek*)

Left: Sgt Bill Peek's enlistment certificate into the Royal Signals. (*c/o Bill Peek*)

Telephone: BARnet 6500   Box 25, Barnet, Herts.

VHS/273   18th August, 1941.

W.H. Peek, Esq.,
20, Hilditch, Street,
Poplar, E. 14.

Dear Mr. Peek,

    Your log of the 13th August at 1920 had some traffic looking very like German Army traffic, i.e. time and number of letters but no 6-letter indicator on 8450 k.cs. This linked up with traffic produced by Budden HS/246, at 2200 hours on 5400 k.cs.

    I have been asked to ask you if you would make every effort to get some more of this traffic and I am asking Budden to produce some more of his so that we can tie the two together again.

    Mr. Budden's address is: H.G. Budden, Esq., 127, Richmond Park Road, Bournemouth, Hants, Telephone No. Winton 2672. I am sending him a copy of this letter for information.

    Will you please mark your logs "Special Watch, G.A. Type traffic"?

                  Yours sincerely,

S/ABB

Right: Sgt Bill Peek's VI letter from Arkley View. (*c/o Bill Peek*)

Below: Sgt Bill Peek's VI record of service. (*c/o Bill Peek*)

RECORD OF SERVICE   ARMY FORM W5258

No. 2600/83   Rank W/SGT

Name PEEK. W.H.

Served in Regts/Corps as follows:

	Regt./Corps	From	To	Assn. joined with date	Remarks by Assn. (if any)
a	R. SIGNALS	2/11/41	3/2/46		
b					
c					
d					

Date 22 MAY 1946

1. This card should be presented or sent by the person named above to the Regt/Corps Association he wishes to join or from which he requires assistance.
2. The Secretary of the Association should stamp and date the card in the relative column when the soldier joins the Association.
3. If you send this card by post, do not fail to enclose your address.

Wt. 40594/221 500M 1/46 KJL/1719/30 Gp. 38/3

Left: RSS VI Ray Fautley (photograph taken in 1942 by his father at their home at 27 Marlow Drive, North Cheam, Surrey). His uniform is that of the Royal Observer Corps, supplied as cover for their VI work. (*c/o Ray Fautley*)

Below: Senior RSS officers: Capt. Tant, affectionately called 'Auntie', in far left back row, and Capt. Bellringer, known as 'ding dong', sitting in the middle of the front row. (*c/o Bob King*)

...wartime meeting of VI group leaders at the Leatherhead regional office of the Radio Security Service. Old-timers will recognize many ...iliar faces, as very many of these amateurs served on the RSGB Council in the 'forties and 'fifties, including at least three former ...sidents (Arthur Watts, G6UN; "Dud" Charman, G6CJ, and the late Gerald Marcuse, G2NM). Lord Sandhurst (centre, standing and smoking a pipe) and a number of "Box 25" officers are also in the group

Above: A rare photograph of RSS VI group leaders in Leatherhead, taken at Highland House, Clifton Road. (*c/o Stan Ames*)

Below: A *Daily Mirror* article, from Friday 14 February 1941, exposing the work of the RSS. (*c/o Ray Fautley*)

Each operator employed in R.S.S. will be placed in one of the following Grades:

Grade A, Grade B or Grade C.

In order to be graded, an operator will have to undergo one of the following tests:

Grade A. Read

69 groups of 5 letter cypher in 3 minutes making not more than 8 errors.

69 groups of 5 figure cypher in 3 minutes making not more than 8 errors.

Block-letter writing is optional, but letters which in the opinion of the examiner are illegible will count as errors. Those who do not write the above messages in block-letters will be expected to read the 5 letter cypher text in the test for Grade B, and write this in block letters.

Grade B. Read, and write in block letters

60 groups of 5 letter cypher in 3 minutes making not more than 6 errors.

60 groups of 5 figure cypher in 3 minutes making not more than 6 errors.

Grade C. Read, and write in block letters

54 groups of 5 letter cypher in 3 minutes making not more than 5 errors.

54 groups of 5 figure cypher in 3 minutes making not more than 5 errors.

As well as the reading tests, an operator irrespective of which Grade test he attempts will also undergo an oral and practical examination in the handling of a National HRO or equivalent communication receiver, designed to show that he is able to get the best results from such receivers under conditions of weak signal strength and interference.

Since no short examination can show unfailingly that an operator is really efficient at interception work, the grading which is based on this examination alone, and not on further knowledge of the individual concerned, will be reconsidered at the end of a month on the basis of the actual work of the operator, and in some cases a regrading to a lower grade might be necessary.

Those in Grades B and C can always apply for a test for regrading to a higher rate. In the event of failure they will not be elligible to take that test again until one month has elapsed.

If those who fail to pass the test for Grade C show to the examiner exceptional promise, they may be engaged on a temporary basis to enable them to make a further attempt. During this period they will be paid the Grade C rate of pay.

It should be pointed out that the object of the examiner is not to fail applicants, but to assess their abilities as accurately as possible, and this will be constantly remembered in the organisation of the tests.

Where, in the opinion of the examiner, an obviously capable applicant has failed in a test owing to some mishap, or through some unusual circumstances, a second or even a third test will be given without delay.

In conclusion it is pointed out to all applicants that the Controller R.S.S. is anxious to enroll good operators and not to lose their services.

FHL/FC
6.10.41.

Note on the grading of operators for the RSS.

Telephones:
BARNET 6500 (4 Lines)
MILL HILL 4271 (4 Lines)

P.O. BOX 25
BARNET
HERTS.

KING H.S.   V/HN/353

27/12/41   HDA   on 6650   at 1015   4 msgs
            SIG   8200   1300   1 & pt.
            SFG   7830   1845   1

SECRET

The undermentioned traffic has been retained for either information
or investigation, for which many thanks.

KING. H.S. V/HN/353

17.11.41. RES 6900 kg/s at 1700 hrs. 1 msge.
           GWE 5200   "   " 1900 "   1   "
           E   5400   "   " 1900 "   1   "

Yours sincerely,
P. H. ROLFE,
Capt., R. SIGNALS,
'HN' REGIONAL OFFICER.

It is with great pleasure that I forward
to you the attached certificate in recognition of the
valued and devoted service which you have voluntarily
rendered to our Organisation during the War.

This certificate is signed by Sir Herbert
Creedy who, during the War years when your work
was of the utmost value, was the head of the
Department to which we were responsible.

I would like to add my personal thanks
for all you have done and for the many hours of
hard work and personal self sacrifice you have
contributed.

Colonel,
Controller,
Radio Security Service.

TRAFFIC RETAINED FOR INFORMATION
FOR WHICH MANY. THANKS.

RADIO SECURITY SERVICE
H.N.
7 - AUG 1941
R. S. S.

KING,H.S.V/HN/353

3.8.41. E 6600 kc/s at 1900 hrs. 1 msge.

A. A. HALL,
Capt. R. Signals,
Regional Officer, R.S.S.
"H.N." Region.

Above left: An example of acknowledgement correspondence to a VI from Arkley, received for all submitted RSS logs. (*c/o Bob King*)

Above right: A signed letter of thanks to RSS VI AW Box from the RSS controller at Arkley View. (*c/o Neville Cullingford, curator of ROC Museum Archives*)

Below: An example of a VI intercept decrypted signal. (*Author*)

447 GROUP II/124
     TETUAN to MADRID
     RSS 642/20/11/41
     RES on 6900 kcs. 1709 GMT.   19/11/41
     182/495

[No.182] For MACO, ref. your M letter No.90 of 16th
November. The essential preliminary both to better
traffic and functioning and to the carrying out of
requirements is a thorough study of the local
conditions in MONEDA [= MELILLA] and A[LBO]RAN by a
technically competent W/T operator. This therefore
can only be tackled after the arrival of the substitute
W/T operator. Please state when his arrival can be
expected. In the case of direct traffic between
MONEDA and MEDIA a cypher clerk for MONEDA would also
seem to be necessary, if the old cypher is not to be
used any longer.

Left: Capt. Morton Evans. (*c/o Bob King*)

Below: The photograph of senior RSS officers was taken at the rear of Arkley View in early 1941. Included are Col. Stratton (main chair) and Morton Evans (who became deputy controller of the RSS by January 1942).
Back row, from left to right: Etherdge, Penham (?), Berkley, Lakin, Vale, Roper, unknown, and Banham.
Middle row, from left to right: Lloyd, Bellringer, Tant, Sabine, Scarratt, Lord Sandhurst, Rolfe, Evans, Rutland, Watherson, and unknown.
Front row, from left to right: Adams, Col. Stratton, Worlledge, Lacey, and Hall, with RSS Steward Paddy sitting on the ground. (*c/o George Busby*)

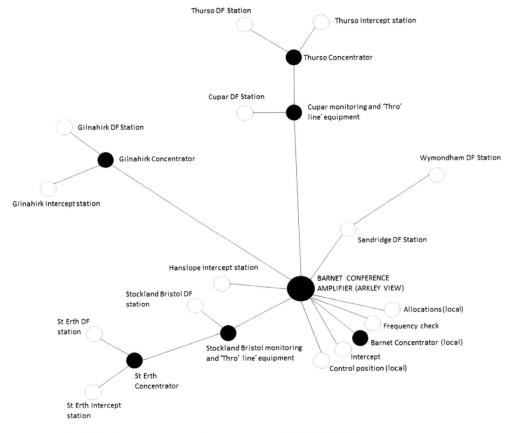

The RSS–GPO telephone conference system. (*POST56/144*)

Crofton Hall Nissen hut, with vegetable and flower garden. (*c/o Alan Sharpe*)

Gilnahirk's RSS station in Northern Ireland. (*c/o George Busby*)

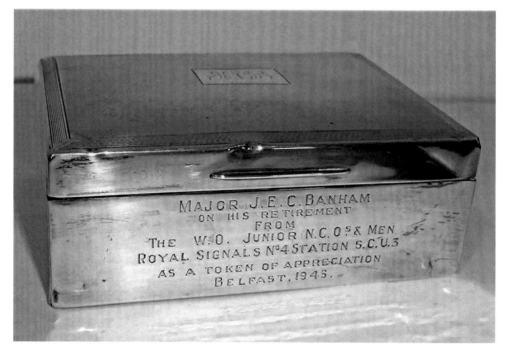

Maj. Banham's (OIC Gilnahirk RSS Station—'Station No. 4') leaving present—a silver cigarette case, from the lower ranks. (*c/o the Banham family collection*)

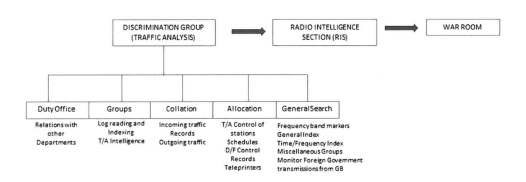

An RSS Discrimination Group organogram. (*Author*)

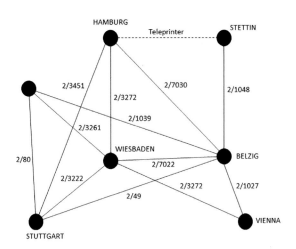

Above: German *Amt Mil.*—fixed wireless stations. (*Author*)

Below: German Westerwald network wireless stations. (*Author*)

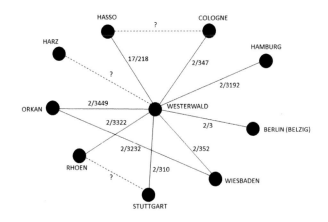

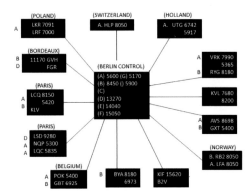

GROUP 2 - BERLIN

	(POLAND)	(SWITZERLAND)	(HOLLAND)
A	LKR 7091 / LRF 7000	A. HLP 8050	A. UTG 6742 / 5917

	(BORDEAUX)		(BERLIN CONTROL)		
B D	11170 GVH / FGR		(A) 5600 (G) 5170 (B) 8450 () 5900 (C) (D) 13270 (E) 14040 (F) 15050	A B	VRK 7990 / 5365 / RYG 8180

	(PARIS)
A B	LCQ 8150 / 5420 / KLV

KVL 7680 / 8200

A B : AVS 8698 / GXT 5400

	(PARIS)
D A A	LSD 9280 / NQP 5300 / LQC 5835

(NORWAY) B. RB2 8050 / A. LFA 8050

	(BELGIUM)				
A B	POK 5400 / GBT 6925	B	BYA 8180 / 6973		KIF 15620 / B2V

Group 2 Berlin (note: the ABCD in the graphics is a measure of the accuracy of interception). (*Author*)

SPANISH CONTROL GROUP No. 1

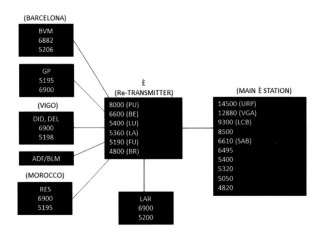

(BARCELONA)
BVM 6882 5206

| GP 5195 6900 |

È (Re-TRANSMITTER)
8000 (PU) 6600 (BE) 5400 (LU) 5360 (LA) 5190 (FU) 4800 (BR)

(MAIN È STATION)
14500 (URP) 12880 (VGA) 9300 (LCB) 8500 6610 (SAB) 6495 5400 5320 5050 4820

(VIGO)
DID, DEL 6900 5198

| ADF/BLM |

(MOROCCO)
RES 6900 5195

| LAR 6900 5200 |

Above: Spanish Control Group No. 1. (*Author*)

Below: Spanish Control Group No. 2. (*Author*)

SPANISH CONTROL GROUP No. 2

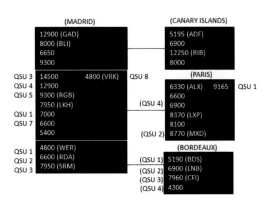

(MADRID)	(CANARY ISLANDS)
12900 (GAD) 8000 (BLI) 6650 9300	5195 (ADF) 6900 12250 (RIB) 8000

QSU 3	14500	4800 (VRK)	QSU 8	(PARIS)
QSU 4	12900			6330 (ALX) 9165 QSU 1
QSU 5	9300 (RGB)			6600
	7950 (LKH)		(QSU 4)	6900
QSU 1	7000			8370 (LXP)
QSU 7	6600			8100
	5400		(QSU 2)	8770 (MXD)

QSU 1	4800 (WER)	(BORDEAUX)
QSU 2	6600 (RDA)	(QSU 1) 5190 (BDS)
QSU 3	7950 (SRM)	(QSU 2) 6900 (LNB)
		(QSU 3) 7960 (CFI)
		(QSU 4) 4300

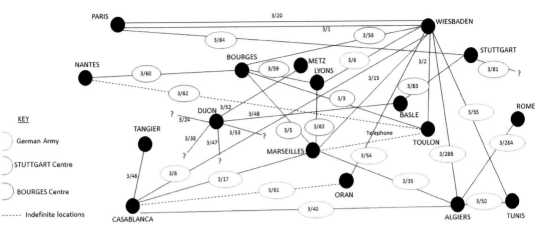

RSS Group 3 services, including German Army W/T links. (*Author*)

A 1946 aerial photograph of Arkley View in Barnet, showing the house and huts at the back—horizontal lines are film scratches, but dark diagonal lines in the field are shadows of antenna poles. (© *English Heritage—c/o Stan Ames and Hertfordshire Archives*)

Name H.KING
Address
File No. Y/HN/353

R.S.S. Log Sheet

BERTIE

Region HN
Group /
Sub-Group OXFORD

120

(1) DATE AND TIME G.M.T.	(2) CALL AS SIGNALLED	(3) MESSAGE AND REMARKS	(4) FREQUENCY kc's	(5) WAVE LENGTH m.	(6) TYPE OF SIGNAL	(7) STRENGTH
9.12.41. 1700	CZE	QSA0 PSE CALL =K =SRI QSA0 =WAT PLEASE NW73 QAX NEXT GBVA	5400		CW	3
1800	E	NIL IIK ND 22 ND 349 RM (PRM BLOTTED E OUT) NOTED THANKS	5400		CW	3
1800	GGG	QTC (LISTENED TILL 1815 BUT ND) STILL WANTED	6200		CW	2
1815	WEB				CW	
	URK	QTC CT 935/71 = (VY HEAVY ATMOSPHERICS) 4880			CW	3
		AOHLC VUBAK =NKUZ MHPXN LTUPK				
		XFGEL WOFYH RDZFZ RZAXP DFJZB				
		TYHNW OPLDU NECIW FSJGS QVYIG				
		DVDQX WBDMJ MHRWW NKLFW UFF=O				
		THZGQ OOVKW CZEHQ MWEKE HZ=ZM ZQDD MIWF VXAOU KOVVW MESKB =NCXX				
	DUF	RPT W35 PSG QSY	5190		CW	2
	URK	=IICT T FX	4900			
		QFK IIH APSY= OYIIR LCHUP FBJJL				
		YJIIHO RIPBG WLYRY MMTUR OMIUQ				
		MFDQY EOVEG DQEZB IUVCU ADWNJ				
						4

U.K. COVERED THANKS (600) after

Above: A completed and Arkley-amended RSS log sheet. (*c/o Bob King*)

Below: St Erth's RSS station staff during the Second World War. (*c/o Jeanette and Michael Chamberlain*)

Above: RSS Operator Louis Varney (G5RV) setting up a DF station. (*c/o Bob King*)

Below: Organisational structure of WNV/FU III. (*WO208/5098*)

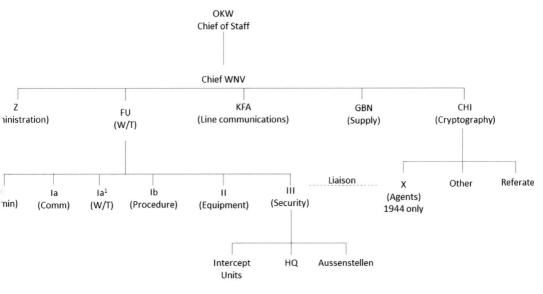

Organisational Structure of the WNV/FU III

OKW
Chief of Staff

Chief WNV

Z
(inistration)

FU
(W/T)

KFA
(Line communications)

GBN
(Supply)

CHI
(Cryptography)

Ia
(Comm)

Ia¹
(W/T)

Ib
(Procedure)

II
(Equipment)

III
(Security)

Liaison

X
(Agents)
1944 only

Other

Referate

Intercept
Units

HQ

Aussenstellen

Organisation and Liaison of WNV/FU III

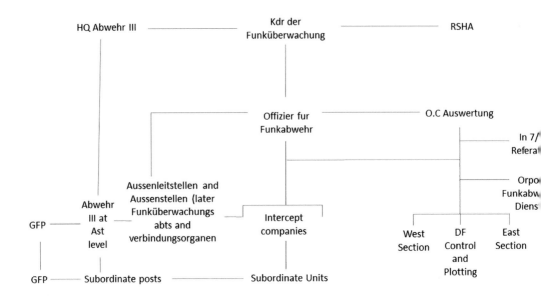

Above: Organisation and liaison of WNV/FU III. (WO208/5098)

Below: Organisation and structure of the *Orpo Funkabwehrdienst*. (WO208/5098)

Organisation and Structure of the Orpo Funkabwehrdienst

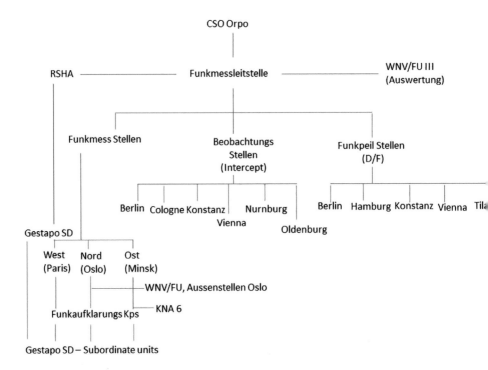

Fixed Abwehr W/T stations in Norway

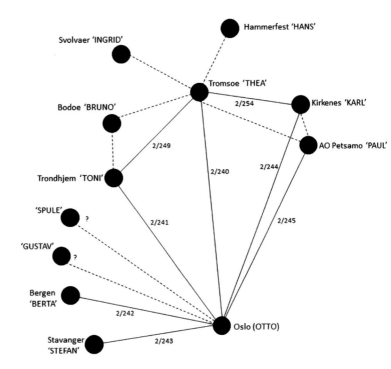

Right: Fixed *Abwehr* W/T stations in Norway. (*Author*)

Below: Intelligence penetration of Turkey. (*Author*)

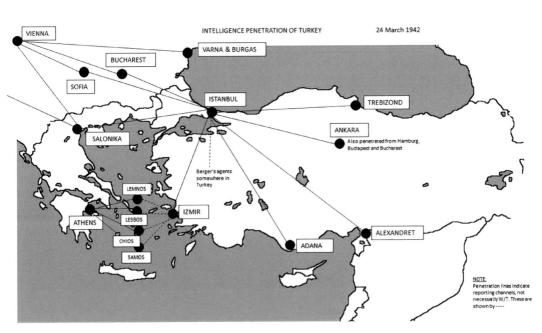

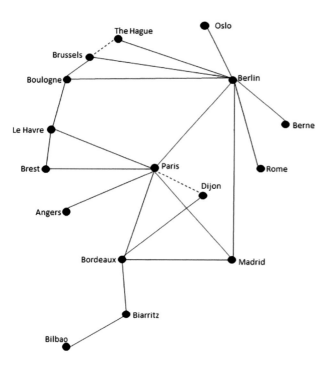

TELEPRINTER COMMUNICATIONS NETWORK USED BY THE
ABWEHR IN THE WEST

26 March 1943

Left: Teleprinter
communications network
used by the *Abwehr* in the
West. (*WO208/5098*)

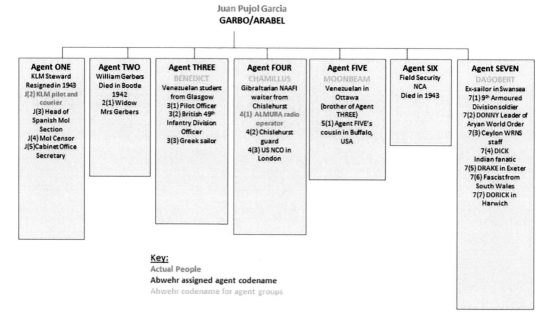

Juan Pujol Garcia
GARBO/ARABEL

Agent ONE	Agent TWO	Agent THREE	Agent FOUR	Agent FIVE	Agent SIX	Agent SEVEN
KLM Steward	William Gerbers	BENEDICT	CHAMILLUS	MOONBEAM	Field Security	DAGOBERT
Resigned in 1943	Died in Bootle	Venezuelan student	Gibraltarian NAAFI	Venezuelan in	NCA	Ex-sailor in Swansea
J(2) KLM pilot and	1942	from Glasgow	waiter from	Ottawa	Died in 1943	7(1) 9th Armoured
courier	2(1) Widow	3(1) Pilot Officer	Chislehurst	(brother of Agent		Division soldier
J(3) Head of	Mrs Gerbers	3(2) British 49th	4(1) ALMURA radio	THREE)		7(2) DONNY Leader of
Spanish MoI		Infantry Division	operator	5(1) Agent FIVE's		Aryan World Order
Section		Officer	4(2) Chislehurst	cousin in Buffalo,		7(3) Ceylon WRNS
J(4) MoI Censor		3(3) Greek sailor	guard	USA		staff
J(5) Cabinet Office			4(3) US NCO in			7(4) DICK
Secretary			London			Indian fanatic
						7(5) DRAKE in Exeter
						7(6) Fascist from
						South Wales
						7(7) DORICK in
						Harwich

Key:
Actual People
Abwehr assigned agent codename
Abwehr codename for agent groups

The GARBO/ARABEL network of agents and sub-agents reporting to the German
Abwehr. (*c/o Nigel West*)

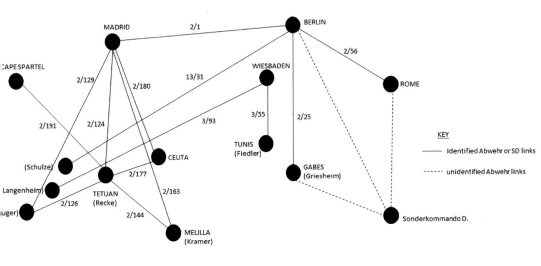

Enemy W/T communications with North Africa, January 1943. (*Author*)

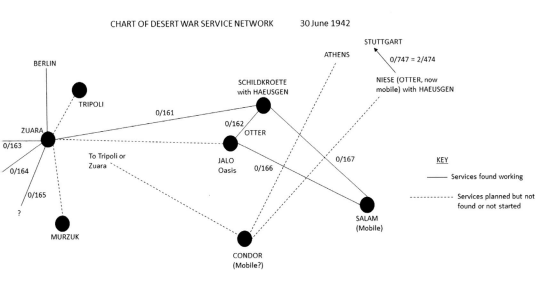

Chart of Desert War Service network, 30 June 1942. (*Author*)

Ray Wright at Sidi Bishr in 1945.
(*c/o Ray Wright*)

A RSS wireless operator
photographed at his W/T set in
Sidi Bishr, Egypt, in 1945. (*c/o
Ray Wright*)

Africa guard detail at the Sidi Bishr RSS compound near Alexandria, Egypt. (*c/o Ray Wright*)

Christmas Day lunch at Sidi Bishr military camp in 1945. (*c/o Ray Wright*)

Above: Three infamous Barnet personalities: Gilbert Ryle, Stuart Hampshire, and Charles Stuart; all three were to become Oxford professors after the war. (*c/o Stan Ames*)

Below: The RSS traffic routeing matrix. (*HW34/1*)

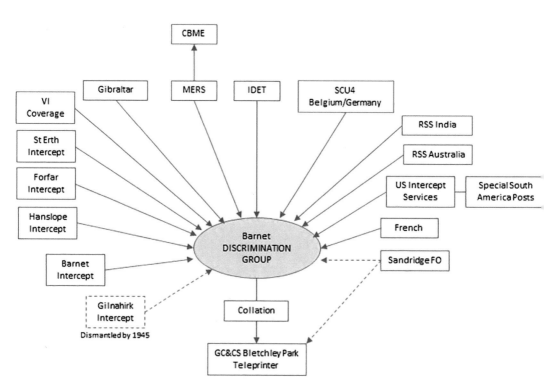

```
14612    GROUP II/124
         TETUAN TO MADRID
         RSS  123/23/11/41 at 1625 GMT.
         RES on 5200 kcs. at 1719 GMT.          22/11/41
         197/155

         [No.197] Consider it expedient to suggest to the Ambassador
         that Consul NOEHRING be allowed to come to MEDIA while
         GUILLERMO is there. NOEHRING would welcome conversation.


14613    GROUP II/124
         TETUAN TO MADRID
         RSS  122/23/11/41
         RES on 5200 kcs. at 1720 GMT.          22/11/41
         198/105

         [No.198] Please state whether a journey to MEDIA for
         discussion there with GUILLERMO could be suggested to
         General ORGAZ.
```

Above: Abwehr VI
decrypted messages.
(*c/o Stan Ames*)

Right: The DELILAH
Secure Speech System,
developed by Alan Turing
at Hanslope Park.

Above: Unveiling of VI plaque at Bletchley Park in 2013 by the Lord Lieutenant of Buckinghamshire. On the left is VI Ray Fautley and on the far right is Paul Cort-Wright, who supported the recording of the RSS BBC documentary *The Secret Wireless War* in 1979. (*c/o Ray Fautley*)

Below: Bletchley Park plaque; despite the plaque, Bletchley Park does not recognise the RSS and its VIs or the wider view of signals intelligence. (*c/o Bob King*)

This memorial was unveiled on July 5th 2013 by
The Lord Lieutenant of Buckinghamshire
Sir Henry Aubrey-Fletcher. Bt JP
to
commemorate the work of 1,500 radio amateurs who
as

Voluntary Interceptors
assisted
the World War II effort through the interception of
German wireless communications

"In the years when Civilisation was a menaced with

destruction they gave generously of their time, powers and

technical skills in essential service to this Country"

Sir Herbert Creedy War Office, 1945

the influential Deputy for Shiraz Habibullah Naubakht and General Zahidi, who commanded the Isfahan area. Mayr had given one of the Japanese W/T sets to an *Abwehr* agent, Berthold Schultze, who had formerly been the German Consul in Tabris.

Mayr was nearly captured after being betrayed by one of his closest associates, but the British managed to get details of the network he was running in every tier of Iranian society. This list justified a significant arrest campaign, which rounded up nearly 150 individuals involved with German intelligence.

Mayr eluded the Allies' hunt, and he had been consistently pressuring his controllers to send him out a dedicated W/T operator that he could use in Tehran. Instead of one W/T operator, he was to receive a group of six German staff, four of whom were skilled W/T operators. Four of the six were SD men, including the group leader, *Untersturmführer* Ernst Blume.

The group was to undertake sabotage operations against the Trans-Iranian Railway network, although Blume was the only one of the group with any formal sabotage training. Mayr was not supportive of this activity. He wanted to use the Fifth Column he had created in Persia to support the German war effort. He thought that sabotage operations would only undermine his work. Mayr convinced Blume and his team to focus on intelligence gathering. Blume was dispatched with one of his W/T operators to the south of the country to report on troop movements, Russian convoys, and the location of Iranian oil wells. This intelligence was relayed back to Tehran via their W/T sets and then onward to Berlin. The team in Tehran would move location for their broadcast transmissions every night to prevent any DF of their signals. The transmissions were intercepted, deciphered, and reported on by the RSS—it was referred to as the 13/39 link to Wannsee. It was operational until Mayr and his SD team were arrested in August 1942 after tip offs from Iranian informers. The arrests did not round up the entire Mayr network, nor even touch another SD network (the Berta Group), which also operated in the capital. The subsequent interrogation detail that was to emerge highlighted some of the deeply political competition between the German Intelligence Services.

> The Mayr case shows the SD working along parallel but at the same time competing lines with the *Abwehr* ... the SD, aided by their apparent greater efficiency in methods, would appear today to be successfully displacing the *Abwehr* in Persia, as it may yet well do in the Middle Eastern area generally.[11]

For many months prior to D-Day, a network of double agents had been recruited and matured under the authority and direction of the Double-Cross (XX) committee led by the Oxford University don John Masterman. The committee, which sat weekly at 58 St James Street, London, included officers from MI5, MI6, the Directors for Intelligence at the Army, RAF and Navy, and Home Forces and

Home Defence. The spies were an eclectic bunch of personalities and nationalities, but they harboured a common goal: to deceive the Germans under the plans laid out under Operation Bodyguard. The network included the following agents: Dušan 'Duško' Popov (MI5 code-named TRICYCLE or SKOOT); Lily Sergeyev (MI5 code-named TREASURE); Elvira de al Fuente Chaudoir (MI5 code-named BRONX or CYRIL); Roman Czerniawski (MI5 code-named BRUTUS, ARMAND or WALENTY); and Juan Pujol García (MI5 code-named GARBO or BOVRIL).

The case officer for BRUTUS in Paris, Col. Oscar Reile, had become an expert in understanding how the BBC was being used covertly to relay messages to the French Resistance and special forces troops on the ground in France. The day before D-Day, fourteen such messages were broadcast by the BBC and Reile's work interpreting these caused the 15th Army in the Calais region to raise its state of alert. Fortunately for the Allies, the 7th Army in Normandy ignored the messages.

Shortly before D-Day, TRICYCLE did a tour of Kent and the south coast to further the deception around the build-up of forces in Southern England to attack the area around Calais. He produced a stream of reports that the Allies were preparing a vast naval force, but tried to draw the Germans off the scent by playing down the immediacy. The Allies were 'preparing and improving cook houses, wash houses, tented camps and landing grounds ... in spite of intensive preparations there are no signs that invasion is imminent'.

In February 1944, TRICYCLE submitted a list of fictitious First United States Army Group (FUSAG) units to one of his *Abwehr* handlers in Lisbon. He continued to furnish his contacts throughout the spring of 1944 with false data and FUSAG units operating on the south coast, preparing for the invasion of France.

The most significant of the double agents was the MI5-run GARBO, ironically a native Spaniard who was a former businessman and chicken farmer. Experiencing the Spanish Civil War first hand, he hated Nazism and Communism. As the war ran its course in Europe, he approached MI6 in Madrid but was not taken on; by 1941, he volunteered his services to the *Abwehr*, via a man called Wilhelm Leissner. After initial training, he was deployed to London, but he actually moved to Lisbon where he began sending a series of bogus intelligence reports about Britain. From 1942, Bletchley Park, through its associated RSS teams at Hanslope Park, had been intercepting signals carrying spurious intelligence on a Madrid to Berlin link from an *Abwehr* agent supposedly in Britain.

Bletchley had been able to decrypt the *Abwehr* Enigma cipher from 1941 and read the messages. The intercept from GARBO was referring to a fictitious large convoy transiting from Liverpool to Malta, encouraging the German Navy to interdict it.

Eventually, the signals were traced to a Lisbon-based operative. He was recruited and was smuggled out of Portugal, arriving in England in April 1942. He was put up by MI5 with his wife, Araceli Gonzalez de Pujol, and infant son in a semi-detached house on Crespigny Road, North London. He was being run by a thirty-four-year-old MI5 case officer, half-Spanish artist Tomas Harris. Between them, they created a fictional network of up to twenty-seven agents, dotted around England and overseas, who were creating intelligence on military dispositions in the build up to the invasion of Europe. GARBO was the only real agent among them. They were as imaginative as a Gibraltarian NAAFI waiter from Chislehurst (code name CHAMILLUS) to an ex-sailor from Swansea (DAGOBERT), and even a Venezuelan student in Glasgow (BENEDICT). He even convinced the *Abwehr* that he had an agent operating in the headquarters of the Supreme Allied Commander South-East Asia (SACSEA) in Peradenyia—in what is now Sri Lanka.

He had convinced the Germans to pay him the equivalent of £20,000 to finance his network, which was to produce a stream of intelligence on any entirely fictional army group. Pujol would get the London Underground into central London every day to meet his handler, Harris, at their Jermyn Street offices to develop their sub-agent network and scripted messages that would be sent on to the *Abwehr*. The intelligence was low grade, but it confirmed to the *Abwehr*, and ultimately the German High Command, that the invasion would come much further north in the Pas-de-Calais region.

By 1943, GARBO's wife, Araceli, was becoming tired of her life in England and her husband's work. She longed so much to return to Spain that she threatened to expose his work as an agent. She had even attempted suicide. GARBO, with his MI5 handler, concocted an elaborate hoax of its own to attempt to turn her around. They created a story around GARBO being arrested and subsequently imprisoned at Latchmere House (Camp 020) and brought her, blindfolded, to him. She was to sign a sworn statement that she would never tell the Germans her husband was being run as a double agent. Harris was later to write 'the extraordinary ingenuity with which he has conceived and carried through this plan has perhaps saved a situation which might otherwise have been intolerable'.

Over the course of the next three years, GARBO and Harris were to inundate the German *Abwehr* with over 1,200 wireless reports and 315 letters that had been written in secret ink, with accompanying cover letters. Each of the letters averaged over 2,000 words. Over 500 of the wireless reports were transmitted between January 1944 and D-Day alone. Harris had concerns that the Germans may be suspicious when just one agent was producing such a quantity of intelligence.

These packages were transferred via a KLM airline courier using a diplomatic bag to *Abwehr* cover addresses in Portugal and Spain, through his controller 'FELIPE'. Replies were picked up from a bank safe-deposit box in Lisbon. This was all overseen by MI6 on the ground in Lisbon. Later on in the war, the network relied on radio and Morse transmissions using an *Abwehr*-supplied code and a left-wing group of sympathisers who had a radio ham as a member.

Just three hours after the invasion commenced on D-Day, GARBO's reporting to his handlers suggested that this was the first the *Abwehr* knew of the invasion, further solidifying his authenticity. On 9 June 1944, after a meeting that GARBO had with some of his sub-agent network, he decreed that the Normandy invasion was a deception for the real thing, which was to take place in the Pas-de-Calais. The German High Command, and even Hitler himself, believed the reporting, which led them to keep twelve German armoured divisions positioned for over 120 days around Calais.

The Special Counter Intelligence Unit (SCIU), devised by MI6's Section V (its counter-espionage arm), was established to penetrate enemy intelligence services in the field. They were aided by MI6's control of Ultra dissemination. The SCIU was generally an SIS unit but run with MI5 and often local field security personnel from the Intelligence Corps. When the SCIU made the assessment that an agent may well be of use in XX deception operations or counter-espionage, they would have been transferred to Army Group for further onward assessment.

By the time of D-Day in 1944, MI5 had deployed a number of officers into the various army groups and staff appointments as counterintelligence liaison. In doing this, MI5 began to assert control over MI6 in the dissemination of ISK and ISOS reporting, collected largely through the RSS teams. Double agents in the field would be controlled by SCI units based with Supreme Headquarters Allied Expeditionary Forces (SHAEF) and 21st Army Group. An equivalent US SCIU was developed, but this fell under the control of the OSS.

Ultimately, during the Battle of Normandy after D-Day on 6 June 1944, the British Sector was small with little CI activity, and this did not change even after the US military break out of Normandy into Central France later that summer. Due to the valued work of the RSS, Bletchley Park and the resultant ISOS reporting signified by D-Day the Allies had knowledge of over 100 W/T stay-behind agents in both Northern France and the Low Countries.

An example of this is a German stay-behind agent known by the *Abwehr* alias EIKENS. As the Allies took Cherbourg on 28 June 1944, he had been spotted transmitting on his W/T set by the RSS between 7 and 20 June. It was known he was in a valuable strategic location from the DF results and he was found on 8 July. EIKENS was the Spanish-born Juan Frutos, and he was to be the first *Abwehr* agent captured in the Normandy offensive, who was turned for counter-espionage work. He had been acting as an interpreter with the US Army. Frutos had been recruited by *Abwehr* officer Erich Buecking in 1935. When he was found by US counterintelligence officers, he had a letter addressed to one of his aliases on his person. Under questioning, Frutos provided the locational details of his two W/T sets and cipher books. After two days of interrogation, he agreed to work for the Allies and was redeployed as an interpreter for the US officer in charge of Cherbourg port. After numerous engagements by SCIU officers, it was deemed that Frutos was unreliable and he was sent back to Camp 020 in Britain, although his work did expose wider *Abwehr* agents.

In France, the stay-behind agent Yves Guilcher (GUILLAUME) was the first to be captured by the Allies after the Normandy invasion in June 1944 and sent back to Britain for interrogation. He had been detained on 10 June by the British Intelligence Corps 19 Field Security Section at his house on 77 Rue Street, St Loup, Bayeux. He had been denounced by Guy Mercader, the leader of a local French Resistance group.

Born in July 1916 in Saint-Brieuc, he had grown up as an orphan and spoke French, Breton, and some Arabic. He served for seven years in the French Army as an electrical technician. In October 1941, he had volunteered to go to Russia with the LVF (*Légion des volontaires français*) to fight the Bolsheviks with the aim to join Charles de Gaulle's forces. He was subsequently sent to Versailles, then on to Poland, where he remained for three months in a camp learning the art of W/T. Shortly after this, he was denounced as a communist, appearing before a German military court where he was sentenced to three months in the salt mines in Krakow.

Guilcher managed to return to Versailles, leaving the LVF and applying for work with the Todt Organisation (the German civil engineering company). Around November 1942, he was recruited by an *Abwehr* agent, and after months of W/T training, he was deployed to the Caen–Saint-Lô–Isigny region. He was assigned the cover name BERGERET at Angers and settled himself into a residential property in Bayeux with 5,000 Francs he had been given on 25 April 1944.

Over the following few weeks, Guilcher was to make trips from Bayeux to Saint-Lô for further instruction by the *Abwehr* officer on the organisation and recognition of British Army vehicles and equipment. He was given a W/T transmitter and receiver set and he fell under the command of the *Abwehr* Trupp 122 at Angers. Guilcher was not given any cover story, nor were any cover arrangements made: 'He was simply told to keep his set in a drawer and to say, if asked, that he was not working for the Germans'.

He had been specially trained on wireless operations for over a year by the Germans and he had been tasked with transmitting information on Allied troop movements in the event of an invasion in and around the town of Bayeux. Under interrogation, Guilcher said that his motives for working for the Germans were to 'avoid having to work in Germany. It was implied that if he did not work for the Germans he would go to forced labour'. Money was a clear motivation.

There had been information from an SIS source in April 1944 that Guilcher was 'working for the *Gestapo* in the Department of the Cotes du Nord, particularly in the Morlaix sector. He has caused the arrest of arrest of 25 patriots, including the rector of St. Brieuc'.

A *château* on the outskirts of Angers acted as the *Abwehr* W/T reception centre, taking messages from spies operating across Normandy and Brittany.

Guilcher had been told there were in the region of 200–300 W/T sets in operation in the region and twenty to thirty in the Normandy coastal region alone. The receiving station for Guilcher's W/T transmissions was on the German frontier near Stuttgart.

During the raid on Guilcher's property, the army search team found the W/T set buried in the garden and a wooden box found in one of his rooms containing blank German message forms, typed lists of phrases and abbreviations, typed lists of frequencies, German message forms in cipher, and instructions on using the set itself.

Guilcher had been instructed to transmit once a week on a Monday or Wednesday at 1.30 p.m. CET. He used a double transposition code based on the novel *Louis XIV* and had a second emergency code supplied using an easily memorised French phrase if the codebook was confiscated or lost. The W/T set was examined 'by the experts from whom we are expecting to have a report in due course'. This would have been the RSS engineering section at Hanslope under Maj. Dick Keen. The set was identical to one seized at Carenten belonging to agent DURANT (MATELOT) who escaped custody.

The interrogation was overseen by Capt. S. H. Noakes from MI5s B1B section along with Maj. E. M. Furnival Jones from the Evaluation and Dissemination Section G-2 (Intelligence) Division of SHAEF. He was initially processed in Normandy by the 101 Special Counter Intelligence (SCI) Unit, who were to recommend that he 'be sent back to the UK, under personal escort ... and a detailed interrogation may well produce information of strategic value of Abwehr confronting us'. He arrived at the notorious Camp 020 at Latchmere House in South London on 16 June 1944, as a Category 'A' suspect. Upon interrogation, he signed a confession that he had been recruited by the *Abwehr* in November 1942. His interrogation reports from Noakes were sent as routine to Hugh Trevor-Roper in the RIS in Barnet.

Only one German agent was to escape the interest of the RSS interceptors. Twenty-five-year-old Dutch-born Danish agent Jan Willem Ter Braak, whose real name was Engelbertus Fukken, was parachuted into Britain in November 1940. He had been sent by the German *Abwehr* and was spotted on his descent from the aircraft near the town of Haversham in Buckinghamshire. The subsequent search by the authorities found his discarded parachute but could find no trace of Ter Braak. He had made his way with his W/T transmitter to lodgings in Cambridge, where he was to spend the next four months living undercover. This was the longest duration any agent had spent in Britain undetected. By the spring of 1941, he was to run out of money and he was to shoot himself using his *Abwehr* issued pistol in a Cambridge air-raid shelter.

These German agents were to be a key aspect of German intelligence activity in Europe during the Second World War. The RSS was to complement the work of MI5 in preventing them getting a foothold in Britain and to assist with monitoring them as Double-Cross agents. The RSS most certainly paralleled the work of the *Funkabwehr* but there were differences. The German air squadrons for close range DF work were not particularly successful, though they could have had more effect on the Eastern Front. The interception and location of VHF transmitters undertaken by No. 615 Intercept Company was a task that RSS was never called upon to undertake.

The *Funkabwehr* also played a much more significant role than the RSS in the organisation of wireless double crosses. It was a much larger organisation than the RSS, and although the number of manned receivers did not greatly exceed that of the RSS, they were more widely dispersed in smaller units. Taking into account the VIs, the two organisations were roughly the same in number. The *Funkabwehr* had more DF stations and deployable mobile units than the RSS.

The eight mobile intercept companies of the *Funkabwehr* would roughly map across to the overseas units of the RSS. They also used a wider array of radio interception equipment than that of their British counterparts. As with most of the German intelligence agencies, the *Funkabwehr* suffered from serious rivalries and petty jealousies both internally through the coexistence of the WNV/FU III and the *Orpo Funkabwehrdienst* and externally in contact with the *Abwehr III* and *Amt. IV* of the RSHA.

Arguably, the most significant difference between the RSS and *Funkabwehr* would be the decentralisation of discrimination, allocation, and cryptographic work to the *Außenstellen* of the *Funkabwehr*. This was forced by circumstance rather than design. Their DF techniques were leagues apart. The RSS had pioneered a centralised system of plotting signals to line and latterly introduced statistical plotting, which gave it significant advantages over its German competitor. But their interception and discrimination methods were largely identical. What is clear is the RSS would achieve many more successes than the *Funkabwehr*, even though it would have far less extensive experience. The RSS would punch above its weight. The network of fixed stations and nationwide VIs gave the RSS great coverage of occupied Europe. The RSS had proved its value against German intelligence, but the Axis powers extended beyond Germany. It would need to evolve a more global footprint to tackle the likes of the Italian and Japanese intelligence networks. The RSS would have to extend its reach overseas.

6

Overseas

Looking back on what was achieved I feel a sense of pride at the small role I was allowed to play in work that must rank among the greatest acts of the war.

Raymond Wright, RSS Wireless Operator
Sidi Bishr, outside Alexandria, Egypt, during the Second World War

At the beginning of the war, MI5 gave instructions to the RSS on the type of messages German Intelligence agents would send and an indication of the station to which they might work in Germany. In March 1940, this information bore fruit when RSS wireless operators located a ship called the *Theseus* off the coast of Norway broadcasting messages back to Hamburg in Germany, and agents operating in Belgium, Luxembourg, France, and Holland.

This vessel was regularly transiting the coast and the cipher being used by the radio operators on board took two months to break after it was first heard. The subsequent traffic suggested the vessel was reporting on neutral shipping heading for British ports. Norway was still a neutral country at this stage of the war. When Norway was invaded, the *Theseus* would dock into Bergen harbour and transmit military and administrative messages back to Berlin. The Admiralty were to describe the *Theseus* as 'a form of Naval *Gestapo*'. The code was worked on by Maj. Ernest Gill and his assistant, twenty-six-year-old Oxford scholar Lt Hugh Trevor-Roper. The fact that the two had broken this significant cipher was not lost on the GC&CS at Bletchley Park, when its commander, Alastair Denniston, found out via information relayed to them directly from Gill on 29 January 1940. Denniston rebuffed them directly, suggesting that it was the role of Bletchley Park staff to decipher codes.

One of the most important intelligence milestones of the Second World War occurred in December 1941. During this month, Bletchley Park broke the *Abwehr* Enigma cipher system. The resulting ISK product was exploited to its fullest extent by the entire British intelligence apparatus around the world. The authorities in the Middle East used this intelligence to map out the *Abwehr* intelligence network covering the region under control from both Ankara and Istanbul. It allowed them to identify unknown *Abwehr* agents and gain an understanding of their operations and morale.

Overseas, the RSS would add a significant weight to the global reach of British Signals Intelligence. The RSS was to be pioneering in its approach in working with and maintaining special sections manned by military personnel. The RSS would maintain interception units in the Middle East and also in North America to sustain coverage of targets operating in Latin America. Its two most active units were at Gibraltar, which had six receiving stations, and the unit in the Middle East, which had fifteen intercept positions. In the Middle East, some of these positions had to be diverted to local priorities, which involved RSS Mobile Units as well.

RSS mobile units were deployed into Europe under SHAEF command during the Normandy campaign in the summer of 1944. Although under SHAEF command (nominally the Chief Counter Intelligence Staff Officer at Army Group HQ), they would be directed and controlled by the RSS back in Britain. Six vans were deployed with 21st Army Group and the 1st US Army Group. The personnel and vans at HQ 21st Army Group were formed up as an MI6 Special Communication Unit (SCU) and the officer in charge of the mobile vans would be responsible for their technical employment. They were to work closely with the SCIU teams in occupied Europe and localised CI teams.

By September 1944, one of the RSS mobile units was stationed in Paris, hunting down stay-behind W/T agents. The Americans would also have similar mobile teams operating in France, who were often a law unto themselves. Lt-Col. Maltby described 'the brisk if somewhat unhelpful wanderings of the American Mobile Unit in France'. Although signals intelligence was shared directly with these American deployed teams by the RSS, they could not be instructed by the RSS about the operations they should undertake.

The overseas detachments of the RSS would fall under the auspice of SCU4 and were to include Middle East Radio Security (MERS) Intelligence Section and the Italian Detachment (IDET), which was formed following the invasion of Italy and ended up in Graz in Austria. Both the MERS and IDET were under the command of the effervescent Capt. Jack Hester.

At Barnet, the Overseas Units were represented by Maj. Poole who would fight their London battles for them, recruiting operators from the Signals Group, procuring equipment from the Engineering Group and War Office. Poole also established an overseas communications system by cable and special radio links.

Communications to the RSS Gibraltar station (under the command of Capt. Preston), from the units deployed in the Middle East, Belgium, and Germany, were via cable and wireless-supplied dedicated teleprinter and typex machines. Direct radio connections with these stations were coordinated from a central W/T station at Barnet, using one-time ciphers or typex according to load and facilities provided. It was the overseas link to the RSS Discrimination Section that was to be the most significant. Directives sent by this Barnet unit reached the Middle East and Gibraltar, as well as the RSS Liaison offices in Canada, which had good working relations with the Royal Canadian Signals, the US Coastguard, and the Federal Bureau of Investigations (FBI).

The value of the RSS sections at Gibraltar and in the Middle East were quickly proven. Gibraltar had had success in exploiting what was referred to as GG/SMA traffic, which conveyed Allied shipping movements around the Straits of Gibraltar to Germany. The Germans had reporting agents in many Western Mediterranean ports, and most of them were in hourly communication with Madrid and onwards to Berlin.

It was under a direct request from Vice-Admiral Sir James Somerville, the newly appointed Force 'H' Commander at Gibraltar, that the RSS provide a decoder to decipher this traffic locally. The Gibraltar section had also had success in exploiting German agent transmissions from Spain, which were well known to the RSS but were difficult to collect from Britain. This was also the case for some German intelligence networks operating in the Middle East, which had poor coverage in Britain. In the early stages of the RSS involvement in overseas intercept, a complete scheme was devised for the overseas wireless intercept extending from Gibraltar to North Borneo was prepared. Central to this programme was a chain of HF DF stations interlinked by W/T and situated at strategic points around the globe, and the cooperation of the Indian and Burmese internal W/T Security organisations as well as those of Canada, Australia, South Africa, and the Colonies. This overseas programme was quickly curtailed by MI6 and a halt put on any significant despatch of RSS teams overseas. Where units did exist overseas, MI6 insisted as a matter of principle that there was to be no cooperation between the RSS and any deployed 'Y' Service units.

Because of its geographic position, Gibraltar was a key intercept site for the Allied war effort. A British convoy passing through the Straits of Gibraltar into the Mediterranean needed to be unobserved by any German agents present near the Spanish coast. Fortunately, from the ground-breaking work of the RSS site, the service had mapped out the *Abwehr* network in Spain, whose traffic they could read in detail. The transmitted messages were intercepted by the RSS Gibraltar station, and the translated decodes forwarded through to the Admiralty within half an hour of its broadcast.

A meeting involving senior SIGINT commanders from the various organisations in July 1941 decreed that RSS Foreign Units should not be accompanied by cryptographic staff, but that cryptography should be carried out centrally by GC&CS at home, and the requisite information communicated to foreign units.

Throughout the war, the French were to become a critical part of the Allied intelligence-gathering effort against German occupation. There was a lot of interactions with the French via a dedicated teleprinter line to Paris. In the middle of 1943, a sequence of meetings were to occur between GC&CS and the French 'Y' Service, often hosted by the RSS. The cooperation was based around access into the Spanish Navy, Army, and Air Force traffic, from the French-controlled North Africa interception sites. They had achieved some good cryptological successes against the Spanish Air Force Wheatstone machine cipher systems. The Spanish employed two military cipher systems (referred to as Clave RED and Clave INSPECTOR). Mr J. E. S. Cooper often represented Bletchley at these meetings and, on one occasion, provided a cardboard model of the Wheatstone machine that could be used to decipher current messages. Bletchley had managed to produce a different decryption method for Clave RED from the French and an agreement was made to send through raw traffic samples to the French 'Y' Service teams in North Africa.

The French lead at these meetings was Commandant Black, who was the chief cryptographer to Col. Louis Rivet, Head of the *Bureau Central de Renseignements et d'Action* (BCRA). The RSS were to appraise Black; they found him impressively competent throughout their dealings with him.

Black headed up the French 'Y' Service in North Africa and had been responsible for intercepting the Spanish Moroccan and the Spanish ISOS and ISK groups, which he exploited to good effect. His team had managed to break the ISOS cipher but not the ISK traffic, and was not made aware that Bletchley could. The Spanish intercept was a duplication of RSS coverage in Britain that was sustained (largely for Admiralty customers), regardless of any progress the French were making in North Africa.

There was a proposal put forward to Black to potentially get the French 'Y' Service teams in North Africa to realign to other priorities because of the RSS duplication on Spanish traffic. It was considered that the French focus on transmissions from Southern France, Italy, and Sicily to assist with scant resources and lack of coverage in these regions of the Mediterranean Theatre. It would have meant an additional thirty receiver positions for interception, skilled discrimination, traffic analysis, and localised cryptographic expertise. As a *quid pro quo*, Britain offered deciphered messages from the Spanish ISOS (not ISK) services that would have amounted to 5,000 groups per day, potentially rising to 8,000 groups per day, which would have been a significant burden on communications capacity but Gambier-Parry was able to commit to providing the necessary W/T communications channel in both directions to cover the traffic load.

It was also proposed that some form of direct liaison occur between the RSS and Lt Van den Boesch (Commandant Black's Technical Intercept officer) on the topics of DF, discrimination, traffic analysis, and allocation. By March 1945, the French had newly formed a dedicated interception unit. From late 1943 onwards, operationally, the two services would de-conflict as routine on W/T plans, even down to passing frequencies in use by agents in occupied Europe.

The RSS had direct liaison officers in the USA, Maj. Maidment and Capt. Lakin, who were based in New York. Liaison officers were also deployed in India, Australia, and with the RCMP in Canada. There was also working-level liaison with a US Coastguard interception effort by the spring of 1945 off the coast of North West Africa.

The RSS special sections, manned by military personnel, were sent as far afield as Egypt, Gibraltar, Malaya, Malta, Cameroon, Tanzania, and Palestine. They also worked closely with local civil organisations in Cyprus, Mauritius, the Gold Coast, and Burma.

A requirement to assist the Russians with their wireless intercept, particularly to augment coverage of the Eastern Front, was discussed at length internally within the RSS/MI8. A proposal was formed in October 1941 to install a British 'Y' intercept station in Russia (either in the Moscow or the Caucasus region). MI8 was keen to get the following requirements:

(i)   German Air low grade M/F raw material.
(ii)   German Air Force safety service M/F raw material.
(iii) German Naval 4-letter raw material.
(iv)   Any further German raw material giving date, time and frequencies.
(v)   German Air Force signal handbooks.
(vi)   German Naval and Merchant Service communications orders, and relevant code books and documents.
(vii) German Air Force and German Air Code (FAUT).[1]

In return, the RSS would give the Russians access to the following:

(i)   Certain German 3-letter air codes.
(ii)   Complete scheme of German Army communication network and call-sign book.
(iii) Information regarding the German knowledge of Russian Military communications as revealed by German Y D/F reporting.
(iv)   German sea rescue code.
(v)   Information of our knowledge of German Naval frequencies and communication routines as revealed by D/F and captured documents.[2]

Much of this dialogue with the Russians was orchestrated by RAF Sqn Ldr Scott-Farnie and discussed at a high level within the 'Y' Committee. The Russian Ambassador to London was invited to inspect the British 'Y' and D/F stations, and to see maps showing the German order of battle. The committee also recommended the Russians send over a wireless expert to begin liaison in earnest. The 'Y' Committee proposed that the Naval W/T station at Murmansk be equipped with communications receivers for interception of M/F and HF as this material 'is of immediate operational value'. To achieve heightened sharing of material with the Russians, the W/T link with the UK would have to be bolstered by the installation of an extra transmitter.

The RSS collected a lot of Russian KGB transmissions during the war, much of it emanating from the Russian Embassy in London, from the DF results. The RSS had made MI5 aware as far back as June 1943. Maltby and others had noted these intercepts because of the technical skill involved in the methods of encrypting the messages. There also were unique in the length of broadcasts, lasting for up to eight hours in each day long cycle, which would stretch the limited RSS resources on this target

RSS involvement in the Far East campaigns was also significant. One 'Z' and two X-type Special Wireless Sections proceeded by sea to Singapore in January 1941 with six Mobile Units equipped with R106 receivers only (no portable DF sets—Ferrets or Snifters). The units were commanded by Capt. McMillan from the Royal Signals and came under the control of DDMI (Malaya) and the Far East Combined Bureau (FECB). The 'Z' and one 'X' Section were located with the Royal Navy W/T station at Kranji in Singapore, the other 'X' Section being deployed to Kuala Lumpur. One of the Mobile Units was deployed to the border with Thailand to intercept potential illicit wireless transmissions and research any new Thai transmitters.

The units developed a close relationship with the Royal Navy, which assisted with DF, although the Navy could only provide single line bearings. The RSS wanted to augment what DF capabilities there were in the region and offered two fixed DF stations (spaced loop type), one for Singapore and one for Northern Borneo. A DF station was also proposed in Rangoon, Burma. These additional three DF stations, working alongside the already established DF sites at Kharagpur, Belgaum, and Abbottabad in India, would, if linked by W/T, cover the greater part of the Far East and India. Two key RSS staff in India at the time were Desmond Downing (G13ZX) and Maj. Etheridge.

The India RSS effort was the result of a direct request from Field Marshal Sir Archibald Wavell, the C-in-C of Allied forces in India from 1941 to 1943. The requirement led to the RSS assisting in the formation of the 'No.1 Radio Security Company', which was largely manned by personnel from the Royal Corps of Signals recruited from the 'Y' Service teams in India, with a total complement around 450 men. The company was ultimately the responsibility of the Government of India who, along with the British Treasury, helped fund its establishment. Prior to the Second World War, SIGINT in India had been the preserve of the Indian Army.

The year 1942 saw a rapid expansion in theatre as the RAF 'Y' Service units were deployed to India to bolster efforts against the Japanese target. By the summer of 1944, there was an intent to repatriate the majority of the trained personnel from the company to bolster the numbers of trained interceptors for the campaign in Europe. The RSS was training up to 400 replacement staff over a six- to nine-month period. These had been drawn from the Ministry of Labour, under a decision sanctioned by the Signals Intelligence Board, and involved the Director of Military Intelligence (India) Maj.-Gen. John Alexander Sinclair. He was to become the head of the SIS after the war. The original RSC came partly from the 'X' Sections in Malaya and were in part recruited from the deployed 'Y' Service personnel in India.

The work in India was deemed to be unique: 'There is no similarity between what is tried to be done against the Japanese Intelligence Service and that which is being done against the *Abwehr*'. Their collection priorities during the Second World War were Afghanistan; Iran external; Russia; IWI; Japanese merchant shipping; Japanese consular, in place of the Japanese Navy; and China.

Each strand of this India collection effort involved four-man shift teams. Their Russian collect enabled the RSS to cover Transcaucasus and Central Asia Military and air formations with ten watches. The above continued commitments would require an increase of forty-four wireless operators into No. 1 Wireless Company. These requests to bolster the ranks of personnel returning to Britain were to fall on deaf ears in the middle of 1944, as the Allies were preparing for the biggest invasion of the war. The Signal Intelligence Board needed to replenish personnel, but they dictated that 'the simplest way of maintaining the Indian Radio Security Company at strength is to provide trained personnel by the same machinery that provided the initial establishment'. Regardless, the RSS wanted Russian traffic to be maintained and improved upon, 'most desirable that Indian interception of Russian traffic should be expanded to utmost in view our inability to allot sets for this work here'.

Under direction from the Signal Intelligence Board both the 'Y' Services and RSS interceptors were to be deployed into the far corners of the world. In February, the board approved the feasibility of sending two W/T operators to Sweden under the oversight of Grp Capt. Frederick Daubney, DDI. A small interception unit working to Force 133 in Istanbul was established under the command of DMI Middle East. In the following tables, detailing the services covered by MERS (Middle East Radio Service (Aegean Group) (from HW51/26)), an asterisk (*) indicates ENIGMA traffic.

CENTRE 1: MYTELENE		COVER NAME: BERTA		
Works To:	Cover Name	Service Covered	Not Covered	Estimated Daily Traffic
SALONIKA	SEBALD	7/78	-	20
ATHENS	ADOLF	7/89	-	15
VIENNA	WIRA/WENDO	7/75	-	3
SAMOS	SUSI	7/47	-	5
CHIOS	CARLO	7/90	-	20
LEMNOS	LEDA	7/49	-	3
SAMOS works CHIOS		7/54	-	2

CENTRE 2: SALONKIA		COVER NAME: SEBALD		
Works To:	Cover Name	Service Covered	Not Covered	Estimated Daily Traffic
SAMOS	SUSI	7/58	-	3
CHIOS	CARLO	7/54	-	2
LEMNOS	LEDA	7/48	-	2
ATHENS	ADOLF	7/95	-	5
ATHENS	ADOLF	2/506*	-	3
VIENNA	WIRA	-	2/538*	-
VERLIN	SCHLOSS	-	2/38*	-

CENTRE: ATHENS		COVER NAME: ADOLF		
Works To:	Cover Name	Service Covered	Not Covered	Estimated Daily Traffic
MYTELENE	BERTA	7/89	-	15
SALONIKA	SEBALD	7/95	-	5
SALONIKA	SEBALD	2/506*	-	3
CHIOS	CARLO	2/987	-	3
SOFIA	SEPP	2/524*	-	3
BERLIN	SCHLOSS	-	2/26*	-
SICILY	?	-	2/167	-
?	?	-	2/510	-

CENTRE: SOFIA		COVER NAME: SEPP		
Works To:	Cover Name	Service Covered	Not Covered	Estimated Daily Traffic
VIENNA	WIRA/WENDA	7/23	-	20
ATHENS	ADOLF	2/524*	-	4
BUCHAREST	BENITO	2/521*	-	4
UKRAINE	?	2/561	-	2
?	?	2/509	-	1
?	?	2/?	-	1
?	?	7/60	-	3

CENTRE: SICILY		COVER NAME: ?		
Works To:	Cover Name	Service Covered	Not Covered	Estimated Daily Traffic
BERLIN	SCHLOSS	2/56*	2/56*	-
MADRID	MEDIA	2/151	2/151	-
ATHENS	ADOLF	2/167	2/167	-
TRIPOLI	TROLI	?	?	-
DERNA	SKORPION	?	?	-
TUNIS	?	?	?	-

CENTRE: VIENNA		COVER NAME: WIRA		
Works To:	Cover Name	Service Covered	Not Covered	Estimated Daily Traffic
SOFIA	SEPP	7/23	-	20
TURKEY	?	7/53	-	2
GREECE	?	7/59	-	1
UKRAINE	?	7/88	-	5
VARNA	?	7/97	-	10
MYTELENE	BERTA	7/75	-	3
BUCHAREST	BENITO	-	7/4	-
SOUTH POLAND	?	-	7/16	-
BUCHAREST	BENITO	-	2/536*	-
ZAGREB	ABAZZIA	-	2/543	-

There had been some local success in collecting illicit wireless transmissions in Hong Kong, but there was no requirement for a DF station there 'owing to local technical difficulties'. The RSS influence into Asia was far reaching, and the organisation was to host two visitors from as far afield as Australia in 1944.

The *Abwehr* had significant levels of interest in Egypt, with its strategic position in the Middle East for the Allies. They had an active wireless link from the Budapest hub to the Japanese Embassy in Cairo, and a 'well-camouflaged W/T station in Cairo' located in the church of a Hungarian priest in the city. Activity in Egypt was run from the Turkey *Abwehr* network, as was much of the Near East. The Germans were very interested in the armament and equipment of the British formations in Egypt, the movement of shipping between Port Said and Haifa, and the disposition of Allied troops within Africa and the Western Desert. The *Abwehr* also had interest in reporting on Allied oil deliveries and oil production in Egypt and, not surprisingly, reports were intercepted, which included the address of the British Staff HQ in Cairo and the organisation of the British Intelligence Services' presence in the city.

February 1941 saw the formation of an RSS Military Unit at Trowbridge under Capt. Hester, which sailed for Egypt in March 1941. Egypt in the Second World War was very much the regional centre of British military power, and the RSS units there were to be the first overseas units established by the service as well as Gibraltar. The RSS wanted something big in the Middle East. The senior officers had realised they would need to commit to the region. Efficiency would never be obtained in RSS work by using small local units, both in cryptography and signals interception. They realised that depth was the essence of the problem.

The Cairo RSS unit was under the command of the then Capt. Jack Hester and Gibraltar was under the direction of Lt Donnan and worked in conjunction with the Army HQ at both locations. Much of the SIGINT focus in the region was around the Combined Bureau Middle East (CBME), which was established in late 1940, based out of the King Farouk Museum on the Suez Road in Heliopolis, just north of Cairo in Egypt. This was opened by Col. Freddie Jacob and was under direction from GC&CS at Bletchley Park, and the personnel would fall under local control for their pay and accommodation. It was intended to replicate some of Bletchley Park's cryptographic work alongside the mainstay of intercept and traffic analysis. It would act as the signals intelligence centre for the whole Middle East, employing signals specialists from the Army, Royal Navy, and RAF until March 1943. The CBME was linked back to Britain via a wireless link to the SIS Section VIII facility at Whaddon.

RSS personnel were not employed at the facility and the CBME was officially an RAF establishment commanded by Sqn Ldr Jeudwine; subsequently, the interception at the facility was undertaken by the RAF Wireless Units stationed there (Units 50 and 53). The CBME would provide the local MI5 (Security Intelligence Middle East, or SIME) section and the local MI6 section (referred to in the cover term Inter-Service Liaison Department, or ISLD) with decrypted intelligence that made a significant improvement to their counterintelligence work at a local level. It was to have a vital knock on effect in shaping the Allied war effort in North Africa.

The RSS were located at the Ma'adi Military Camp in an affluent tree-lined southern suburb of Cairo on the eastern bank of the Nile, which was conveniently also home to the Combined Services Detailed Interrogation Centre (CSDIC). Many of the interrogation cells at the camp were wired with eavesdropping equipment installed by engineers from Dollis Hill. One of the RSS wireless operators based at the Ma'adi camp was Peter Stewart, who had joined the RSS in 1941. He had taken his original wireless training on a six-month marine wireless operator training course at Liverpool Wireless School, and graduated in October 1940, going on to join the Marconi Wireless Company as a junior wireless operator. He went on to join the RSS, where his first role after moving from Arkley View to Hanslope was to train French-Canadians in Morse before they were deployed behind enemy lines in France. He went on to volunteer to go overseas. Prior to being deployed they were housed in tents in the grounds of Hanslope Park and given weapons training (with their standard issue Lee–Enfield rifles), physical fitness, and unarmed combat training. The deployed personnel were sent to Avonmouth and embarked on the troopship *Esperance Bay*, which had over 2,000 troops on board, making living conditions and hygiene challenging. The vessel sailed via Durban in South Africa, where they were transferred on to the *Nieu Amsterdam* troopship. From there, they transited via the Suez Canal to Egypt, where they served at the Ma'adi camp. The intercept station was partially excavated below ground and encased in sandbags for protection from aerial Luftwaffe attacks. The men slept under canvas in the desert, while the officers were based out of a nearby villa.

When the Axis forces were beaten out of Libya, Stewart and three of his RSS colleagues were sent on an assignment to Appolonia in Cyranaica on the North Libyan coast, a distance of over 700 miles on war-ravaged roads and desert tracks in a mobile radio intercept unit, which they amiably referred to as the 'Gin Palace'. They were to stay in a deserted farmhouse and establish a radio link to

Allied agents operating in Crete and on the Aegean Islands. These agents were operating under restrictive conditions, using limited-range radio sets and often under surveillance, so contact was difficult.

After significant winter rainfall, the camp at Ma'adi was flooded under 2 feet of water when the local canal burst its banks on the night of 31 December 1944. Alongside other RSS staff, Stewart was relocated to the RSS station at Sidi Bishr, near Alexandria, where he was to serve until the end of the war.

The RSS facility at Sidi Bishr, a couple of miles east of Alexandria, comprised of around fifteen to twenty receivers and had a number of skilled wireless operators such as Charles Emary (G5GH) and Ray Wright. They would transmit their logs back to SIS Section VIII at Whaddon, the small village not far from Bletchley. Emary was originally in charge of the Station 'X' radio station in the tower of the Bletchley mansion between 1939 and 1940. He had also been involved in training SOE wireless operators at Thame Park. The output from the Sidi Bishr RSS interception site was sent to Britain via a radio link located in a villa just outside the camp perimeter, using an American 399 transmitter, part of a broader American HF mobile link in the region. There was also a separate RSS DF station about 5 miles from the main station.

The MERS interception priorities were the following—Italy (especially Northern Italy), Yugoslavia, Bulgaria, and Aegean services. MERS had originally been established by the RSS to find illicit W/T sets, as it was in Britain, but it soon evolved into its own distinct unit, under Hester's leadership, to intercept *Abwehr* W/T traffic and its Turkish and Aegean networks. It quickly broadened its coverage to exploit the German Balkan and Italian networks.

Hester worked closely with the CBME cryptographic section, which would read transposition ciphers on the spot and send the product back to Britain. The MERS could exploit around three-quarters of the total Aegean networks traffic. MERS could also intercept some ISK traffic, which was inaudible in Britain and transmitted back to the GC&CS at Bletchley. It would thus have expanded the RSS coverage of the ISK traffic in the Balkans, Turkey, and Italy.

Hester was to create MERS detachments as far afield as Derna and Benghazi in Libya, whose intercepts would be relayed back to Cairo for deciphering locally or for forward transmission back to the GC&CS. He was supported at Sidi Bishr by Maj. 'Topper' Brown, Capt. Charles Peck, and Capt. Mountford. MERS, at the height of its production, could intercept in the region of 200 messages per day.

Infamously, the GC&CS Middle East unit were permitted to decrypt their own ISOS hand cipher intercepts. This went against protocol. In a memo from Col. Worlledge to DDMI(O) in June 1941, Worlledge was adamant that any cryptography undertaken on German intercepts was to be achieved in Britain, not at an overseas unit:

We will under no circumstances agree to Group material being subjected to local cryptography, or to any local distribution of the results. It would be quite impossible to maintain the essential secrecy of ISOS material were we to reverse this decision...meanwhile I am taking such steps as will prevent Hester's organisation applying local cryptography to Group material.[3]

The memo goes on to agree the RSS control:

It was agreed that RSS foreign units should not be accompanied by cryptographic staff, but that cryptography should be carried out centrally by GC&CS, at home, and the requisite information communicated to foreign units.[4]

Worlledge wanted to maintain and fully utilise the cryptographic excellence at Bletchley. Anything that was undertaken to decipher locally would dilute the capabilities the British had to read the *Abwehr* ciphers.

Worlledge generated a significantly weighty argument to sway the opinions of DDMI(O). He had quickly realised that a cryptography team in England, with access to the information produced by a German outstation derived from a relay link nearer home where the cipher had already been broken, would have a great advantage in tackling the cipher of the outstation itself. The teams in the Middle East dealing with ISOS material undigested could be very misleading and dangerous. If the stations wanted to undertake local cryptography, there would have always been a danger of overt local action in spite of orders, losing the Allies this unique source of intelligence.

In July 1941, MI6 promulgated a directive for the overseas Special Wireless Sections (with regard to the ISOS and IWI traffic):

1. Control of foreign units of the Radio Security Service in future must be centralised in the HQ of the RSS at home.
2. The RSS foreign units should not be accompanied by cryptographic staff, but that cryptography should be carried out centrally by the GC&CS at home, and the requisite information communicated to foreign units.
3. No further foreign units to be despatched until those in existence proved their value and that the authorised establishments should be kept in abeyance.

These decisions had been made because DMI wanted command and control to be decentralised to the local headquarters (in this case, DMI Middle East, DMO&I India and Burma, and DDMI Malaya). It was widely considered that it would have been impossible for any wireless interception in the Far East to be effectively controlled from Britain. The RSS teams in the Middle East did have permission independently to decipher wireless traffic locally. It had been found to be of immense local value to operations in theatre. They had not had any reportable output from Bletchley ISOS traffic.

All the relevant ciphers had been broken at Bletchley, and from June 1942, the CBME team was to take on responsibility for deciphering the Group VII traffic locally. The RSS was to rely on the MERS in Egypt for much of its strategic and tactical material on the *Abwehr*. As Hester became aware of the abilities of CBME cryptographers to exploit the traffic locally, it stimulated MERS to rapidly produce more and better traffic. Many significant Aegean network links (which had been difficult to intercept to the low frequencies used) were being collected almost in their entirety. New Balkan links were also being found. Over time, with the increasing workloads and intercepted traffic, the MERS, CBME, and ISLD teams developed a close working relationship. ISLD would have translator staff deployed into the CBME. In June 1942, the CBME cryptography team had eleven personnel of all ranks. The deciphering would be done by the ISOS team at the CBME and then the output translated by the ISLD translators and it would be teleprinted direct to the ISLD. As time elapsed, the German decodes and keys would be signalled back to Bletchley.

It would become a well-oiled machine, but it did have cause to be interrupted, as was the case in July 1942 during the Rommel advance into Egypt. The ISOS team moved to a military camp in Gaza and then subsequently on to Sarafand. Their intercepts had to be sent from MERS via bag, and the subsequent decodes teleprinted to the CBME. During these transitions, the teams were often short of equipment and stores, to a point where they had run out of the transparent paper used for stencil decoding work and had to rely on the bromo toilet paper as a necessary replacement. Sarafand in Palestine had been a significant wireless interception site since the early 1920s for the Army.

Ray Wright, an experienced W/T operator, was selected to go to Sidi Bishr along with a pool of other operators from RSS stations around the country. Around twenty of them were assembled at Arkley where they spent a few weeks training, having medicals and inoculations, and then given a period of leave before being deployed to Egypt. They embarked on a vessel at Newhaven to go via the Channel to Dieppe, and subsequently put on to a French train to Toulon in the south of France. Here they boarded a French passenger ship called the *Champollion* for a five-day crossing of the Mediterranean to the Egyptian port of Alexandria. The route through France, and by sea to the Middle East, was known as the MEDLOC route. It was designed to minimise the risk from German U-boats. The RSS personnel would then have been moved from the ports, often via the Ma'adi military camp to Sidi Bishr. There were two main RSS huts on the camp, one referred to as the Operations (Intercept) hut, which housed the receiver banks, and the other adjacent 'Intelligence' hut where the messages were analysed and processed. From there, the signals were taken by despatch rider to Alexandria, where they were transmitted back to Britain.

There was a very large army transit camp at Sidi Bishr where troops were coming in and going out most of the time. It was fairly secure and the entry gates were controlled by a couple of Military Police who seemed to be more concerned with the appearance and dress of those passing to and fro than security. Within the perimeter of this camp there was a P.O.W. camp, mainly the remnants of the German Afrika Korps who were patiently waiting repatriation to their homeland. Also tucked away in the rear of this large camp was SCU4 (Special Communications Unit No. 4). This was surrounded by a substantial perimeter fence and guarded day and night by armed sentries.[5]

The guards were from East and West Africa regiments and none of them spoke English. They probably represented our greatest physical danger, especially when approached at night. You would approach them out of the dark and walk towards the floodlit gate area and immediately hear the ominous click of the safety catch coming off, before the challenge. The response to the challenge was a greetings word, either *Abadi* or *Jambo* depending on whether the guards were from East Africa or West Africa. Straight forward enough one would think, but far from it. The African troops wore the same uniform with the wide brim hat and they looked exactly the same, so you took a chance when you gave the password. If you got it wrong you hastily gave the other one and hoped for the best. Communication with them was nigh on impossible, and they took their duty very seriously.[6]

Inside our perimeter fence there were the usual buildings, an admin hut, stores, ablutions, a dining hut and accommodation huts. Then there was another fenced off area known as the compound which comprised two huts. One was the operational hut and the other the 'I' room (intelligence). The operational hut was where the interceptors worked. No one was allowed to enter the compound unless you worked there and those who worked in one of the huts did not normally enter the other hut within the compound. There was also a teleprinter facility within the station. Outside of the station there was a radio link station and a D/F facility which was staffed by SCU4 but once again unless you worked there you never visited it.

Life within the camp was very much what you made of it. There was really no social life and you did not leave the station and mingle with the other troops in the larger transit camp. This was mainly because of the nature of our work. However, there was an opportunity to go for a swim, as the Mediterranean was within walking distance although there was not much of a beach, mostly a rocky foreshore. On a full day off one could walk to a rail stop and go into Alexandria by train, which most of us did. There were good shops and restaurants in Alexandria. When on leave most of us went (in civilian clothes) much further afield, either to Palestine, Syria or down the Nile to Luxor, the Valley of the Kings. Most of the unit members had tastes which tended to set them apart, and serious study of the ancient cultures of the region were popular.[7]

Since enlistment we had no military training but most had been in one or other of the Cadet Corps so some of the basic elements were known. It was thought that a little extra training might be useful and fortunately the admin sergeant had been in the Airborne Division, including service at Arnhem, and he gave some useful instruction in unarmed combat and in the use of small arms, pistols and the stengun.

Food in the camp was monotonous and largely comprised a canned product labelled 'M and V' (meat and vegetables) which was served up usually as a stew. Initially the cooks and mess hall staff were local Arabs who were under the control of a soldier who ensured that they arrived for work on time and carried on doing it until they were ushered off the camp. A valuable local staff member was the *dhobi waller*. He had his own tent and his lantern lighted tent could be seen in the distance late into the night. He offered two forms of clothes washing service. There was the 'Company Dhobi' paid for by the admin which provided a 3 days service. Then there was the 'Flying Dhobi' which was a one day service, washing given in first thing in the morning was washed, starched and pressed by evening, and you paid him just a couple of piastres. We mostly used this service.

The food situation improved when the services of the local Arab cooks were replaced by a couple of German POWs from the nearby camp. They used their imagination with the supplies they had to work with and we were pleased with the result. They seemed to enjoy being with us during their working hours. Not only was it a break from containment inside their own camp but it meant that they ate our food and were paid for their services in a useful currency, *viz.* cigarettes. This was a highly tradeable currency within their camp. Despite the fact that the Afrika Korps and the Eighth Army had been knocking seven bells out of each other for the past few years, now that it was over we found the German POWs quite nice fellows. Nevertheless they never moved away from the kitchen area and were escorted in and out of our camp. Fresh water was one thing we missed most of all. All local water had to be boiled and it never really got cold.[8]

By the late summer of 1943, the RSIC agreed that part of MERS should be moved to Sicily, and Hester coordinated an advance party to the island to reconnoitre reception conditions there. He suggested they would need just three weeks to establish the unit there as soon as the order was given. The RSIC wanted this to be done with the utmost urgency. They would act in correlating the interception programme with the course of impending military operations. As military operations in Italy advanced northward, it was vital the RSS push a forward interception unit towards the Alps. Towards the end of 1943, a small intercept team was sent to Bari to attempt better collection of the Yugoslav networks.

There was a drive from the RSS and MI5 at this stage of the war to get hold of wireless equipment from any disrupted German intelligence networks to be brought back to the RSS for engineers to deconstruct them to enhance the Allies knowledge for interception: 'Every possible step should be taken by section officers to recover equipment in use by existing cells when they are closed down. A considerable amount of equipment will be collected by security officers in the course of their duties'.

Hester was concerned that this would stretch the already fragmented MERS to breaking point. Since being established, MERS had experimented with a number of intercept locations, but most of the effort was centred on their two sites in Cairo and outside the town of Al-Arish. The manpower and equipment at Cairo were in short supply, and the unit could not adequately take on any additional interception duties without impacting its current workload. Hester had had to refuse tasks to intercept Yugoslavian cross-link traffic due to lack of operators. He would need reinforcements from Britain to meet any additional demands. Hester also argued that the MERS team had a reliance to be close to the CBME cryptographic unit. They also needed to be centred on Cairo for access to the Allies communications links, supply lines, and direct access to the military commands that wanted the intelligence reports.

On operations in Italy with the MERS detachments, Capt. Hester was involved directly with the infamous 30 Assault Unit (30AU), a covert commando intelligence gathering unit set up by Ian Fleming, the author of the early James Bond books. During the Allied push through Italy, Hester and 30AU raided the German Embassy in Rome, collecting valuable W/T equipment, although there was 'nothing new or of interest'. He had been given apparent intelligence from the RSS on the equipment at the embassy. The confiscated HF equipment was given careful examination and was considered to have been constructed by an amateur, possibly one of the operators themselves.

Prefixes for CBME—raw Typex traffic back to Britain

FENCE	German Naval 4 letter traffic
RATIO	Italian Naval 5 letter
TOWER	Italian Naval 4 letter
ACRID	Italian Naval 4 letter
NIECE	Italian Naval other figure
VICAR	Naval traffic lights (in G. settings)
SURLY	Certain German traffic as indicated direct to RN at Alexandria
TALON	French Naval
GIDDY	
BLOOD	
MIRTH	Used for German High Grade material typexed to UK
WRATH	
FACET	
AWAKE	Italian Military
PULSE	Vichy French Military
BOGUS	Used by Heliopolis for certain Playfair traffic
SCOOP	

SUGAR	German Air 3 letter traffic, can be used indiscriminately with SCOOP for GAF material
BLAZE	
FLOCK+	French Air
LADLE	Italian Air (Athens and Eastern)
COVEY	Censorship material
BULGY	Italian Diplo (5 letter, alternate consonant/vowel throughout)
UNITY	Italian Diplo (other 5 letter and Air)
LEAFY	Meteorological
YEAST	RSS traffic (only to be used if sent by Heliopolis on RAF link)
GUILE	Miscellaneous
ETHIC	Used by Sarafand for Djibouti traffic
PRIDE	Used by Sarafand for Iraqi intercepts

+ as this is the telegraphic address for the Baghdad Signals Unit, UK have been asked to change it, but so far no reply has been received

(From TNA file HW51/56)

The RSS sections in France were often offered the opportunity to interrogate captured agents to collect vital intelligence on wireless broadcasts. In a note to the RSS in August 1944, Lt-Col. Maltby was asked: 'Are you interested in a man, a Belgian, who has been working for four years with the Gestapo in Belgium on DF'ing? He has been working the Pernod and Luth sets for the Gestapo and has escaped. He is now in the hands of the Maquis, whence it may be possible to extract him...' Maltby gave a short positive response back: 'Yes please, we should be most interested to interrogate this man'.

Resources for the MERS facilities in Egypt were restrictive even in early 1941. Requests had gone back to Britain for more skilled wireless operators. They were in short supply, but a telegram from the Air Ministry in January 1941 highlighted that the regional collection on Italian traffic was to be its priority and 'strong reinforcements are on the way to fill present deficiencies'. Work was underway through 'Y' Service training pipelines at RAF Cheadle on the German Airforce (GAF) traffic and VHF communications. Resources were not forthcoming immediately:

[However] personnel and equipment ... can be despatched as they become available either to complete your establishment if deficiencies exist after present reinforcements reach you ... in view of German development we are sending by quickest means one officer (Waters) for Combined Bureau with one year's experience GAF tactical traffic. He will bring complete dossier of codes, aids and recognition of units and notes on signal procedure.

Occasionally, the CBME cipher specialists in Cairo would get a request for a decode to be passed immediately back to Bletchley, often messages that contained valuable cribs for Enigma keys. On one occasion, the team had to relay information on a low-grade network that had appeared on the Eastern Front, with the intent that Bletchley would convey this directly to the Russians.

As the war ran on, the CBME component was to move on but various other SIGINT collection sites were maintained by the military, including the Navy sites at Sidi Bishr (Alexandria) in Egypt and Malta, and the RAF at Port Fuad in Egypt. The Army 'Y' Service, in addition to the site at Sarafand, maintained a site in Istanbul and in Malta.

The mobile units as they progressed through the spine of Italy, following the Allied offensive, came to a pause in Northern Italy or Austria, the Army concentrating at Pfannberg in Austria and the RAF at Graz in Austria and Conversano in Italy. Just before the end of the war, the RAF was to move its 'Y' Service collection units to Udine in Italy.

The flow of Japanese diplomatic and illicit wireless traffic was a source of concern for the RSS as the war progressed in the Pacific. There was little evidence of illicit agent derived traffic across the Pacific. US traffic would flow to Japan via diplomatic cipher channels in South America from the main station in Santiago. This was switched to Argentina and it would become the only source of Japanese traffic, often said in plain English-language broadcasts.

There was no detectable Japanese illicit activity in mainland USA during the Second World War. The US Federal Communications Commission (FCC) were said to have a 'very efficient..and wide network of intercept and D/F stations'. Working alongside the Canadian Army during the early years of the war, the FCC picked up transmissions from a controlled German agent operating in Canada for which neither intercept service was aware. Likewise in Hawaii, FCC operations were replaced by an Army intercept service and they proved no evidence of illicit Japanese traffic being transmitted.

In India, during the spring of 1943, Axis-controlled agents were being dropped behind Allied lines by parachute equipped with radio sets. One such agent, an Indian Army signaller, gave himself up when he landed with all his accompanying radio sets, cipher equipment, and documents. During detailed interrogation, he revealed he was a member of the first radio class for Indian agents who had been tasked with gathering intelligence on Allied troop dispositions, aerodrome activity, and attitude of the local populace to subversive work. He exposed the names of other agents operating in the region who were subsequently rounded up. The cipher he was to use was that of a simple *Abwehr* cipher already known to the RSS. He was told to transmit in his native language with the rest of his deployed team. His control stations were at Rangoon and Shwebo in Myanmar.

CSDIC interrogations and seized documents had highlighted that the SD had left behind sixtyagents in Rome to carry out espionage and sabotage tasks. The agents had been divided into four main groups with its own separate and distinct W/T communications network and had deposited large caches of sabotage equipment around Italy, including even at the German Embassy. Although this network was sizeable, the RSS assessment was it could only be dysfunctional. The SD had been very well penetrated by the RSS interceptors, so knowledge of their operations was detailed. Many of the SD agents who had been poorly trained and just wanted an excuse to get across to the Allied lines.

The RSS had a significant role to play in Gibraltar. During 1943, the land campaigns in Sicily, North Africa, and Italy had almost freed the Mediterranean for Allied ships. British Intelligence had continually lobbied the Spanish Government to force a closure of the German reporting station at Algeciras and reduce the number of German personnel in their collection stations south of the Straits. The Spanish 'acted in as dilatory and half-hearted a manner as possible and have assisted the Germans with reports and in other ways'.

Much of the wireless traffic from these German *Abwehr* stations consisted of details of merchant shipping movements and typically small warship movements such as minesweepers. It was clear to the RSS that their collection in the region was very incomplete as they were missing a lot of naval movements through the Straits.

> The deterioration in the reporting of the different Stellen varies. It is most marked at Algeciras. A year ago Madrid received from Algeciras some 20 messages a day on an average, and harbour reports were given in extreme detail, all the merchant ships being identified, and information could be passed on by Madrid within the hour. Now SIRENE passes anything up to 6 or 7 reports in the day and, while the delay in forwarding from Madrid varies enormously, the average is certainly 3 or 4 times as long … the stations at Spartel, Tres Forcas and Alboran have altered little as their personnel has remained unchanged. The other stations have lost the efficiency of their night-reporting service though their daytime standard is, on the whole, maintained.

The *Abwehr*'s priorities for the Straits of Gibraltar were threefold: firstly, the passage of convoys (especially troop movements) and the strength of their escorts—the sailing of convoys from Gibraltar and the direction taken; secondly, movements of warships, especially the larger classes and capital ships; and thirdly, movements that may give a pointer to future intentions of the Allies such as the movements of landing craft (and also the arrival of convoys from the Atlantic to Gibraltar and the inward passage of convoys).

It was clear that much of the reporting by these *Abwehr* stations was incorrect and this intelligence was being passed up to the higher echelons of the German military, who would be making inaccurate assessments of Allied naval posture in the Mediterranean. One such example was highlighted:

... the weekly situation report to Istanbul by Berlin gives 5 battleships in the Mediterranean though there are in fact only two, the French LORRAINE, and the WARSPITE in dock in Gibraltar. It is known that the High Command have accepted that number of battleships and have this been led astray.

The RSIC report goes on to suggest that 'although the reports may, and do, give individual items of considerable importance to the German long-term planners and total picture of movements of troop and store convoys, major warships and landing craft is sufficiently inaccurate to be likely to produce a false impression of our strategic intentions'.

In August 1944, a couple of Australian officers visited the RSS, and they were to return with a recommendation that an interception service, run along similar lines to the RSS, be established in the country. The Australian Army had agreed to assist with this and help in the detection of any illicit wireless transmissions from Japanese agents. There had been little evidence of Japanese agents operating within Australia, but the security service had come across the Japanese training Chinese nationals in the country to undertake radio transmissions on their behalf. There was even evidence of a German agent operating as a sergeant within the American Army in Australia.

The Australian Army Signals teams would provide personnel for interception, discrimination, and mobile units where required. They would work directly with the security service who would cooperate the moment an agent was located inside Australia. Two signals groups were set up in Australia: the Central Bureau, which was attached to the Allied Commander of the South West Pacific area, under the command of Gen. Douglas MacArthur, and the Royal Australian Navy/United States Navy Fleet Radio Unit in Melbourne (FRUMEL), under the command of Adml Nimitz. It was the Central Bureau that had the role to research and decipher any intercepted Japanese military radio broadcasts.

Lt-Col. Sandford of the Central Bureau had been appointed from the UK to control the RSS work in Australia. Sandford was responsible for the cryptanalytical part of the work and would act as a liaison bridge back to Britain but also provide a link via cipher channels to teams in India and the British Security Coordination (BSC) working out of the Rockefeller Centre in Manhattan, New York. The BSC, an arm of MI6, was founded in May 1940 as simply the regional SIS station in North America. Although actually run by a Canadian, William Stephenson, its covert aims were to gather intelligence and to assist with the flow of munitions to the war in Europe from America. Many of the staff at the BSC were Canadian nationals, although interestingly, the head of propaganda for South America was British but born to a German father and British mother who had lived in Brazil for more than twenty years. MI5 had once considered him to be a dangerous Austrian spy.

By September 1944, the RSIC and Maltby were to shape plans for forward deploying RSS Mobile Units into Belgium and France or even into Germany if the German Army was to capitulate. It would fill a gap in the intercept of low-frequency traffic inside Germany, which would not be accessible from British aerials. Maltby wanted the unit to consist of eight double-banked positions and would have a direct W/T communications bridge back to the RSS HQ in Barnet.

The RSS worked closely in conjunction with MI5 throughout the war. They were also to have a close working relationship with the BBC Monitoring service at Caversham Park, for which the BBC was paid a subsidy. They were to rely heavily on the RSS DF system for DF of any radio stations they wanted locational information on.

RSS reports from intercept of Russian traffic from the Eastern Front were referred to as MAX reports and covered an area from Leningrad to Iran. This strand of intelligence was discovered from ISOS reports in the winter of 1941–1942, produced from traffic from an *Abwehr* outstation operating in Sofia, known as *the Luftmeldekopf*, connecting to a well-placed agent in Russia. *Luftmeldekopf*'s W/T station was given the code name SCHWERT by the RSS and was controlled by Maj. von Wahl (known as 'Wagner') operating in Vienna, but the station itself was run by Maj. von Kahlen in Sofia.

The station was transmitting daily operational intelligence summaries to the *Abwehr* station in Vienna about progress on the Eastern Front, and this traffic was producing a steady stream of intelligence for the RSS interceptors. The reports were being relayed by a number of methods, including teleprinter, telephone, and even by hand. By March 1942, nearly 300 RSS reports were generated from these MAX reports. The total number sent was estimated to be between 30 and 50 per cent more than this total. They were said to be 'singularly accurate in forecasting Russian operations'. Of course, at this stage of the war, the Russian Front was still the major interest of the Germans.

It was widely suspected at the time that the MAX reports originated from a Russian double-cross operation. British intelligence made the decision to expose the material to the Russians, and in October 1943, SIS representatives in Moscow gave them a summary of intercepted MAX reports, which engendered a limited response back from them. Post-war interrogations undertaken on members of the *Abwehr* station established that these MAX reports were indeed sourced from a Russian Double-Cross operation, by an agent who had infiltrated a group of White Russians.

There was a strong bond between the RSS and the Polish throughout the Second World War. As previously mentioned, Maltby and Jameson Till were to be instrumental in supporting the PMWR unit at Stanmore and develop what SOE and the Polish 2nd and 6th Bureau were trying to achieve in the clandestine wireless war against German occupation. Col. Heliodor Cepa was responsible for developing this relationship. These groups were jointly working on creating the 2nd Bureau wireless intercept stations in the summer of 1945. These were known as JULIA, TEKLA, and KRYSIA.

Polish 2nd Bureau—wireless intercept stations		
JULIA	Hours of work	0800–0900 MET
	Frequencies	Central: 6610, 7002, 7523, 8418
		Julia: 6960, 7580, 8700, 9550
	Callsigns	Central: RHZ, SI2, BQ1
KRYSIA	Hours of work	1800–1900 MET
	Frequencies	Central: 6610, 7002, 7523, 8418
		Krysia: 7925, 8240, 8483, 9280
	Callsigns	Central: 09N, FGZ, DA3
TEKLA	Hours of work	1300–1400 and 2300–2400 MET
	Frequencies	Central: 6707, 7440, 7997, 8554
		Tekla: 6603, 7337, 7623
	Callsigns	Central: Y3G, ZH5, A1I

These three stations were located in Central Europe, in the same area as stations KASIA and EMILIA, which already existed at the location. There had been debate a few weeks prior to this between Maj. Jameson Till and the CSC on the sanctioning of Polish clandestine stations at Aarhus in Denmark, namely the proposed FLORA II station. The RSS and CSC did give authorisation to the Polish 2nd Bureau for them to communicate with a new wireless station called ZIMNY on the North Baltic coast. The RSS was also to help support the training of Polish clandestine wireless operators, even orchestrating a series of exercises in Scotland using the mobile unit SCR.299. The senior RSS officers were cautious about how far they could go with developing the operational capabilities of Polish Intelligence.

In correspondence in May 1945, it was noted that 'great caution must be exercised in regard to the training of Polish operators for clandestine purposes'. The RSS were informed of the route the mobile unit would take across the border and back, and even the power output of the aerial being used and frequencies employed. The exercise was being coordinated as the Polish C-in-C had promised the British War Office that they would have two more Army Divisions ready to deploy by the end of June 1945, and there was a requirement to train their wireless personnel in intelligence gathering. Jameson Till had discussed at length with Leonard Williams, Chairman of the W/T Board, who had approved the RSS support for the Polish exercise.

The two-month exercise involved a vehicle-mounted system and two fixed stations at Chipperfield and Connington. The Polish wireless operators were to be divided into three groups under the command of the following NCOs: Sgt Janaszek, Sgt Beidrzycki, and Cpl Podkul.

One of the RSS operators who followed the journey of SCU4 into southern Europe was Don Wallis (M0ZDW). He had been recruited into the RSS following some sage advice from his brother-in-law, Archie James, who was working for the service at the time it was headquartered at Wormwood Scrubs. He was duly called to Arkley View for an interview with Capt. Bellringer and offered a job, with the support of his father who was trying to steer him away from service with the RAF. Within a week of accepting the RSS job, he was at Arkley starting his training:

> I was posted to St. Erth station near Penzance with some really first-class operators, some ex-Cable & Wireless and many amateurs who helped me in many ways. My next move was a posting to SCU4 for overseas duty in Italy. We left from Liverpool on the Duchess of Richmond troop ship in convoy via Gibraltar and Valletta for Naples. Then on by road to Rome where I met up the lads who were in the advanced group who had set up the station.
>
> We were billeted in Bruno Mussolini's Villa ... here the intercept work was similar to St Erth we did not know who or what we were receiving! I thoroughly enjoyed Rome and we celebrated VE day there. Soon after we moved the complete station to Austria, part by train and part by road. I was on the train living in a cattle truck together with our HROs. The Station was set up in a village school with Huts for our banks of HRO receivers at Deutsch-Feistritz north of GRAZ.
>
> Very different traffic was being logged here. We enjoyed the skiing and ice skating on the local frozen lake. Here I had a spell on the Radio Link with UK, using a vibroplex bug key, an AR88 as monitor and the HRO. The procedure was the same as the Germans used (five letter groups and same preamble) and I can still remember the Call Signs we used: JLQ and BSH. At the end of operations we returned to the UK by train.[9]

The overseas units made a huge contribution to the RSS and the wider British intelligence insight into German and other Axis intelligence service operations overseas. The work was built on the value of partnerships and the strength of deploying RSS personnel as liaison officers. MERS gave unique access into the German activity in the Balkans, Turkey, Italy, and the Aegean, producing a significant strand of ISK traffic. Sidi Bishr was to be one of the most vital British intelligence-producing stations during the Second World War, and their work was to continue against the Jewish insurgency in Palestine after the war had ended.

The building of a global network for SIGINT collection was to epitomise a new era for British Intelligence. Approaches taken in the Second World War were to shape the way the newly formed GCHQ was to tackle the post-colonial drawdown of the British Empire and develop new initiatives for the Cold War.

7

Pedigree

In the years when Civilisation was a menaced with destruction, they gave generously of their time, powers and technical skills in essential service to this country.

Sir Herbert Creedy, Under Secretary of State for War (War Office 1945)

One of the most significant components of the RSS was found in the RIS, run by Hugh Trevor-Roper. It was nominally under MI6 control, but Trevor-Roper and his team of academics stayed at Arkley. From the very beginning, Trevor-Roper was an analyst in the RSS and he had a good appreciation of the intercepts and what they meant. Bletchley Park also had analysts doing this work, but the RIS had an innate ability to penetrate the depths of the *Abwehr* and *Sicherheitsdienst* intelligence services. Hugh Trevor-Roper, Charles Stuart, Stuart Hampshire, and Gilbert Ryle were all to go on to become professors in a variety of academic disciplines.

After MI6 took over the RSS, they were placed in Section V in St Albans and overseen by Maj. Felix Cowgill as Section Vw. Section V were the group responsible for all ISOS decrypts and controlled its distribution. The products were originally stored at their St Albans Registry, located in a house called Brescia. Over the course of the Second World War, Section V was to move into central London. As time went on, friction began to appear between Cowgill and Hugh Trevor-Roper due to Cowgill's excessive security requirements and holding back vital information; eventually, they placed the RIS team directly under the control of 'C', the head of SIS/MI6. Patrick Reilly, the assistant to 'C', the head of MI6, was to state that the RIS was the most powerful intelligence tool available to the Allies. An example of this was an RIS report that indicated an *Abwehr* station in Belgium was asking for Allied clothing, equipment, and items such as identification passes. The RIS advised that the Germans were intending to equip 'line-crossers'. This was just a few weeks before the infamous Battle of the Bulge. No one at the time seemed to have picked up the implications of this intelligence.

The RIS was disbanded around March 1945, and the section split up. Three of its members joined the War Room, and Capt. Ryle remained in Barnet under formal transference to the RSS, been given the title RSS(I). His role was to collect all background intelligence relevant to the work of the RSS, and also to make sure relevant W/T intelligence got to areas of the British military and intelligence organisations where it was valued. In reality, the recreation of a specific intelligence wing with Capt. Ryle was just a reinstatement of the RIS by another means.

The Discrimination Group at Arkley View in Barnet was to become the hub of the RSS, by which the organisation would have as its centre of gravity.

One of Bletchley Park's most famous members of staff, Gordon Welchman, developed a new approach to analysing the metadata behind the German wireless traffic. The technique was to become known as traffic analysis and was to help the Allies map out the German Intelligence services networks with some ease. The metadata of a radio transmission (what we would refer to as a message preamble, message origination and destination, date and time stamp) could be recorded and was used over time to map out the active radio networks. It would give insights into the command centres who controlled the radio network and who the individual operators were, and allowed the teams at Bletchley to be able to pick up differences in operational activity by monitoring the patterns of intercept from the VIs. Amalgamated, all this information would be valuable, without even exploiting the content of the radio transmission. It was pioneering work.

The work of the RSS was invaluable to the task of breaking the Enigma ciphers in Hut 6 at Bletchley Park. It opened up some new insights into the inner workings of the German *Abwehr*. It has been estimated that over 268,000 messages from the RSS were decrypted at Bletchley (97,000 in *Abwehr* hand cipher and 140,000 enciphered from an Enigma machine, the rest from the *Sicherheitsdienst*).

It was the log sheets that were the core of the interactions between the interceptors Arkley View and Bletchley. It was two-way process between those collecting the transmissions around the country and overseas and those that analysed the material. These log sheets give a clear indication on how advanced the collaboration was in the routine adjustment and reprioritising of intercept operations (through the RSIC hub). By 1941, Arkley View in Barnet was processing 10,000 log sheets per day, emphasising how industrial the process was.

One of the most notable achievements of the RSS was the development of the new general search capability to discover new and important radio transmissions. One such stream of traffic, carrying radio traffic between Tokyo and Budapest, had coded material embedded within it, which was proven to be of immense value to the Japanese section at Bletchley Park.

The RSS had also pioneered, through the work of Maj. Keen, a technique to statistically plot DF bearings. By the end of the war, the vast swathe of material the

RSS had collected was of immense value to the GC&CS, most notably the information collected on Russian radio networks. Around 50 per cent of the RSS was directly engaged in the interception of German intelligence traffic for the GC&CS at Bletchley.

Year	Total number of messages sent to BP
1941	58,000
1942	180,000
1943	253,000
1944	368,000
1945 (to the beginning of May)	147,000

Year	Agents sent to UK and captured	Caught by ISOS	Reflected in ISOS
1940	26	0	4
1941	23	6	9
1942	29	5	7
1943	22	3	13
1944	12	3	2
1945	0	0	0

Year	Agents detained or brought to UK	Per ISOS	Reflected in ISOS
1941	28	7	9
1942	41	15	7
1943	54	21	18
1944	41	9	13

The decrypts of the German Secret Service (*Abwehr* and *Sicherheitsdienst*) messages were referred to by the nomenclature of ISOS (Intelligence Service Oliver Strachey) and ISK (Intelligence Service Knox), which related to the senior staff members of the sections. Strachey was head of the *Abwehr* decrypting section, focused on their hand ciphers. Dilly Knox led the section responsible for breaking the *Abwehr* machine ciphers from December 1941. But it was the ISOS material that was the real game changer in the Second World War. It was of immensely practical value to the Allied intelligence machinery. It was significant for a number of reasons:

1. It led to the identification and arrest of spies.
2. It filled in (over the course of time) a large detailed background picture of the *Abwehr* and SD organisations, their methods of working, their technique of espionage, their cover addresses, their secret links, the identity of their officers, and their relations with other parts of the German military machine.
3. It supplied information regarding the technique of sabotage, especially against British shipping, and thereby assisted in the development of countermeasures by the Security Service.

4. It provided information of operational value, e.g. the formation or assembly of *Abwehr* commandos before and in the neighbourhood of a projected German advance.
5. It provided political information, e.g. the nature and extent of Spanish collaboration with the Germans.
6. It provided valuable material concerning the German organisation and its detailed working, which was used with good effect in order to obtain information during the course of interrogation.

Another smaller series of reporting was issued by the GC&CS at Bletchley, which was referred to as the ISOSICLE and emanated from the decryption of *Sicherheitsdienst* (Amt VI) and SIPO (*Sicherheitspolizei*) hand and machine-enciphered messages. They were typically disseminated to Section V of MI6.

Without the successful interception of German wireless signals, Bletchley's cipher specialists would have lacked the raw material to penetrate, decipher, and analyse Enigma. The whole British and Allied SIGINT effort in Britain would total some 50,000 men and women at its peak, and the RSS's contribution, certainly to the MI5 deception operations, was vital.

After the end of the war, RSS VIs would be responsible for laying the foundations of the modern-day GCHQ. The GC&CS was to formally change its name on 1 April 1946 to GCHQ. Many of the RSS staff were recruited and offered posts at Eastcote.

W/T Sitation Report 25th April 1945
   Group 1

The HAMBURG station is still active but has sacrificed some of its less important and more irregular contacts and is now working with only about a couple of transmitters.

   1/102 (multiple service) Hamburg to various outstations in Denmark has shown increased activity.

   Several of the answer stations on Group 1 have been instructed to send blind if they do not hear control, showing that HAMBURG hopes still to receive, though it may be unable to transmit. This may imply that the control hopes to move to a new location.

Group 2

Station BURG is now dead. All its services faded out between the 16th and 20th April. Its round-robin transmissions have been taken over be WIESE.

   Service 2/1027 (formerly BURG-WIESE) has revived from a station in the HAMBURG-KIEL area to WIESE. The Spanish stations area working normally, with Station JAKOB at MERANO acting as control-station <u>vice</u> BURG.

Station KONRAD is dead. Station WILJA is active, though less so than recently, in a 'Redoubt' area, possibly still at STRAUBING. Station SONJA (Sigmaringen) closed down on the 20th April and came up on the 22nd, perhaps at LECH in the Vorarlberg. The agents of KONRAD and WILJA do not appear to be working to any other control. Some agents are calling their old controls in vain.

The Kdo and Trupp services on the Western Front are functioning at a low ebb.

The Italian network is normal and very busy.

Balkan networks are fading out.

Norwegian W/T servies are active.

Besides the service between HAMBURG area and WIESE, there appear to be either one or two new services working between North Germany and South Germany.

Group 13

The main Group 13 transmitter moved from Berlin, probably on the night of Saturday 21st April. Many of the less important services which worked from Berlin have not been heard since, but the network of services which worked to the control c/s CAG are mostly still active.

Bearings on CAG suggest that the transmitter is operating from the AUGSBURG/SALZBURG area (further bearings being taken both on CAG and CAG_1)

The station at PRAGUE is very active and has taken over from Berlin the more important of the services that worked from there outside the CAG network.

The STUTTGART centre (mainly agents in West) has not been heard. The station in Czechoslovakia (Pilsen area) is active but may have moved to the South.

Group 13 services working to the Iberian peninsula—13/11, 13/12, 13/122, 13/202, 13/212, 13/272 are all active.

Group X

These services have shown a falling-off in activity except for X/160 (Tromso to Greenland) and X.5604 (Bremen area to Madrid area)

Group 14

Group 14 control at BERLIN (DFE/DFI/DOG) was last heard working normally at 1900 GMT on Friday 20/4/45. The transmitters at NAUEN usually working on Group 14 material have not been heard since.

On Saturday, 21/4/45 an unusual transmitter on a very low frequency (DKD on 69.7 kcs) was heard sending traffic blind addressed to 14/75 answer which is thought to be in Munich area. This answer was heard on Monday 23/4/45 sending blind to MADRID but has not been heard again. Various outstations (MADRID, LISBON etc.) were heard attempting to contact control without success, throughout Saturday and Sunday.

During the morning of Tuesday 24/4/45 a station was found using the callsign 'DFI' but without any Group 14 callsigns. The station was slightly off the normal DFI frequency and the signal was hand sent. No contact with any other station was made. Bearings indicated SALZBURG area and this station is possibly the same as 14/75 answer mentioned above.

This station was again heard calling 'DFI' early Wednesday morning without result. Only one answer station (MADRID) attempted to contact a hypothetical control. Spanish interworking continues normally while FAR EASTERN services have been unheard since Friday.

The present situation appears to show that an outstation or a group of outstations is trying to re-establish a control in the are MUNICH–SALZBURG–LINZ. It may then be possible to make contact with outstations in neutral countries and unoccupied GERMANY.

Radio monitoring and the RSS was the mainstay of Hanslope's work throughout the war, but the Park was to be involved in other clandestine technical operations. Towards the end of the war, there was a push to encipher secret British telegraph signals, and a new system referred to as ROCKEX was developed.

The Germans had an interception transmitter based near Eindhoven, which at the time was capable of collecting telephone calls being transmitted from Britain across the Atlantic. Beginning work on this problem in 1943 was Bletchley Park's Alan Turing, who had pioneered the cryptological breakthroughs into the German Enigma cipher machine. Turing was to lead the design and development for a portable secure speech system, which was to become known as DELILAH.

This had followed a visit to the USA by a British Joint Staff Mission, which included Turing, in late 1942, where they had been taken to the Bell Labs to see the design of a new US secure-speech system in development.

Previous work to build a secure-speech system for the British government had produced a system called SIGSALY that, weighing in at nearly 50 tonnes, was so large it was housed in the basement of the Selfridges store on London's Oxford Street. It would provide a secure communications link between British Prime Minister Winston Churchill in No. 10 Downing Street and US President Franklin D. Roosevelt in the White House in Washington, DC. The Allied leadership needed something much more portable.

Turing lived in Shenley Brook End village with a Mrs Ramshaw, and for two days a week, he would cycle to Hanslope Park to develop the DELILAH system with a small team of specialist engineering staff, which included Lt Don Bayley, REME, an electrical engineer who had recently graduated from university. The team also had an ATS operator and mathematician called Mary Green, who had done some pioneering work with Maj. Dick Keen on DF, and Robin Gandy, another mathematician who originally came up with the name DELILAH.

By the autumn of 1944, Turing was working full time at Hanslope Park on the project, occupying a room on the top floor of the Hanslope mansion house before relocating to a cottage in the garden. The DELILAH prototype was ready for the summer of 1945, although it was never used operationally as the war came to a close before it could. When it was first tested, the scrambled voice that was transmitted was collected and recorded to a 16-inch disc by the PWE 'black propaganda' broadcast facility at Milton Bryan. Possibly because of the excitement of the event, Turing's braces snapped and Harold Robin, PWE Chief Engineer, supplied him with some bright red cord from a packing case to hold up his trousers. The project was to be the first example of the digitisation of voice in the world.

> Research on DELILAH has been in progress since the beginning of May 1943. Up to now the work has all been concentrated on the unit for combining the key with the speech to produce cipher (or scrambled speech) and for recovering the speech from the cipher with the aid of the key.
>
> Alan Turing's DELILAH Report, 6 June 1944
> TNA file HW62/6

Not all the RSS work went to task. Plan Flypaper was one of the abortive attempts by the RSS to mount a more aggressive posture against Germany. The DASD German radio amateurs had been permitted to continue their peacetime activity during the war but under stricter controls. They were occasionally given specific exercise scenarios to work through on the wireless sets, which may be tasks that would be given to them during a war emergency. Flypaper was established to find out more about the members and activities of DASD (referred to as 'D' stations) as well as providing these German radio amateurs with a means to establish communications with Britain should any of them choose to switch sides.

The operation was to begin on 8 October 1944 under strict conditions. A number of G7 call signs were established to provide a channel for a surrender submission from some or any part of the crumbling German military in 1945. The operators were advised the following:

> … under your instructions you are forbidden to call German stations … you should avoid making appointments with D stations unless there are apparently exceptional reasons and a report should then be sent in as soon as possible … although so far the hoped for reaction has not taken place, in that no one wishing to communicate with the British government has used you, it is felt that the scheme should be continued for an indefinite time … unless careful listening

is done, it will be difficult for such stations to get hold of you and they may also be somewhat deterred if they only hear you working a string of genuine German stations.[1]

Although a number of foreign amateur wireless stations were contacted, nothing significant was to emerge from the work up to its closure on 10 June 1945. The skills of the RSS operators were never in question and '... each member has shown such initiative and determination to maintain a high standard of security'. It has been argued the project failed because of the rigid rules and guidelines the operators were set:

1. Ordinary amateur procedure will be used with a few exceptions noted below.
2. Each station must stick to its allotted call sign.
3. The frequencies used must be those agreed by the W/T Board, as given on the attached sheet.
4. Power not to exceed 50 watts.
5. So far as possible stations in densely populated areas should be avoided so as to minimise complaints from the public and in all cases steps must be taken to reduce key clicks.
6. CO de G7F- calls will be used. The word 'TEST' will not be used.
7. There will be no time restriction, but the operators taking part will obviously have to make arrangements between themselves and through a central control. In particular it is intended to have a round table G contact on Sunday at 11 a.m. (BST). Whichever operator is acting as control will call CQG de G7F- and will make contact with each other operator in turn and then put all stations in contact with one another successively.
8. No German amateur will ever be called but if a German amateur calls one of the network, he will be answered. Contact with enemy stations should be kept as possible consistent with the use of ham chat. In particular such expressions as 'dear O.B.', and '73's' should be avoided; also such phrases as 'tks for the FB QSO'. It must be remembered that our network admits that it is officially controlled (see below) and as such is bound to be subject to regulations and monitoring.
9. In the event of anyone asking for QRA, only the county shall be given as a reply.
10. There must be no third-party traffic and no personal messages which can possibly give the indication of the identity, occupation or address of the sender, nor even any expression which could confirm the county as permitted to be given in paragraph 9. Operators should endeavour to avoid mannerisms which might enable listeners to identify them as pre-war amateurs.
11. In the event of an operator asking for a QSL the reply to be given is 'Sorry cannot QSL'.

12. In the event of any station asking one of our group whether his station is licensed (or any similar phrase), the reply to be made is 'Here O.K. official station'. The word licensed is not to be used in this connection.

13. No 'handles', i.e. personal names or nicknames are to be used.

14. Stations must close down if requested by any service or authorised station. It must be appreciated that the activity of this group is absolutely the last radio priority on the air.

15. The subject of the weather is completely banned. If one of the group is asked about the weather he must reply 'not allowed'.

16. There must be no reference to enemy action, such as bombs, bomb damage, planes, air-raid warnings or the like, either directly or indirectly. Equally there must be no reference to the passage of allied planes, troops or convoy movements etc. In fact, the full principles of Signal Security must not be lost sight of.

17. The traffic between stations can include discussions on radio conditions, equipment, aerials and the usual chat of this kind. If any of the stations are using special service equipment they must devise a notional set to describe, if questioned.

18. In discussing radio conditions, no reference whatever must be made to the conditions for receiving any stations other than those of known amateurs.

19. A log must be kept showing the date, time, frequency and call sign of any station called whether contact is made or not. It is not necessary when working within the group to keep a log of the actual traffic passed, but anything unusual should be noted in case a private or foreign station comes up using one of our allotted call-signs.

20. In the event of a station coming up using a G call sign, even one of the G7 series, the station is to be worked and no comment made. The station might well be in enemy territory and using a G call sign as camouflage. The incident is to be reported as soon as possible by telephone to the control as explained in paragraph 23.

21. In general the reply to any question over the air or otherwise as to the nature of our stations is to be to the effect that 'this is an official station permitted to use amateur calls and procedure. It is operating for practice purposes'.

22. No R/T will be used in any circumstances.

23. In the event of any enemy station calling one of our group and offering a message to a third party or a Government department; the message should be accepted and acknowledged and the enemy station should be instructed to come on the air at the same time next day or as convenient but not within 24 hours.[2]

Plan Flypaper

The frequencies which were permitted by the W/T Board were as follows:

3.5–4.0 mc/s
7.0–7.3 mc/s
14.0–14.4 mc/s
28.0–30.0 mc/s

Call signs permitted to be involved in the plan:

G7FA	Lt Colonel Kenneth Morton-Evans
G7FB	G. R. Lee
G7FC	Stan Riesen
G7FD	A. S. McNicol
G7FF	W. J. Burton
G7FG	H. W. Stacy
G7FH	A. C. Simons
G7FI	Captain Robin W. Addie
G7FJ	Captain Louis Varney
G5FJ	Not allocated
G7FK	Not allocated
G7FL	Not allocated
G7FM	Not allocated

One thing Flypaper did highlight, however, was that the DASD operators who were district leaders or those included in the organised practice groups attached to those leaders were permitted to make direct contacts with amateurs in Allied countries. Flypaper helped generate an organisational structure for the RSS of the German DASD amateur groups and those that acted as controllers within the radio networks. The RSS were to identify fifteen known pre-war German amateurs on the network and a list of forty-eight other operators who were unknown to the service. In 1945, as the war was coming to a close, German intelligence was seeking information for six (the Lower Rhine, Westphalia, Bremen, Baden, Harz, and Hesse Districts) of the DASD District leaders to establish their preparedness for an invasion.

Kenneth Morton-Evans, who was to be the driving force for the Flypaper work, surmised: '… some Germans were worked several times … but none ever said much. We of course, from time to time announced that we were transmitting with the full authority of the British Government. Anyway, no flies stuck to us but it was fun'.

Another unsuccessful project by the RSS was the Wilton Scheme, which operated from March 1945 up until its termination on 24 May 1945. British

Intelligence feared the Germans would use Allied POWs as hostages, so the RSS was tasked with attempting to get contact with prisoners at camps across Europe. A team of eight G7 call sign RSS wireless operators were used for the operation, and although many prisoners had designed and built very effective wireless receivers and transmitters, no contact was ever established.

A success that is often not discussed among the RSS was the effect the wireless intercept and subsequent intelligence derived on German sabotage plans against Allied merchant shipping. Up to January 1943, German intelligence had scored two significant sabotage successes: the attack on the *Grelhead* in December 1941 and the *Erin* in January 1942. They had had a partial success in causing an explosion on the *Ravensport* in January 1943, which was only managed to be saved by being towed to shallower waters, from a SIGINT tip off by the RSS. For the rest of the war, German intelligence carried out no successful sabotage attacks against Allied ships. A table below highlights some of the failed attempts as a result of RSS intelligence:

Method	No. of Ships	Tonnage
Bombs removed from ships after warning	2	3,666
Towed to shallow water before explosion	1	1,787
Bombs prevented from being taken on board	1	Water tanker
Sabotage definitely abandoned owing to strictness of watch after warning	2	10,496
Sabotage attempts laid on but abandoned possibly owing to precautions taken	12	19,094 plus 7 unspecified
Sabotages attempts reported to the Germans as achieved, but no bombs discovered after search, possibly owing to precautions taken	9	25,406
TOTAL	27	60,449 plus 8 unspecified

There were a number of other occasions where an attempt by German Intelligence was intended, but the vessels were never fully identified. The RSS were to report 'there was also the occasion in December 1943 and January 1944 when bombs were put in cases of oranges. Although some warning was received by special intelligence, it was not possible to take action before the ships had sailed and it was decided to allow the ships to continue their voyage and take a chance; a policy which was justified in the event'.

By May 1945, the RSIC was to initiate discussions on the future of the RSS. The committee was keen that the RSIC was to not go out of existence completely but to be adjourned *sine die*, with a formal recommendation to that effect to the higher RSC. The committee stated at the time that the 'GC&CS would be worthless unless fed by RSS, and RSS work would be equally pointless unless its material were dealt with by GC&CS'. Maj. Ryle was to submit a formal note of resignation as RSIC to the chairman. The minutes of the meeting closed with the statement 'sherry and biscuits mitigated the solemnities of the meeting'.

By July 1945 there were fifty-five DF sites in the UK: RSS, seven sites controlled by Barnet (Arkley View); Royal Navy, fourteen sites controlled by Scarborough; Army, ten sites controlled by War Office 'Y' Group (Beaumanor) and four sites controlled by Forest Moor; and RAF, five sites controlled by Chicksands and fifteen sites controlled by Cheadle.

A plan was needed to draw down the scale of the DF effort and to centralise resourcing and funding. A paper outlining a proposal for a central exchange was crafted by Maj. L. B. Firnberg from the GC&CS, but 'this would call for a degree of inter-service cooperation which it would be idle to expect'. Future priorities for a new centralised DF system and British network would be coordinated by GCHQ continuing to use signal-to-line methods. The estimates of how well performing these DF stations would be at triangulating signals would be based on check bearings using commercial stations utilising fixed Berne List call signs (the estimates being published by GCHQ). When the RSS was finally disbanded, it still had six DF stations at its disposal: Lydd, St Erth, Wymondham, Gilnahirk, Forfar, and Bridgwater. These were controlled by Barnet until the end of 1946. In October 1946, it was agreed the stations would be subsumed under the control of Scarborough, but the transition was not enacted until 24 March 1947. Scarborough DF was brought under the command of 'T' Group GCHQ, with the short title T48. The overseas DF networks in Germany, Cyprus, Malta, Habbaniya, and Austria continued to operate on their parent single-service systems.

In September 1945, there was beginning to emerge some significant duplication in the coverage of Russian wireless networks between the RSS and the GC&CS. Morton Evans and the GC&CS had to fully coordinate to exchange traffic logs, network information, and cipher details as routine. Similar problems had also occurred in overseas theatres and were only partially solved by more effective liaison. Problems were beginning to emerge.

After the Second World War, the RSS role to support British intelligence operations was diminishing, and the organisation was to be subsumed into the new government Signals Intelligence organisation GCHQ at one of its wartime stations on Lime Grove in Eastcote, North West London. At this stage, SCU3 was still some 1,200 strong and SCU4 overseas had a total headcount of around 400. The total number of VIs at the end of the war was 600, of whom 450 were considered active, committing over 3,000 interception hours a week collectively.

Eastcote had been chosen as an outstation for Bletchley Park in April 1943 where the infamous Enigma Bombe processing machines were located and tasked by the Park. It was to become the largest Bombe outstation, with over eighty Bombes *in situ* by the end of the war. Eastcote was to be the first post-war location to be selected for the GC&CS, which was to become GCHQ. They were to move in early 1946 in a number of stages, the last group was to relocate in April 1946.

The recommendation came from a lengthy review of the security service MI5 in Britain and a report from Sir Samuel Findlater Stewart, which was issued in November 1945. Findlater Stewart was a senior civil servant, a chairman of the Home Defence Executive and former permanent undersecretary for India. He had been commissioned to undertake a review of Britain's future needs for SIGINT by Prime Minister Winston Churchill. He was encouraged to make recommendations for any organisational changes that might be required, and the concluding report was entitled 'Defence of the Realm and Nothing Else'.

The review was very discrete, with only two copies of the report on the RSS made—GCHQ was not formally allowed to have one. His recommendation was that 'the takeover should be as such as to preserve the special personality and technique of RSS and to make possible smooth expansion in emergency'. He identified one of the main issues in retaining the organisation was funding. The 'cost fell under three headings, the amount of money needed to administer the organisation including individual expenses and honoraria; the cost in manpower and money of the directing staff in GCHQ; and the cost of the equipment, issued free to the members of the organisation and maintained at SIGINT expense'.

Findlater Stewart's conclusions were as follows:

1. The technique developed by RSS in war and the experience gained in operating it ought not to be lost.
2. Full cover is not needed in peacetime.
3. The aim should be to carry out 'test audits' and maintain a skeleton record and a cadre of operators.
4. RSS should not exist independently of the SIGINT organisation.
5. It should be amalgamated with SIGINT and sufficient staff, apparatus and records should be taken over to enable the special personality and technique of RSS to continue in existence and to expand smoothly in emergency.
6. We recommend that provision should be made, as occasion requires, for a seat on the governing Board of Signals Intelligence for a representative of MI5 whose task it would be to ensure that the requirements of counter-espionage and security were not lost sight of.[3]

A lengthy memorandum crafted by Gambier-Parry on 18 December 1945 to Edward Travis constructed the process of implementing these conclusions, and outlined the tasks, organisation, cost, and size of the future RSS. The implementation of these conclusions were finalised by June 1946. A number of RSS Traffic Analysis staff and other roles were transferred across in June 1946. GCHQ was keen to learn how the RSS search techniques had evolved over the course of the war. In April that year, a number of GCHQ staff were sent from Eastcote to Barnet to study the General Search methods for nearly a month.

In June 1946, the VIs, as a collective, and thirteen RSS controlling staff, including Maj. Bellringer, were transferred across to GCHQ at Eastcote. They were moved into the control of 'T' Group into a subsection referred to as T45 with a target cadre of 750 VI operators; by the end of 1946, the total had reached 704. There was some consternation across GCHQ of the value of many of these 'amateur' operators being given roles in the new GCHQ. One particularly sour note was a paper written on 25 November 1946 by Mr R. Frawley, a member of the General Search section (S54A) in 'S' Group, who articulated their concerns of the differences in approaches between the two teams 'inadequacies ... were being tolerated unnecessarily and the yield on their operations was not commensurate with the effort on S Group'.

The agreed proposal (ratified by the then GCHQ Director Edward Travis on 13 November 1948) to retain elements of the RSS was widely received across the post-war intelligence community. The review accepted that the organisation compliment the current manpower resources at the new GCHQ 'nominally 16 teams at the current size of 650 VIs (against an establishment of 750) ... it agreed that the organisation provided a reserve of trained operators'. Travis was to recommend the following that the total strength of VIs to be reduced to 250 (as recommended in the report) plus 150 members retained for the SIGINT organisation. He also wanted the VIs to be on a firmer footing with GCHQ and to fall under the chain of command of the head of the General Search Branch (known then as S54), Mr C. L. S. Williams. The VI section would be referred to as S54v.

Each RSS operator would receive two letters, one outlining the changes and the other covering the fact that their services would no longer be required or inviting them to volunteer for the new role in GCHQ. Many were discharged under King's Regulation (KR) 1940, Paragraph 390 XVVIII (a), with the words, 'Services being no longer required for the purpose for which they were enlisted'. During 1949, the existing establishment of S54v was drawn down from 400 to 200, including numerous staff who acted as directing staff.

Post-war Britain and its SIGINT service had to reprioritise its effort and resourcing, and this review period instigated by the Findlater Stewart review lasted some three years. SIGINT continued to change and the new GCHQ had to rise to the challenge. Part of the RSS and 'Y' Service drawdown was to establish the overseas posture. The SIGINT collection units were dispersed in accordance with the various strategic military campaigns, including the Middle East, continuing through North Africa, the Mediterranean and Italy, finishing up in Austria. There were also units in Germany (as a result of the main Western Front campaign) and in the Far East (from its start point in India).

The overseas/SCU4 RSS units were taken over by the Army. NORDET in Germany and IDET in Austria were subsumed into the local Army 'Y' Service units. This was mirrored in India where the Abbottabad station was to take over the RSS tasks, although the No. 1 RSC was absorbed into the DDY set up. It was only in the Middle East did any of the RSS vestiges survive, where the MERS continued at Sidi Bishr, providing valuable SIGINT collection against the main target at that time, the Jewish dissident organisations in Palestine. It would later move from Egypt to Cyprus.

It was critical for the future of intelligence cooperation that all three services continue along Second World War levels of interoperability and trust. The Findlater Stewart review recommended that the new director general of the security service 'have contact with the Government Code and Cipher School on a prescribed working level'. This was interpreted to mean having an MI5 liaison officer (MI5 nominated Capt. A. S. Martin for the role) at Eastcote who could also represent MI6 on any direct counter-espionage work. The review had recommended that the RSS be discontinued as a separate entity and that sufficient staff and equipment be retained and amalgamated into the new GCHQ. It was clearly stated that 'special provision should be made within the new amalgamated organisation for the personality and technique of the Radio Security Service to continue in existence'. The government and its intelligence services wanted to keep the RSS skills and techniques it had pioneered on traffic analysis, discrimination, and DF into the new post-war age.

Treasury was to approve that an additional 115 staff would be added to the establishment of GCHQ at Eastcote and 160 to the establishment of the Foreign Office intercept stations, most of whom went to Hanslope Park. This would be nearly twenty-four full-time teams and an additional fourteen VI 'nominal' teams employed on General Search tasks for GCHQ and the Foreign Office. At this time, the opinion was that ninety-one teams would be needed to give, 'full round-the-world cover on all Morse bands and that a regular line of clandestine transmissions should most certainly be detected'.

By May 1948, a new 'Clandestine Radio Committee' was established, filling the void left after the war from the demise of the RSIC. It had representation from MI5, MI6, and GCHQ. Discussions, just like with the RSIC, were largely focused on interception priorities.

There have been many books, Hollywood films, and public interest in the code and cipher work at Bletchley Park in recent years, but there has been scant attention to the work of the signals collectors of the GPO, 'Y' Services, and the RSS. It has often been said that it was the *Abwehr*/RSHA messages that helped Bletchley Park solve the Enigma cipher. Once the teams could decrypt the traffic, they could read the German traffic often quicker than it was received at its destination.

The ability to read this material would play a vital role in the Allied deception plans, most notably the work of the XX Committee and their double agents like Garbo. It was to shorten the war significantly and save many thousands of lives during the Allied landings in North Africa, Italy, and France.

SIGINT post-Second World War Manpower (November 1946)				
	SCU 3, 4, and 10	No. 1 RS Company India	Total	
			Operational	Admin
Officers	98	17	105	10
Operators	1,377	350	1,810	-
Engineers	83			
Admin	471	83	-	554
Civilians	105	-	75	30
VIs	1,050	-	1,050	-
TOTALS	3,184	450	3,040	594
	3634		3634	

The RSS complement by September 1946 would total 744.

At the end of the war in Europe, those RSS staff who were still operating as VIs would receive a certificate signed by Permanent Undersecretary for War Sir Herbert Creedy from the War Office. It was an official thank you from a grateful nation. A select few were lucky enough to receive a BEM. For many in the RSS, they felt it was a token gesture for a service that was to deliver one of the greatest intelligence coups of the twentieth century.

As GCHQ took hold at Eastcote from 1946 onwards, there was a reluctance to discontinue the services of the VIs. A new unit was to be created, called the Government Communications Voluntary Radio Service (GCVRS). To qualify for this, a W/T operator would need to be able to read Morse at twenty words per minute and be able to commit to undertake sixteen watches per calendar month (each watch being at least one-hour duration and performed on a separate day). If enrolled, they would be entitled to a general expense allowance of 12s a month, which would cover all out-of-pocket expenses incurred by the operator. The GCVRS would follow the same procedures of General Search as the RSS did during the war.

In a letter from January 1949 between the director of MI5 and Sir Edward Travis, the then-director of GCHQ, they articulated the dilemma of taking forward some of the Findlater-Stewart recommendations:

> Our concern, however is not with the situation resulting from the Findlater-Stewart recommendation—indeed I am quite confident that the plans you describe for building up General Search will meet our immediate needs—but rather with the situation which would face us in the outbreak of war. Then our joint problem would be not merely searching for but covering and exploiting what we must assume would be extensive secret networks. This sudden expansion of clandestine activity would undoubtedly coincide with increased demands upon your resources from the Services and the Foreign Office and it is hardly reasonable to expect that they would be in a position to spare sufficient of their Y resources to meet the situation. I believe that until there are in existence

independent intercept resources recognised as responsible for the development
and coverage of clandestine transmissions and capable of quick expansion
should the need arise, our war-planning cannot be considered complete.[4]

The GCVRS was comprised of small groups each with an independent group
leader, who would have three distinct classes of operators, referred to as Voluntary
Radio Operators (VROs):

GCVRS Structure		
GVRO (Group Voluntary Radio Operators)—Group leaders	HVRO (Honoraria Voluntary Radio Operators)—Employed staff, paid Honoraria	PVRO (Part-Time Voluntary Radio Operators)
Complement: 18	Complement: 11	Complement: 181
Flat rate of 18 shillings per week	Monthly Honorarium of £25	Received flat rate of 9*d*/1- hour watch (providing not less than 8 watches/month)
	Conditioned to 24 scheduled 8-hour watches/month (total of 264 watches per year)	Undertook 16 one-hour watches per month. Regarded as self-employed by GCHQ
Total cost of GCVRS in 1954–55 measured around £9,800		

The role of the GCVRS was to provide a cadre of partly trained operators on
the outbreak of war, provide cover on the ground wave of agent transmissions
emanating from the UK, and provide cover to the regular intercept stations
dotted around the country. As the Cold War went on, the value GCHQ got from
the GCVRS diminished. There were increasing limitations in what could be
shared directly with the operators working from home, 'due to advances in the
radio transmission methods and procedures adopted by agents'. A memo on the
GCVRS in 1957 concluded that the 'value of the VRS in an anti-clandestine role
has become negligible and out of proportion to the cost of operating the Service'.

GCVRS Manpower (as of 31 October 1954)						
Group	Region	Total	HVRO	GVRO	PVRO	Others
A	South and SE England	62	4	4	14	40
B	SW England and S Wales	35	2	4	11	18
C	Midlands and E Anglia	36	-	3	19	14
D	Northern England	37	1	5	1	30
E	NE England	6	2	1	1	2
F	Scotland	13	-	1	9	3
G	N Ireland	14	1	-	13	-
Independent members too isolated to group		6	-	-	-	6
TOTALS		209	10	18	68	113

After consultation with MI5, GCHQ made the decision to disband the GCVRS and the concept of using Voluntary Interceptors to monitor clandestine communications was to cease. MI5 was to state that the Russian Intelligence Services, its main target at this stage of the Cold War, favoured sending important communications to Moscow through the Diplomatic Bag or through the medium of the wireless transmitting station installed at the Soviet Embassy in London.

The RAF under authority from the Air Ministry was to maintain its RAFVRS, however. Its main function was to provide an adequate reserve of wireless operators form the support and reinforcement of the Signals Branch of the RAF. The RAF needed around 200 skilled W/T operators who would sign on for a minimum period of five years, in the age range of eight to forty-five who could sustain a Morse speed of twenty words per minute.

The RAFVRS would contain both RAF and civilian personnel held on the complement of the 'Reserve Centres' who were responsible for the administration of the service. The RAFVRS was headquartered as part of the Home Command Group HQ.

Once recruited, the operators were duly tasked to undertake wireless reception duties in their own homes in accordance with specified programmes. They had to commit to at least sixteen one-hour periods of search each month. The RAFVRS Airmen were paid over £3 allowances a year, to cover 'maintenance of a radio receiving set, power supply and incidental expenses'. The civilian operators were only paid 12s a month.

What is clear is that without the successful interception of Axis radio transmissions by groups like the RSS, Bletchley Park's code-breaking specialists would have lacked the raw material to penetrate, decipher, and analyse the infamous Enigma traffic that would change the course of the Second World War. At the height of the war in the middle of 1944, the RSS was intercepting in the region of 14,000 messages a fortnight. Without the skills of the full-time and volunteer interceptors, civilian and service alike, listening for sustained periods to weak Morse signals, Bletchley would not have been able to develop its decryption expertise.

As the Second World War ended and a new world order was beginning to become entrenched, it was clear that signals intelligence would play a key role in understanding our adversaries. What Britain had learnt in creating and running the RSS was to help shape the fledgling GCHQ, one of the key intelligence arms of the British government for the following decades of the Cold War and beyond.

The RSS/VI poems

I must go back to the set again, to the Superhet and the phones
And switch off the broadcast music, the announcer's measured tones
And search again on the short waves, with loud calls blending
For the dim sounds of the Morse code that a far foe's sending

I must go back to the set again, for the time has come to seek
In the QRM and the QRN for my allocated squeak
And all I ask is a steady note, through the ether speeding
At a fair strength, in a quiet spot, at a nice speed for reading.

Attributed to Norman Spooner, a Bournemouth VI and Group Leader

Portrait of a General Search Op at Changeover
Tired was he, and worn and weary
Like the old man in the story
Who had staggered many furlongs
With the weight of all the nations
Resting on his bending shoulders.

Tired was he but watching, anxious
Rest the signal should escape him
And be lost to Gilly's General Search
Upward must our curve be bending
Upward! Upward sighed the Corporal
Keep it upward spoke the Major
(very fierce and very warlike)

Thus our weary listener struggled
Struggled hard to please the Corporal
Struggled to placate the Major
Did his best to get that signal
And the message that it carried.
When the job was safely copied
Handed to his telex brother
He laid down his phones and pencil
Walked and bussed to well earned slumber
And to dreams of curves and figures

Gilnahirk W/T operator Bright 29/10/1943 (c/o George Busby)
Originally written on the back of a QSL card

'If I should die, think only this of me
That there's some blade of Irish grass
That is forever England
That there shall be in that rich earth
A T/P Op concealed
Twas blocking bad that killed the lad.
Tis right should be revealed.

Those curly wisps, those pencil strokes,
Fancy alone could tell,
The difference twist the E's and G's
They sounded deaths dark knell.

The O's and U's he wished would loose
Their wild superfluous twines
Adopt the copper-plate-like charm.
That is our dear Irvine's.

At last his strength at lowest ebb.
He sent on bended knee,
And finally crossed the Great Divide
'My Country, twas for thee!'

With apologies to Rupert Brooke—adapted from his Second World War poem
'The Soldier'
Written by Cyril Hartley, an RSS Teleprinter operator at Gilnahirk, who could
not adapt to the RSS 'blocking' technique and subsequently did not qualify as
an RSS intercept operator

Notes on Detection of Illicit Wireless 1940: Illicit Wireless Intercept Organisation

General instructions.

The following instructions are issued as a result of experience, suggestion, and enquires in peace and war, up to date.

Object of the Organisation

The object is to intercept, locate, and close down illicit wireless stations operated either by enemy agents within the United Kingdom or by persons, not necessarily enemy agents, operating transmitting stations without being licensed to do so under Defence Regulations 1939.

SECRET   Copy No. 21

(Not for publication—Crown copyright reserved)

NOTES ON THE
DETECTION OF
ILLICIT WIRELESS
1940 THIS DOCUMENT IS THE PROPERTY OF HIS MAJESTY'S
GOVERNMENT

SECRET

NOTES ON THE DETECTION OF ILLICIT WIRELESS

By Lt.-Col. Adrian Simpson, CMG, RE, AMIEE,
Late Deputy Managing Director, Maroni's Wireless
Telegraph Co. Ltd, and Director of Wireless
Telegraphs to the Government of India.

NOTES ON THE DETECTION OF ILLICIT WIRELESS

1. It is hardly necessary to emphasise that these notes are highly confidential and that the illicit use of wireless transmitting apparatus is an offence against No. 8 of the Defence Regulations 1939.
2. In the last war, the science of wireless was comparatively speaking in its infancy and it would have been quite impossible for any enemy agent to have attempted to make use of wireless as a method of secret communication, with the hope of success. He would have been located by our Direction-Finding Stations within a matter of minutes and would have been rounded up and under lock and key within a matter of hours.
3. One case actually occurred in 1918 when a small but over enthusiastic section of Territorials with more zeal than discretion, proceeded to carry out a night practice with some captured German apparatus near Hampton Court. They were located and rounded up by a squadron of cavalry within three quarters of an hour and spent an uncomfortable night in the guard room before their *bona – fides* were established.
4. The position to-day is very different. The science of wireless transmission has developed at such a phenomenal rate that the practical difficulties of detecting a skilled agent have increased out of all proportion.
5. The reason for this is simple. In the last war, we had to deal only with medium and long waves, which could be D.F.'d with considerable accuracy and rapidity. Not only this, but also their employment entailed much greater power and larger aerials, a fact which would have rendered an agent who might have wished to establish an illicit station far more liable to detection by a casual observer than is the case to-day.
6. Mainly owing to the introduction of short waves, the whole problem has become an exceedingly complex one, owing partly to the vast increase in the number of wave lengths available, and the enormous number of stations of all nationalities operating on the ether at all times of the day and night, there by tending to cloak an irregular or illicit transmission on low power and partly owning to the long ranges which can be obtained with a very small expenditure of energy, coupled with possible complications such as the use of single side band transmission. And last but not least the exceedingly small dimensions of the apparatus, which need not occupy a space much greater than say a large sized dictionary, or a 3lb biscuit tin.
7. Add to this the facts that short waves are far more difficult to D.F. with rapidity and accuracy, that they are seriously interfered with by physical objects such as balloon barrages, overhead trolley bus wires, even lamp-posts and trees, etc., that an outside and therefore visible aerial is no longer necessary and some idea will be obtained of the extreme complexity of the problem before us.

8. In notes of this kind, a certain number of technical references are unavoidable and whilst some readers are first-rate radio experts, others have not had the advantage (or disadvantage) of an extensive training in wireless and technicalities will therefore be avoided as much as possible.

9. As already pointed out the present day wireless transmission problem is a very complex one, but fortunately, from the particular aspect from which we are called upon to view the question, it may be somewhat narrowed down, if we are prepared to assume, as we can reasonably do, that, as a general rule: -

    (a) Only low power will be employed;

    (b) Bulky or intricate apparatus will be involved;

    (c) Complicated aerial systems will not be used owing to the ease with which they can be spotted.

    (d) Only continuous waves will be employed;

    (e) Morse keying at hand speed will in all probability be favoured in preference to   telephony, which for any given range, requires more power and is therefore more likely to be detected.

10. If we accept the above premises we are able to arrive at certain general conclusions; 'general' because while wireless waves no doubt obey certain rigid laws, our knowledge of these laws is unfortunately far from perfect and we can only draw inferences, which are true in the majority of cases.

11. As you all know, wireless transmitters send out what for the sake of convenience may be described as a composite wave, which for practical purposes can be resolved into two components, namely the ground ray and the reflected ray.

12. The ground ray, as its name implies, tends to follow the curvature of the earth. In the case of low power short-wave stations, as its intensity is small, it is rapidly damped out and can only be heard at comparatively short distances. This distance depends largely on the physical properties of the earth's surface. For instance, the ground ray will carry much further over sea than it will over land.

13. The so-called reflected ray on the other hand, leaves the transmitting aerial at an abrupt angle, travels upwards until it meets a series of conducting layers, known as the ionosphere, from one or other of which it is reflected downwards, coming to earth again over an area, the nearest part of which may be several hundred or even thousands of miles from the point of transmission. This distance in miles between the point of transmission and the line at which the reflected wave returns to the earth's surface is termed the skip distance and it should be remembered that this skip distance tends to increase as the wavelength decreases.

14. Within the skip, signals may or may not be audible. The under surface of the ionosphere is not smooth and some scattered reflections may come back into the skip area. In general, it is not possible to obtain good D.F. bearings on transmitting stations when the D.F. station is within this skip.

15. Very short waves are not reflected by the ionosphere but pass through it and are lost in space. Such wavelengths, however, can only be used in a manner somewhat similar to that in which visual lamps or helio signalling can be used, i.e., the path between sender and receiver must be fairly clear of optical obstructions.

16. Without entering into a detailed technical discussion as to the reasons which have led to the following conclusions, it is fairly safe to say that wavelengths of six metres and under are not likely to be used in the present state of development, since waves of this order would be liable to atmospheric refraction and they would not be suitable for reliable communications, except at very short ranges.

17. Wavelengths of the order of seven to fourteen meters might well be employed for communications across the North Sea, say from the English to the Dutch or Belgian coast, on the assumption that both the transmitting as well as the receiving

stations are situated right on the coast. A few miles of land intervening on either side would necessitate the use of longer waves. These wavelengths will certainly require to be watched for back radiation over the land could be made extremely weak and our permanent D.F. stations would probably hear nothing whatever. The signals would, however, be picked up locally by any trained observer with a suitable receiver.

18. Wavelengths of fifteen to twenty metres are very suitable for regular reliable ground ray communication from coast to coast. There should be no marked fading between say, fifteen and twenty metres at any time and these wavelengths must be closely watched by local observers, as it is more than probable that signals on these frequencies would only be audible in the vicinity of the transmitter.

19. Ground ray communication on wavelengths of the order of twenty to seventy metres is not likely to be used as this band would almost certainly suffer from sever fading during the daytime. On the other hand, this wave band (twenty to seventy metres) is extremely important for reflected or ionosphere ray communications.

20. As we go up the scale of wavelengths however the value of the ground ray for communication purposes commences to predominate and speaking very roughly, one may say the "skip" effect ceases to have any practical value for reliable communication for wavelengths of one hundred and twenty metres and upwards and the ground ray will then become the predominant factor.

IONOSPHERE OR REFLECTED RAY COMMUNICATION

21. As just indicated, the wave band twenty to seventy metres is extremely important for reflected ray communications, particularly for distances such as we are called upon to envisage—that is to say from England to Germany and Central Europe.

22. The shortest wave reliably received by reflection from the ionosphere will depend on the time of day or night, season, sunspot cycle and other factors which we need not consider here. Suffice it to say that during the winter season the figure will be approximately twenty five metres *during the day* and is very seldom ever likely to be less than twenty metres at any time. (On disturbed days, the figure may be forty to fifty metres). At night, the shortest wave for normal reflection will increase probably reaching values of sixty to seventy metres.

23. Assuming therefore an efficient receiving station somewhere in Germany, it should be quite possible to select a suitable wavelength, having regard to range and seasonal conditions, which would give a regular reliable service. If such a station were to be established in a carefully chosen locality in this country, it would very likely not be heard at all at our permanent interception and D.F. stations. The apparatus required would occupy very little space and only a comparatively small aerial would be necessary. The station could be situated in the centre of a densely populated area, or alternatively it might well be installed in a small car with a portable aerial which could be fixed to a convenient tree or chimney. Indeed, on the shorter wave twenty to sixty metres quite a small aerial is all that is necessary. A vertical rod 12ft long, attachable to the car or even a good car radio fixed aerial would be sufficient.

GROUND RAY

24. We will now leave the skip effect and come back to our friend the ground ray, for as already pointed out, as we increase our wavelength and reflected rays from the ionosphere will tend to become weaker, particularly during the daytime, as

compared with the ground rays over the normal communication ranges for which these wave lengths are used.

Moreover, the apparatus tends to become considerably more bulky, a larger amount of primary energy is required, thereby rendering the signals easier to detect, while the aerial becomes correspondingly bigger and more difficult to hide.

25. Generally speaking, therefore it is unlikely that wavelengths of over say one hundred and twenty metres will be used for ordinary illicit communication—and by that is meant the sort of communication that an enemy agent would endeavour to establish for the purpose of sending information *out* of this country.

26. It is not wished to convey by this statement that the enemy will not try to use medium and long waves—in fact, we have definite indications that he will do so for special purposes. All that is suggested is that short waves, low power, and a small aerial are more likely to be used by the gentleman who wants to hide himself in a thickly populated area. This is a fair assumption because an agent who wants to send out information, which in turn argues a regular scheduled service, will not want to increase his own difficulties and consequently the risk of discovery, by installing a medium or long wave station somewhere out in the wilds to which he would have to convey his information before he could dispatch it.

27. There is, however, one important exception—the so called illicit beacon station— and we may as well deal with this at once. Beacon stations, as you probably know are wireless transmitters designed to send out a characteristic signal – usually of a repetitive nature – which act as navigational aids to aeroplanes fitted with direction finding apparatus. Such a station, secretly installed in one of our large manufacturing towns or near an important military objective, would, if it were not detected, enable enemy planes to fly straight to their objective.

Alternatively, such a station erected near the coast or on a vessel within the three-mile limit would furnish and excellent land fall or jumping off point for attacking aircraft.

28. To this you will probably reply: 'Here! Wait a minute you told us just now that medium and long wave stations are much more easily detected because they have to use more power and can therefore be more easily located by our D.F. stations and because the apparatus and aerials are necessarily larger and can be more easily spotted. Furthermore, a beacon station to be of *maximum* value must be fairly near its target which would in most cases be in a thickly populated area. Why then should they use such stations and so increase the risk of discovery?'

The answer is that they cannot help themselves, at any rate in the present state of development. Owing to the high noise level in an aeroplane, fairly powerful signals are required if they are to be received at a sufficiently long range to be of practical navigational value to the plane flying at a speed of anything from 200 to 300 miles an hour.

29. For reasons which it is unnecessary to enter into here, it may be said that any station which the Germans are likely to have erected for this purpose will, at any rate for the present, work on a wavelength of not less than three hundred metres and not more than one thousand seven hundred and fifty metres; and whilst admittedly the risk of location and detection is much greater than that of a low power short-wave station, it is never the less not so great as would at first appear, if you consider the circumstances. Assume that an agent knows his job and can find, let us say, an old disused factory with a medium-sized chimney stack in which to hide his aerial, or alternatively a private house with a good television aerial on the roof (the down leads of a television aerial would, suitably connected, make a very efficient transmitting aerial for this purpose) situated near the target and on the correct line of approach. Even a broadcast receiver aerial can be used. A good

aerial for the purpose would be a long broadcast aerial, attached to a high tree or chimney top, broken by an insulator to comply with the P.M.G.'s Regulations limiting the active length to 100ft; for the purpose of illicit transmission this insulator could easily be bridged over in a way which would be invisible from the ground.

30. All he has to do now is to get his transmitter installed, which he can test out on a non-radiating closed-circuit aerial and he can now sit down quietly and wait for zero hour and nobody any the wiser. When a raid is signalled on that particular objective, and there are a hundred ways of doing this, all he need do is switch on his transmitter, operated by an automatic device which will repeat a pre-arranged signal and then retire quietly to the nearest dug-out. In effect, this means that the beacon will only be on the air for perhaps fifteen or twenty minutes at the outside and although the D.F. stations may succeed in locating the area it is going to be an extremely difficult job, especially in a black out, to locate the actual site.

31. The importance of dealing with the beacon problem will naturally be appreciated, as all our elaborate arrangements for plunging the country into absolute darkness will not be of very much avail if the enemy is to be allowed to erect wireless beacons in or near our big cities, which in these circumstances would remain, from a wireless point of view, almost as brightly illuminated as they are in peace time. Having reached this stage let us now try to summarise the position and see where it is leading us.

32. We can conveniently summarise the position by saying that there are four main forms of illicit transmission for which we have to keep watch:

(i)   The beacon gentleman operating on from 300 to 1,750 metres.

(ii) The agent whose duty is to warn the enemy when our own bombing squadrons are taking the air.

(iii) The Intelligence agent whose duty it is to collect information and convey it to the other side.

(iv) The agent whose duty it, may be to communicate from the shore to submarines and sea-going craft.

33. Let us take these in order:

(i)   *Beacon stations*—Owing to the wavelength employed and the fact that more power is necessary to obtain the requisite range, these stations will probably be picked up at once by our interception and D.F. stations, who will be able to give us the approximate area where the station is located, but we shall be lucky if our regional G.P.O. vans (which form part of the technical organisation) are able to locate the actual premises from which the transmission is taking place—bearing in mind that they may have to operate during a complete black-out, that the station will only be on the air for a few minutes at a time and will not be heard again till the occasion of the next raid or the next wave of attack.

In other words, it will come down in the end to a question of local initiative and organised local intelligence, assisted perhaps by technical experts and specialised apparatus, before the station can be finally localised and put out of action. It is not suggested that the machinery of our technical organisation would not be able to locate the station too, if left to itself, but it is suggested that the desired result will be brought about very much more rapidly if local knowledge and intelligence is brought to bear. And in such circumstances the time element is vital, as it may well mean the saving of many lives as well as the preservation of valuable property.

(ii) *Air raid warnings conveyed to the enemy*—Here again the prevention of leakage of information to the enemy must mean the preservation of valuable lives and machines and in as much as short waves (probably of the order of twenty to seventy metres) are almost certain to be used to take advantage of the skip effect, it follows that the first intimation of the existence of such stations will very often come as a result of local observation.

(iii) *Leakage of general information*—Here again the same remarks apply, only even more so, because it is highly probable that the station will be situated in a densely populated district, where the ground wave, which is all we have to warn us of the presence of the station, will probably not be audible over a radius of more than ten miles, if as much.

(iv) Shore to ship—In this case we again may have to rely on local observation to tell us that an illicit station is working in our midst and as we may be dealing here with waves of the order of say twenty metres down to five or even three metres with a station situated very near the coast and very little back radiation from our friend the ground ray, we shall have to rely to a very large extent, if not entirely, on local information to enable the technical machinery of the War Office and the G.P.O. (that is to say the whole system of D.F. stations, interception stations and mobile vans) requires to be supplemented and assisted by a body of trained observers as well as an organised system of local intelligence to examine and co-ordinate the information collected.

34. It is in this duty—one of paramount importance—the collection and co-ordination of local intelligence—without which the technical organisation cannot hope to succeed—that the Police are now being asked to assist us. And when it is explained that ultimate success will depend to something like eighty per cent, on organised intelligence and twenty per cent, on technical machinery, you will appreciate the vital importance of the work you are being asked to undertake. Resourcefulness, a keen power of observation and unlimited patience are the necessary ingredients of success. Two examples may be given; - In more than one instance it was observed that a certain light circuit was nearly resonant and became incandescent each time the key of the transmitter closed. In another instance quiet enquires into certain of the many motor repair shops, scattered over the countryside, with very little apparent business and installations inconsistent with their visible needs, have led to surprising results.

35. It is for this reason and for the benefit of those readers who are not acquainted with the technical aspect of the problem that an attempt has been made to explain in general terms the salient features of the problem, for it the Police are to help in this very important work it is necessary to have a clear understanding of what that problem is.

36. To seek an analogy, the whole business is rather like a shooting party to which the host has invited a number of guns.

The partridges or pheasants, as the case may be, are our illicit birds.

The guns represent our technical organisation and if you like the host is the Government.

The vans are, if you please, the beaters; the observers are the dogs, and the Police the keepers.

True, the party may go out with a number of beaters and if they are lucky they may put up a few coveys, but on the other hand, they may walk over the birds or there may even be no birds at all on the bit of a shoot. If, on the other hand, the host is a wise man he has so organised his shoot that beaters have been over the ground beforehand with the dogs – they have collected all the intelligence available as to where the birds are and are able to place the beaters to the best advantage.

37. So much for the problem itself. Now as to its solution.

The first problem is to cover the country as far as possible with a twenty four hour watch.

This means forming an observer corps of trained listeners to supplement any organised listening that can be undertaken by the Police, and obviously from their intimate local knowledge, the Police are far and away the best judges as to the qualifications and character of any individuals in the district who are prepared to off their services.

As far as possible men should be chosen who are ex-Fighting Service, Mercantile Marine, or G.P.O. operators with a good knowledge of Morse, or who have made radio their hobby in peace time. Of the latter, the men who have belonged to purely listening societies may possibly be of more value than the average member of the R.S.G.B. who, as a rule, is prone to have been more interested in using his own transmitting set than in listening to others. However, this may be—and it is only put forward as a suggestion—the thing is to get together a corps of listeners or observers who are accustomed to listening in and who, after a short time, will be capable of discriminating between various types of transmission and of recognising an unusual or suspicious signal as soon as they occur. Whilst many men will be found to be in possession of receiving sets well adapted for the purpose, others will have to be supplied with sets on loan. All listeners will have to be supplied with log-forms on which to report the results of their work.

38. It is proposed to divide the whole country into nine regions and to place an Army Officer of the Radio Security Service (M.I.8, W.O.), in wireless charge of each region.

   (i) He will be responsible for the selection of civilian observers, having regard to their character, reliability and qualifications.

   (ii) He will see that all listeners, whether members of the Forces or civilians, are supplied with special forms for logging intercepts, showing call signs, frequency, nature of signals, etc., etc.

   (iii) He will arrange for the transmission of one copy direct to the H.Q. of the R.S.S. with the least possible delay, anything of a suspicious nature being forwarded by telephone, in code if necessary, or by tele-printer if available.

   (iv) Any deductions or suggestions which the Officer i/c District is able to make will be forwarded in the form of a report in duplicate for instructions as to what action (if any) is to be taken.

   (v) He will arrange for the calibration of all receiving sets in his district.

   (vi) He will endeavour to arrange for the receipt of reports from trustworthy dealers regarding any unusual enquires or sales of parts of transmitting apparatus, power valves, X-ray or electro—therapeutic apparatus, or other information of a suspicious nature.

   (vii) He should endeavour to obtain from local electricity supply companies reports of an unusual consumption of current.

   (viii) He should have access to all reports from informers in the district regarding individuals suspected of illicit transmitting. Such reports are now being forwarded by *Chief Constables to the Director of Security Services (D.S.S.), and this should continue to be done, but where technical details are available, such as frequency, call sign, etc., etc., such information should be communicated immediately to O. i/c Region, R.S.S.

   (ix) He will be furnished with a complete list, containing names and addresses, of all individuals in his district who have held transmitting licences in peace time, as well as a list of any exemptions from the closing down order.

   (x) He will be responsible for the issue of any wireless instructions which it may be necessary to circulate from time to time.

   (xi) He will arrange for watches to be kept in his Region, on frequencies to be laid down, having regard to the number of men available and the individual apparatus in their possession.

(xii) Generally speaking he will act as wireless intelligence officer and be responsible for the Region of which he is Officer i/c.

(xiii) In suspected cases of illicit transmitters and even in cases where transmission is actually taking place no direct police action should ever be taken without previous reference to the D.S.S. The only exception to this rule is where an obvious beacon has been located or is some other very urgent and special circumstances where a Police Officer and /or the Officer i/c Region may be called upon to exercise his own initiative. The reason for this will be readily appreciated by the Police, for it is analogous to the case of keeping a criminal under observation instead of arresting out of hand, in order to find out with whom he is associating. It is the same thing with wireless—we can sometimes find out much more by letting him go on for a time so as to ascertain with whom he is corresponding and if we are lucky, what he is saying.

39. It goes without saying that the Police will assist the R.O. in the exercise of his duties by informing him of all suspicious cases of a wireless character, in addition to forwarding their official report to the D.S.S. as hereto fore.

40. In cases where a search is decided upon by the D.S.S. it is the duty of the R.O. to obtain and provide the Police with any technical assistance which may be required.

41. At this juncture let us suppose we have a had a bit of luck—that we have located one of these gentlemen and have decided to raid the premises.
    To start with this can be done either under No. 88A(1) of the Defence Regulations (Search Warrant), or if the case is urgent under No. 88A(2) (Superintendents' Authority). In both cases the suspected offence is against No. 8 of the Regulations dealing with the possession of illicit wireless transmitting apparatus or parts thereof.

42. In the event of an offence against the Regulations being established as a result of the raid, the individual or individuals concerned should be arrested and a full report sent to the D.S.S. immediately. No charge should be made pending receipt of further instructions from the D.S.S.

43. In making a search of this nature it is of the utmost importance that the Police Officer conduction the charge should be a radio expert or that he should be accompanied by someone with the necessary expert knowledge. And again, it is extremely important that the suspect should not have the slightest inkling that he is under observations during the preliminary stages, for it would only be the work of a few minutes to take the whole bag of trick out into the garden and bury it. You might search till the cows came home and find not traces. The importance of both these points cannot possibly be overstated, because, as has already been pointed out, the apparatus you are looking for may, in the case of a short wave set, i.e. not bigger than a good-sized dictionary, or about the size of an ordinary office filing tray.

44. It is more than probable that both the aerial and the apparatus may be installed between the ceiling of a flat and the floor of the flat above and all the operator has to do whenever he wishes to work the set is to plug his key into what appears to be an ordinary lighting point, switch on the current and proceed to transmit.
    This will give some idea of the thoroughness with which a search of this kind has to be conducted whenever the evidence justifies it.

45. And this is one more reason for going slow in the majority of cases before action is taken, as it is necessary to be pretty sure of one's facts before going in and pulling a man's home to pieces. Preliminary discreet enquiries will often decide whether the individual, from his previous history and qualifications is likely to have a transmitter or be able to work one. But as you will have observed, the enquiries must be very discreet.

46. However, having decided to raid the premises and obtained the blessing of the D.S.S. and the necessary warrant (say a Superintendents' Authority), what is the best way to do it?

    The first thing to decide is when to enter. And this is very important. It is best to avoid entering when the suspect is at work because if he is actually transmitting he may be able to send a danger signal intimation that he has been caught, which would nullify the possibility of using him and his set if de elected to turn King's Evidence.

47. And here let a word of warning be added. The police Officer in charge of the investigation should make such arrangements as will enable him to swear on oath that no person left the premises during the interval between the cessation of transmission, i.e., between the moment when signals ceased and his entry into the house, otherwise the suspect may escape under No. 8 (2) of the Defence Regulations 1939, by swearing that some third person was committing the offence without his knowledge. In such a case, even a Dictaphone record of the actual signals might fail to secure a conviction if it could not be sworn that no person had quitted the premises.

48. Now let us imagine we have gained access to the premises. What are we going to look for? Unless the man is a lunatic or a complete fool at his job, we are certainly not going to see a neat little transmitting set laid out on the sitting room table with key complete and an obvious di-pole aerial on the roof. We will in all probability see nothing but an innocent receiving set. First of all, we must examine that set and make sure that it is a receiver. The next thing to do is to search thoroughly the premises, including the furniture, fireplaces and all papers and correspondence. The presence of a calibration chart or an invoice for a quartz crystal, of a transmitting key, a microphone, or a pair of headphone (he is unlikely to use a loud speaker for reception from the other side in order to avoid drawing attention to himself), or a scrap of coded message may give the whole show away. And then lastly, if you are still convinced that there is a transmitter somewhere, set to and trace to its source every bit of electrical wiring in the house, even if it means pulling up the floor boards to do so. And don't forget the garage and car if there is one.

    If nothing if found after this, the only thing to do is to apologise as sweetly as possible and go home.

BORDER LINE CASES

49. A word should now be said regarding the type of case with which all are familiar—the case which, owing to a lack of definite evidence, scarcely seems to justify the issue of a search warrant and a police examination of the premises.

    In normal times, one might be inclined to adopt one of the following courses:

(a) Ask the Police to be good enough to send a Police Officer possessing the necessary radio knowledge to interview the person in question; or

(b) Ask the G.P.O. to send a Radio Interference Officer, ostensibly to examine the suspect's licence and apparatus on the grounds of an alleged report of interference, but in reality, to have an excuse to examine the premises.

(c) Arrange for an excuse to enter the premises under No 85 (1) (B) of the Defence Regulations, ("Land" includes buildings: see No 100 of the Defence Regulations.)

50. Cases of this kind are occurring daily in which, due to ignorance or a too vivid imagination on the part of the informant, some perfectly innocent and respectable individual is accused of transmitting without a licence and since the war broke out, a very large number of perfectly innocent cases have been satisfactorily disposed of

in one or another of the above-mentioned ways without giving offence or causing inconvenience to the individual in question.

51. Actually, none of these methods is satisfactory, for, in one or two cases, objection to entry into the premises has been encountered (as to which see No. 82 of the Defence Regulations), and time has been lost in obtaining the necessary authority, thereby affording ample opportunity for the disposal of incrimination evidence before further action could be taken.

    Owing to the extremely small space occupied by modern low power short wave transmitting apparatus, all evidence of its existence can easily be cleared away in a matter of a few minutes, and therefore it is essential to devise some *modus operandi* to meet this point and which, at the same time, will cause a minimum of inconvenience or offence to the individual in question.

52. To overcome the difficulty it is recommended that in such cases the suspect should be visited, of course without an previous warning, by a Police Officer, accompanied by a G.P.O. Radio Interference Officer, ostensibly to investigate an alleged complaint of interference and that the Police Officer should go armed with a Superintendent's Authority under No. 88 a (2) of the Defence Regulations 1989, which should not, however, be produced or used unless objection is raised to entry, or unless after entry has been effected, evidence is forthcoming which, in the opinion of the Police Officer and / or the G.P.O. Officer, justifies a detailed and exhaustive search of the premises.

53. When carrying out a search, there is one other aspect of illicit transmission which must not be lost sight of. It is all the more important as it is not covered by the present regulations, although it is believed that steps are being taken to amend them.

    The reference is to the question of radiation from diathermic apparatus, X-ray equipment and the like.

    Unfortunately, for our point of view, one cannot prevent medical men, dentists and others, from possessing equipment which forms part of their regular business, but at the same time it must be borne in mind that in the wrong hands such equipment is a potential danger, as it can be transformed into a wireless transmitter in a few minutes.

54. Finally, there is the question of infra-red ray radiation and that question has arisen as to whether powers should not be taken to limit this as well.

    An infra-red beam transmitter can easily be made up from a suitable type of focussing electric torch, fitted with a screen cutting off visual rays and passing infra-red. Suitable screens are sold by many photographic dealers and in fact a thin sheet of ebonite makes an excellent filter.

    An ordinary torch gives strong infra-red emanations, which can be picked up by a simple and lightweight detector attached to an aeroplane, actuated by one of the types of photo-electric cells particularly sensitive in the infra-red region.

    Conditions during a "black-out" are, of course, very suitable for the operation of such a device, and the operator would be very difficult to locate from the ground.

55. And now let a warning be given of a few common pitfalls to avoid.

    In times like these, whey spy fever is rampant, every report while it must be investigated, should be treated with the utmost reserve, the informer's evidence carefully sifted and his *bona fides* established. Recent experience has shown that a large majority of informer's reports are due to over-zealousness or to too vivid an imagination and in some cases to malice.

    His or her grounds of suspicion must be carefully examined and wherever possible information on the following points elicited by questioning:

    (a) If seen, what did the apparatus look like, and in what respects did it appear to differ from an ordinary receiver?

(b) If signals are alleged to have been intercepted, it is important to know:

   (i) When heard—time and date?

  (ii) On how many occasions?

 (iii) Telephony or Morse? Text, if possible.

 (iv) What language?

  (v) Wavelength (if known)? If not known was it near and other station on the scale?

 (vi) Call sings used (if any)?

(vii) Relative loudness of signals?

(viii) What make of receiver was being used, when the suspected signals were heard and what kind of receiving aerial?

56. Another common pitfall, which is a frequent source of genuine error, is to be found in the report by an informer that Mr X has been heard transmitting—whereas Mr X has probably never seen a transmitter in his life and has merely been listening quite innocently on his broadcast receiving set. What has actually happened in this case is that in tuning from one station to another he has perhaps for a minute or two to some station sending Morse, and of course, Morse had come out of Mr X's loud speaker. This has perhaps been heard through an open window or a thin wall and the enthusiastic informer immediately sends in a report accusing Mr X of illicit transmission.

57. On the other hand, it must not be assumed that because an individual does not possess transmitting apparatus he, or she can automatically be entirely exonerated; while it is true that such an individual could not be charged under No 8 of Defence Regulations, it does not necessarily follow that they are not using their wireless receiving set for, let us say, promoting pro-German propaganda. This must constantly be borne in mind, for while a well organised watch can make things very difficult for the person who desires to transmit information, there is nothing that can be done to prevent information reaching this country by wireless, and then, after being received on an ordinary everyday receiver, being used for improper or subversive purposes. In a suspected case of this nature all that can be done is to have the individual in question kept under close observation in order to obtain a check on activities and his associates.

58. One word of conclusion. It is hoped that what has been said will make it plain why it is so imperative to establish throughout the country a body of picked Voluntary Interceptors, or listeners. If another analogy may be permitted, this short-wave transmission business is rather like a mashie shot at golf. The ball goes straight up in the air and comes down again at some distance. Our job is to try and pick up the divot.

59. As has already been said, the country is being divided into nine Regions, which correspond with the G.P.O. Regional Centres. This division has been decided on mainly an account of the existing distribution of trunk telegraph and telephone lines, upon which the question of rapidity on inter-communication depends.

60. Each Region will again be divided into a number of groups, each such group consisting of a number of Voluntary Interceptors, under the direction of a Group Commander, who will be responsible for his area, and for the organisation of individual members of his particular group.

    When the organisation is complete each Group Commander will be in direct contact with the Regional Officer, appointed by the War Office, irrespective of the actual county boundaries in which the group in question happens to be situated.

RSS Timeline

March 1939

The War Office MI1(g) (until transferred to MI8(c) in November '39) set up three fixed and four mobile intercept stations using GPO operators. From June '39, VIs were recruited from radio amateurs. The only agent detected at this time was SNOW as the others were using micro dot techniques.

September 1939

Six agents were known to be working under the Hamburg control. Four were interned, but a Swedish woman (later arrested and detained because she was not leading to other agent's capture) and SNOW, a Welsh electrical engineer, worked for the UK. GW (of MI5) was sent with SNOW to a Hamburg meeting where GW was accepted by the Abwehr. The Abwehr also put SNOW in touch with CHARLIE, who agreed to work for the UK.

1940

State of Stations, VIs and personnel: HQ Personnel—about thirty, VIs about 150; HQ—five single positions; Ballygomartin, Northern Ireland—four positions; Thurso—one DF; Lydd—three DF; Sandridge—one DF; Cupar—one DF; St Erth—two DF; and Bridgewater—one DF.

March 1940

The RSS, as it was now called, intercepted Hamburg-working *Theseus*, a ship in the North Sea, and agents in other European countries and also broke the simple ciphers in use. SNOW was the only agent transmitting in the UK and Strachey was put in charge of RSS material at the GC&CS with the RSS responsible for interception. Swinton was put in overall charge of MI5 and SIS.

April 1940

The fiasco over BISCUIT in the North Sea rendezvous was resolved in July 1940 when SNOW introduced BISCUIT to the Abwehr in Lisbon (87–88). Several hundred messages per week from the Abwehr's main links in Europe were deciphered but the Enigma encipherments had to wait another year before being solved.

May 1940

Barnet intercept station opened with twelve double positions.

September to November 1940: ten agents were landed from four dinghies; four landed by parachute. Only one escaped capture, Ter Braak, a Dutchman, who committed suicide in Cambridge in April 1941. The state of his transmitter indicated that he had failed to contact Germany. Three saved their lives by working for MI5. SUMMER (a Swede) who landed near Aylesbury on 6 September 1940 was the first agent to bring a radio set with him. He operated from the police station with a radio amateur present to supervise his Morse. Later, his location is given as being near Cambridge. TATE (a Dane) arrived soon after SUMMER and operated near Barnet from October '40 to May '45. He was awarded the Iron Cross, as was GARBO. GANDER (a German) was used for a few weeks and then detained.

September 1940

The Abwehr sent many agents as refugees or business people through legitimate channels from Lisbon. The first was GIRAFFE, who operated for a while before joining the Free French Forces. In June–July 1941, three more were sent: FATHER (a Belgian pilot), CARELESS (a Polish pilot), and SNARK (a Yugoslav woman).

November 1940

Ballygomartin, NI, closed down. St Erth increased to six positions. All nine VI regions reached a strength of about 1,000.

December 1940

TRICYCLE, a Yugoslav commercial lawyer with a German degree, had a distinguished career as a double agent. Seamen were also enlisted by the Abwehr but were of limited value and several were caught. In the spring and summer of 1941, the Abwehr infiltrated agents among the refugees arriving from Norway. In five out of six cases, ISOS decrypts led to the arrest of several Norwegians.

January 1941

Thurso increased to four positions. Swinton decided that the RSS should be taken over by the SIS. The transfer was affected in May. Technical improvements now began in the RSS and the GPO agency was terminated. The best GPO operators and radio amateurs were enlisted into the Royal Signals as 'specials'. A long-running battle ensued between MI5 and SIS for control of the RSS. GIRAFFE fell next because the Germans were dissatisfied with the poverty of his reports. In the spring of 1941, the SIS representative in Lisbon reported that SNOW had admitted to the Germans that he was working for the British. The truth was not established but it was felt that he must be dropped and was detained.

February 1941

Unit training at Trowbridge for Egypt.

March 1941

Unit embarked for Egypt.

June 1941

Hanslope opened with thirty-two double positions. VIs, by this time, comprised over 1,500 members. HQ personnel now about 150 strong.

October 1941

St Erth increased to twelve positions. Thurso increased to twelve positions.

January 1942

Gilnahirk opened twelve positions. Mobile DF units were now at Barnet, Newcastle, and
Gilnahirk. There were overseas units at Gibraltar (six positions), Cairo, and some personnel in Tehran.

January–October 1942

The RSS intercepted thirty-seven reports from a station in Portugal given the name OSTRO. He was a Czech businessman who was sending imaginative reports, supposedly written from agents in the UK, to the Abwehr, who valued his work. SIS decided eventually to take no action.

End of 1942

Units organised in India.

December 1942

FRITZ or FRITZCHEN was the only parachutist to arrive during 1942, and he landed near Ely. A great deal was known about him from more than 160 Abwehr messages starting on 27 April describing his training and background. His training call sign was FFF and he was known to RSS operators as the Three F Man. ISOS revealed that he would probably be carrying an English radio, with German parts, and was trained in secret writing. MI5 looked forward to his arrival and he obligingly telephoned the police from a nearby farmhouse to be collected. His story tallied perfectly with what was already known and he served well as ZIGZAG. In order to fulfil his assignment, the Mosquito works at Hatfield had to be 'blown up'—at least for aerial reconnaissance purposes.

1943

Forfar opened with thirty-two double positions. Barnet now had thirty-two positions. Barnet training school for operators organised. An intercept unit, with twelve positions, was founded in Rome. HQ staff now numbered about 250. A mobile DF unit was now open at Bristol. A research station opened at Barnet. ISOS was able to be certain that despite grounds for distrusting BALLOON, MUTT, and JEFF, and the risk in letting ZIGZAG return to Germany, the double agents formed a reliable and efficient espionage network in Britain and that no uncontrolled agents were operating. BRUTUS had to be used with great caution, but in '43, it was found possible to get the Germans to accept a substitute operator, and in early '44, they were arranging to send him money, a new transmitter, and a camera. Between January '44 and D-Day, 500-plus messages were exchanged between London area and Madrid, where they were retransmitted to Berlin and hence RSS could follow their progress. GARBO and BRUTUS, along with several other agents, played an important part in the D-Day deception plans. It was difficult to assess what the Germans thought of TATE as his control in Hamburg used a landline to Berlin. TATE moved from Barnet to Kent in June to transmit deception details. ARTIST, who was a most valuable traitor working inside the Abwehr, was arrested in April '44 and is believed to have died in Oranienburg concentration camp.

March 1943

GARBO made his first transmission with a transmitter he had obtained from an unlicensed radio amateur friend (or so he claimed to the Germans). In May, the Germans sent GARBO a cipher that GC&CS had not broken with a new transmitting plan, which required GARBO to use military procedure while the Abwehr continued with radio amateur procedure. GARBO's link with Madrid was made difficult as signals were submerged in other military traffic. It is a tribute to the RSS operators that they shortly picked up GARBO's signals and reported them as a new suspect station. The Germans reverted to the previous plan.

December 1943

Hugh Trevor-Roper (later Lord Dacre), in a TV broadcast on 17 April '79, gave details of the part the RSS played in tracking the effectiveness of operations CICERO and MINCEMEAT. Apparently, Hinsley *et al.* found no reference to this in the official papers. In fact, only the harm CICERO may have done to the Allied cause is mentioned.

1944

Mobile DF unit with small intercept staff later goes to Normandy. An intercept unit with twelve positions was sent to Brussels at the end of 1944.

February 1944

TREASURE (a woman agent) confessed that she had concealed from her controller a special check, which was to be used in procedure if she was under control. She was replaced with an MI5 operator.

June 1944

TATE provided false information about the fall of V-weapons. ZIGZAG, the last spy to reach England, parachuted into Cambridgeshire on 27–28 June with two radio sets, cameras, and a large sum of money. He had previously returned to German for a period. In November 1944, twenty-three agents were captured in Italy. Valuable XX agents were PRIMO, ADDICT, and AXE; this last received the Iron Cross for his work in Florence.

1945

Unit from Brussels went to Minden. Unit from Rome went to Graz in Austria. Gibraltar closes down. Detachment at Cairo and Alexandria move to Cyprus and hands over operation to 'Y' Unit. Hanslope closes down.

1945–1946

Graz handed over to Y units. Minden taken over by Y units.

June 1946

All RSS stations closed. Selected Discrimination Staff re-employed at Eastcote with GCHQ. Research station with some personnel, Barnet mobile unit and Training School with some staff taken over by GCHQ.

RSS Roll call

This list has been compiled over a number of years by RSS amateur VIs. Some on the list are shown as SCU 1, 2, 8 etc., but only SCU 3 and 4 were RSS employed in intercept, direction finding, and studying the Abwehr. They all came under the command structure of Brigadier Gambier-Parry—the other SCUs covered a wide range of duties, mainly centred on Whaddon village.

NAME	UNIT	CALLSIGN	LOCATION/DETAILS
ABEL F.	SLU8		
ACKERLY John	SCU1/8		
A'COURT Reg	SCU3		Arkley
ADAMS Jimmy R.	SCU3	GM5KF	Arkley Discrimination Group
ADAM J.	SCU3	G15AJ	Northern Ireland VI
ADDIE Capt. Robin	SCU3	G8LT	Hanslope (then GPO HQ E in Chief)
ADLINGTON W. E.	SCU3		Gateshead op (Middlesborough)
AINLEY Jim			
AKIN George E.	SCU3	G8DN	Hanslope Park (source G8VG)
ALLEN T. P.	SCU3		Belfast VI
ALLEN Wilfred A.T.	SCU3	G5GT	Hanslope Park
ALLINGTON Capt.	SCU3		
ALSTON G.	SCU3		Thurso D.F.
AMON John			
AMRIDING E.	SCU3		Thurso 41–43 Forfar 43–46
ANDERSON A. E.	SCU8		
ANDERSON J.	SCU3		Thurso D.F.
ANDERSON Vic	SCU2		
ANDERTON J. H.	SCU3		Hanslope
ANGEL Charlie	SCU10		

ANNERLY Mr & Mrs	SCU3		Arkley Group 2
ASH A. G.	SCU1		1944–46 Hanslope, Forfar & Barnet
ASKEW Bob (P. H.)	SCU3	G8TP	Hanslope
AULT	SCU1		
AUSTIN George	SCU3	G8GA	Arkley
AYES Tom Cpl	SCU3		St Erth
BAILEY Mrs	SCU3		Arkley Collation
BAKER Les	SCU12		
BALDWIN Eric	SCU1		
BALL Ralph	SCU4		Hanslope etc. 44–45 GPO
BAMBER Lt	SCU3		Arkley at some time & went to Gib.
BANCROFT	SCU3		Hanslope
BANHAM Capt. J.	SCU3		Arkley
BANNER George			
BANNISTER Horace	SCU3	G8OM	Hanslope DF & Engineering
BARKER Johnny	SCU3		Arkley Sgt in Arkley View
BARLOW Ken	SCU4		
BARNES Cpl Chris	SCU8		
BARNET Mr	SCU3		Arkley Group 2
BARR R.		N Ireland GI5UR	VI
BARRATT Don			
BARTLETT Herbert	SCU3	G5QA	Arkley (May have been VI only)
BARTLETT Sid			Arkley Group 2
BARTON	SCU1		
BARWICK Bert	SCU4		
BARWISE Cpl			
BATES			
BAYLIS Percy	SCU1	G3PQ	Hanslope
BEACOM William	SCU3		Arkley Collation
BEAN Ron	SCU4	G3QI	Arkley
BEARD CQMS	SCU4/10		
BEARDWOOD Harold	SCU3	G5ZB	Hanslope
BEAUMONT Tom H.	SCU3&4	G6HB	Hanslope
BECKETT S.			
BECKETT Ted	SCU8		
BEDWORTH Sgt	SCU3		Arkley
BELLRINGER Maj. H.	SCU3		OIC Enlisting VI Section, RSS
BELSEY Geo W.	SCU3	G4PX	Hanslope
BENNETT Ronald	SCU4/10		
BENT Fred			
BENTLEY Jim	SCU3		Hanslope 44–46

BERESFORD Miss	SCU3		Arkley Collation
BERNARD R. A.	SCU3		Hanslope (Merchant Navy)
BESWICK George	SCU3		Forfar in 1945
BETTS J. J.	SCU3		Hanslope
BEVERIDGE-SMART	SCU3	ATS	Arkley DF
BIGGAM John	SCU4		
BIGGS Sydney	SCU3	G2FWZ	Hanslope Gilnakirk intercept
BIGLEY Walter	SCU3	G2AUA	Hanslope
BINNS Fred			Hanslope (source G3HEZ)
BIRD	SCU3/4		
BLACK Jim	SCU3	BRS5204	Arkley Discrimination Group
BLACKFORD Bob			
BLAIR Gavin	SCU3		Arkley
BLAKE Ray	SCU8		
BOFFIN		G3HS	
BOTT Frank	SCU3	G5VB	Hanslope Engineering
BOWERS John	SCU3	G4NY	Hanslope
BOX A. W.			VI
BRADBURY Cecil A.	SCU3	BRS1066	Arkley Discrimination Group
BREMNER David	SCU3		Hanslope
BRIGHT Civ/Lt	SCU3		Arkley i/c special ops
BRINDLE Jim	SCU3	G3QP	Hanslope
BROCK Harold	SCU3	G3FD	Arkley Collation/Discrimination
BROOKES CSM	SCU12		
BROOKES Peter	SCU3/4		Hanslope/Egypt/Palestine/DWS
BROWN Cpl Archie	SCU3	G2WQ	Gateshead CMU
BROWN Joe	SCU12		
BROWN Sam	SCU8/1		
BROWN Topper	SCU4	G0HEZ	Hanslope Capt
BRUTON Jack A.	SCU3/4		
BRYCE L.	SCU3		Thurso 41–43 Forfar 43–46
BUCKINGHAM S.	SCU3	G5QF	Arkley
BUDDEN Joe?	SCU3		St Erth
BUDGE A. &/or D.	SCU3		Thurso DF
BUFFAM Fg Off. A.	SCU8		Also SLU8
BUICK Ernie	SCU3	G3XJ	Hanslope also VK2BM
BULL John			
BURDICKIN Jack	SCU12		
BURK	SCU12		
BURTON	SCU12		
BUSHAWAY	SCU12		
BUSHELL Ambrose	SCU3		Hanslope

BUTTERWORTH H. R.	SCU3	G2HDO	Hanslope
BUTTON Noel	SCU3	G3BG	Hanslope
BYFORD Lawrence	SCU12		
BYRNE			
BYWATERS Harry	SCU4		
CADDY J.	SCU1		
CALEY John	SCU8/7	G2FSS	
CAMERON CSM Lewis	SCU3		Thurso 41–43 Forfar 43–46
CAMPBELL Archie	SCU3		Hanslope Sgt Gp 7 (Violet)
CAMPBELL H.	SCU3		Thurso 41–43 Forfar 43–46
CAMPBELL H. S.	SCU3		Thurso 41–46 Forfar 43–46 SCU4
CARDER Bert H.			
CAREW Andy	SCU1		
CARLISLE R.	N Ireland	GI6WG	VI
CARTER Sgt L.	SLU8		
CARTER W. (Nick)	SCU3	G2NJ	Arkley & St Erth DF
CASSELS Jock	SCU3		
CASSERLEY Ted			
CASTLE Jack	SCU2		
CAVALLS P.	SCU3	G5SF	Hanslope
CHALMERS			
CHAMBERLAIN Joe	SCU3		St Erth
CHAMBERS Eric H.	SCU3	G2FYT	Arkley Discrimination Group
CHAMBERS Joan	SCU3		Arkley Group 2
CHANDLER T. W.	SCU1	G3EBJ	Nash/Weald/Europe
CHAPPLE S. W.	SCU3	G6SC	Arkley
CHARLESWORTH	SCU12		
CHARMAN Dud	SCU3	G6CJ	Hanslope engineer/Group leader
CHEER John A.	SCU4/10		
CHEESEMAN Ben	SCU3		St Erth
CHEW Alison	SCU3		Arkley Group 2
CHITTLEBURGH Bill	SCU3	G6ID	Hanslope
CLACY Stewart	SCU3	G6CY	Arkley Group 2 & Allocation
CLARK Ham		G6OT	RSGB Treasurer
CLARK Nobby	SCU3		
CLARK Norman W.	SCU12		
CLARK R. F.	SCU3	G5PY	Arkley
CLARK Sgt S. L.	SLU8		
CLARRICOATS John		G6CL	RSGB Secretary
CLAYFORTH F.	SCU3		Gateshead op (fm Pudsey)
CLAYTON Fred	SCU4		
CLELAND C. B.	N Ireland	GI2CN	Northern Ireland VI

CLIFFORD K.	SCU3		Hanslope
COCKAYNE R.	SCU3/1		Hanslope & Whaddon
COCKREM Hugh	SCU3	G3ZC	Hanslope
COLE Reg	SCU3	G6RC	Hanslope
COLE-ADAMS Lt-Col.	SCU3		Arkley—Admin
COLEMAN H.	SCU3		Hanslope
COLES CSM Jack	SCU4/10		
COLLINS Alfred	SCU3	2FII	Hanslope (G4QO) Gp7 Violet
COLLINS C.	SCU3	G8SC	Arkley
COLLINS J. B.	SCU12		
COLLINS R.	SCU8		
CONSTANTINE W.	SLU8		LAC
COOMBS D. J.	SCU8		
COOPER E. C.	SCU1		
COOPER James	SCU3	GM2UD	Hanslope (servicing at Arkley)
COOPER Lt-Cdr	SCU1		
COPEMAN	SCU2		
CORDINER F. J.			Hanslope
CORNISH Cpl	SCU3		Arkley Collation
CORNISH Cpl Ron	SCU3		St Erth DF
CORR Brian	SCU4/10		
CORRIN William			
CORRY Neil	SCU3	G2YL	Home South VI (from Tadworth)
COSADINOS John	SCU3		Gateshead op (fm Manchester)
COURTENAY Capt. R. R.	SCU1		
COWDEN Robert	SCU3	GI2BZV	Hanslope or N Ireland VI
COWEN James	SCU3	GI5OY	N Ireland VI
COWHIGG Dave	SCU8		
COWIE			
COX Cpl A. M.	SCU1		
COX Sgt J.	SLU8		
CRAIG David	SCU3	GM3AWF	Hanslope
CRAIG, Jnr, T. S.	SCU3	GI6TC	N Ireland VI
CRAWLEY Helena	SCU3	G2DDY	Orkney VI
CRAWLEY Leslie	SCU3	G3DT	Orkney VI
CREED Peter G.	SCU3/4		Hanslope
CREMIN Sigmn	SCU1		
CROOKS Sgt	SCU4/10		
CROOKS J.	SCU3		N Ireland VI
CROPPER Joe J. W. C.	SCU3	G3BY	Hanslope
CROSS Cpl E. A. G.	SCU1		
CROSS Ronnie	SCU3		Sandridge & Thurso DF

CROWE Bert	SCU3	G6CO	Hanslope
CURTIES Sgt Leonard	SCU4		
CURTISS	SCU8		
DE CAUX Harry	SCU12		
DE SOUSA Jim	SCU12		
DAKIN Geo	SCU3	G8DN	Hanslope
DALBY Les	SCU3	G5KN	Hanslope
DALE E.	SCU8		Sgmn
DALEY Don	SCU1		
DAVEY Sgt	SCU3		Arkley Collation
DAVIDSON Gerry			
DAVIES K. W. J.	SCU3		Hanslope (Press operator)
DAWSON Trevor	SCU4		
DEADMAN Jack C.	SCU4/10		CSM
DEAN Geoff	SCU3/4	G3NPO	Arkley and Hanslope, MERS
DEELEY Harry	SCU4/10		
DELAHUNT Roland/Ron	SCU3	G4QD/G4DR	Arkley Discrimination Group
DENNIS C. P. O.	SCU3	G3BEE	Arkley Group 1 Discrimination
DENNY Malcolm			
DERRICK Chas F.	SCU4		
DEUCHAR W. G.	SCU3/4		
DICKSON Joe	SCU12		
DIXON George	SCU3	G2DQL	Hanslope
DIXON Mike	SCU3		Arkley Group 2?
DOBSON Peter	SCU4		
DONALDSON	SCU3		Navy/Arkley Research Op.
DONNAN Lt	SCU4		OC RSS Gibraltar Station
DORMAN Steve	SCU1/3		Whaddon
DOUGLAS Andy	SCU4		
DOWNING Desmond		GI3ZX	Arkley Allocation
DRAKEFORD Les	SCU3	G 2 D W B / G3AGD	Arkley Group 2 (BRS 4200)
DRAPER H.	SCU3	G4BU	Hanslope
DREW		G3MD	RSS—VI
DRUMMOND Jock	SCU3&4		Gateshead op (from Dundee)
DUNCOMBE-ANDERSON	SCU1		Major
DUNN Lt David	SCU4/10		Hanslope (source G3HEZ)
DUNN Jock	SCU1/8		
DURANCE Don	SCU3	G4EXX	Thurso DF
DURRANT Fred	SCU3	G5PD	VI
DWYER	SCU3		Arkley Collation

DYER E. G.	SCU3	G4IJ	Arkley
EASON Bill	SCU1	G4MQN	Whaddon 1941–46
EASTWOOD Harry	SCU3	G4GS	Hanslope
ECCLES John	SCU1/8		Whaddon
EDDY Pam	SCU3		Arkley Group 2
EDWARDS Eddie	SCU3		Arkley Discrimination Group
EDWARDS George	SCU3	G2UX	Hanslope/Wymondham/St Erth DF
EDWARDS John	SCU3	G3SR	Hanslope Gp7 Violet
EDWARDS S. F.	SCU3	G2FQX	Arkley
ELMORE Wilf	SCU3		Arkley—Tant's special op 44–46
ELLETT Chas Jasper	SCU3	G3ARJ	Hanslope BRS 3585
ELLICE Jock	SCU12		Far East
ELWELL Capt. Bob	SCU3		Hanslope
EMARY Charles	SCU4	G5GH	RSS in Alexandria, Egypt
ESSEX Frank	SCU3		Hanslope (from Merchant Navy)
EVANS John	SCU3	G2RV	Hanslope
EVANS Ron	SCU4		
EVANS	SCU3		Arkley Military discipline! CSM
FAIRCHILD Cyril T.	SCU3	G3YY	Arkley View Discrimination
FARNEY Dick G. R.	SCU4		
FAUTLEY Ray	SCU3	G3ASG	VI Essex
FAWCETT Mrs	SCU3		Arkley Collation
FAY Peter	SCU3		
FENTON W.	SCU3		Thurso 41–46 Forfar 43–46
FERGUSON D.	SCU3		Forfar 43–46
FERGUSON R.	SCU3		Thurso 41–43 Forfar 43–46
FINCH Charles	SCU3		St Erth
FISH Eddie	SCU3	G2HCZ	Arkley Discrimination Group 5/8
FISH George	SCU3	G4LO	Hanslope
FLETCHER Tom	SCU3	BRS2763	Arkley Discrimination
FOSTER Eric	SCU3/4		Arkley & VI 41–43
FOSTER John	SCU3		Forfar & Gibraltar
FOULKES R. T.	SCU3		Gateshead
FOULKES Reg	SCU4/10		
FOX Graham	SCU3		Arkley research
FRAGLE Leslie	SCU4		Gibraltar 2600470(2607726)
FOYLE Ken	SCU4		
FRAPE	SCU3		Gateshead op
FRENCH H. A. (Herbie)	SCU12		Also SCU7 & 7X (professor)
FRESHWATER Sgt	SCU3	BRS4785	Arkley Admin
FULCHER Gordon			SAS
FURZE Major	SCU12		

GALE Ted	SCU4		
GALPIN Reginald	SCU3	GW2FWD	Hanslope, St Erth & Gilnahirk
GAMBIER-PARRY	SCU3	G2DV	Brigadier
GAMMON Peter	SCU3?	G3VB	
GARDENER Ed L.		G6GR	RSS? President RSGB in '44
GARLEY Leslie	SCU3	GW5ZL	Hanslope
GARRETT Jack	SCU3		St Erth
GARTON Ronald	SCU3	2FZV	Hanslope also St Erth?
GATESD Don	SCU12		
GEORGE Fred	SCU3	G5FG	Hanslope
GILBERT Ray	SCU3		
GILFINAN John		GM3BQN	
GILMOUR Hugh	SCU3/4	G3AUV	Arkley & Middle East
GILPIN Bernard	SCU2		
GIRDWOOD Cpl D.	SCU3		Thurso 41–43 Forfar 43–46
GLEDHILL Dan	SCU3	G8QJ	Arkley
GODWIN W. S.	SCU4/10		VI
GOODACRE	SCU3		Arkley Oaklands training Sgt
GOODFELLOW W.	SCU3		Thurso 41–43 Forfar 43–46 SCU4
GOURLEY Peter	SCU3	GM3LO/ G3LO	Arkley Discrimination Group
GOVER Alan	SCU3	G4AU	Hanslope
GRAHAM Albert		G3AIT	
GRAHAM Peter	SCU3	G3GLK	Arkley Discrimination Group
GRAHAM W.	SCU3	GI5GV	Northern Ireland VI
GRANT Sgt Alec	SCU3		Thurso 41–43 Forfar 43–46
GRATRIX Les	SCU3		Arkley Discrimination Group
GREENSLADE Trevor	SCU3		Arkley Hanslope
GREGG C.	SCU3		Hanslope
GRIFFITHS Ray	SCU3	G2DFH	St Erth DF
GRINYER CQMS	SCU3		Arkley
GROVES Stan	SCU3		St Erth
GYLE Jimmy	SCU4/10		
HALL Mrs	SCU3		Arkley Collation
HALLWOOD Joe	SCU1/8		
HALSTEAD Fred	SCU3	G3ASD	
HAMAUI Edwin	SCU3		Arkley Discrimination group
HAMILL Chas P.	SCU4/10		
HAMILTON Jack	SCU3	G4DN	Hanslope
HAMILTON Sgt	SCU3		Arkley Gp 2
HAMMOND A.	SCU3	G6AH	Arkley research op
HAMPSHIRE Stuart	SCU3	Knight	Ark. Fellow All Souls Ox.

HANDCOCKS M. E.	SCU3	G5HN	Hanslope
HANLEY Cliff	SCU4		
HARDIE John	SCU3		Arkley Group 13
HARDING Harold	SCU3	GW2HH	Hanslope
HARDINGHAM	SCU3		Arkley Oaklands training later Lt
HARE Bunny	SCU4		
HARLAND	SCU12		
HARROWER Alex	SCU3	GM6NX/ G3ESF	Arkley discrimination group
HARVEY Arthur	SCU3		Forfar in 1945
HARVEY R. J.	SCU3	GI5DU	Northern Ireland VI
HASTINGS Capt.	SCU1		Whaddon
HATTON Harry	SCU8		
HAWKER Pat	SCU3/4	G3VA	Hanslope
HAWKES Johnny	SCU3		
HAYES	SCU3		Arkley Collation
HEAP Harry	SCU3	G5HF	VI in Manchester & Chelmsford
HEARN Les	SCU3/4		
HEFFERMAN Jim	SCU3	G4BX	Arkley
HEFFERON	SCU3		Arkley Collation Sgt
HENDERSON J.	SCU3		Thurso 41–43 Forfar 43–46
HEPPLE Edith	SCU3	ATS	Arkley DF (ref G2BTO)
HERDSON Tom	SCU3	G6ZN	Arkley & Hanslope
HESTER Lt-Col. Jack	SCU4		OC RSS ME—Rome O/C SCUs
HILL Wm	SCU3	G2RU	Hanslope
HILLIARD Ted	SCU3		Arkley Discrimination (Press)
HOEDL Earl	SCU3		Hanslope
HOFER John	SCU1		Whaddon MT, L.Horwood 43–45
HOLMES A.	SCU3		Thurso 41–43 Forfar 43–64 SCU4
HOLMES Ernie	SCU12		
HOLT Eric	SCU3	G5OZ	Hanslope
HONEYMAN Tom	SCU4/10		
HOOLE Ken	SCU3/4		Gateshead
HOOSEN Ted	SCU3	G3YF	Arkley
HOPE Bob	SCU3		Arkley
HOPE S.	SCU3		Hanslope?
HORNBY	SCU1		RSS Cpl
HOSIE Bob	SCU3		Hanslope? Cpl at Forfar in 1945
HOULDSWORTH Ernie	SCU3	G6NM	Hanslope (First op with G2DTD)
HOWARD J. (?)	SCU3		Arkley Group 2 > 8
HOWARTH Sgt Ted	SCU3/4		St Erth Alex.
HOWELLS Gwyn			RSS

HOWES William	SCU3	G2CF	Hanslope
HOWIE Tom	SCU3		Forfar operator (Royal Signals)
HUDSON Harry	SCU3		Arkley Allocation
HUDSON Jim	SCU3	G4NS	Hanslope? at Forfar in 1945
HUDSON John	SCU3/4	G4ARB	Arkley, Forfar, Thurso M. Navy
HUMPHISON Fred	SCU12		
HUNT Alan	SCU4/10		
HUNT Cyril	SCU3		Forfar in 1945
HUNTER	SCU3	G3AZ	Hanslope
HUNTER	SCU3	G3IMV	
HUNTER	SCU3	G6HU??	Hanslope
HURST Fred	SCU1/8		
IMRIE John C.	SCU3	GM4GK	Arkley Discrimination Group
INCE Stanley	SCU3	G6LC	Hanslope & Arkley
INDGE K. A.	SCU3		Hanslope
INGLIS Eric	SCU3/4		Arkley, Nordet, MERS
IRONFIELD Wm	SCU3	G4GM	Hanslope
IRVINE Miss	SCU3		Arkley Collation
IRWIN Arthur R.	SCU3	GI5TK	Northern Ireland VI
IVES Phil O.			RSS
JACKSON Cpl A. M.	SCU3		Thurso 41–43 Forfar 43–46
JACKSON Alan	SCU3		Hanslope Eng in '44 (knew Turing)
JACKSON Fred	SCU3	G5FJ	Hanslope
JACQUES Bill	SCU12		
JAMES Archie			RSS
JANES	SCU3	G2FWA	RSS Leatherhead
JEFFERIES Charles E.	SCU3	G5JF	Hanslope
JEFFERS Harry Jeff	SCU3/4		Arkley Forfar/Italy Training Barnet
JENKINS Charles	SCU3		Arkley
JENKINS Frank		G3AXT	
JENKINS W.	SLU8		
JENKS Ronald	SCU3/4	G2DYZ	Arkley and various
JESSUP Geoff	SCU3	G3AMG	Hanslope
JOBURNS	SCU1		RSS Cpl
JOHNSON CQMS	SCU8		RSS SLU8
JOHNSON D.	SCU3		Thurso 41–43 Forfar 43–46
JOHNSON Johnny	SCU4/10		
JOHNSON P. H.	SLU8		RSS Sgt
JOHNSON S.	SCU3	GI5SJ	Northern Ireland VI
JOHNSTONE D. K.	SCU3		Thurso 41–43 Forfar 43–46
JONES Alun Merddyn			RSS
JONES Dr Robbie	SCU3		NW regional VI

JOYCE T. L.	SCU3		Hanslope
KAY			RSS
KEEN Maj. Dick	SCU3		Hanslope etc. DF expert
KELSALL Capt. Jack	SCU3	G3AQQ	Arkley CO training & at Bletchley
KENNEDY T.	SCU3	G6UC	Gateshead (HRO set Maintenance)
KENNEDY	SCU3		Arkley research op
KENWORTHY Bob	SCU3		Hanslope?
KENWORTHY	SCU4		
KEYS	SCU12		
KILLICK Dave	SCU1/8		
KILSHAW W. T. Bill	SCU8		
KING C. R. (Bob)	SCU3	G2FMT	Hanslope (source G8VG)
KING Gordon	SCU3	G4VFV	Hanslope Engineering
KING Bob—Noz (H. S.)	SCU3	G3ASE	Discrimination (BRS 4786)
KINGHAM Kay	SCU3		Arkley Discrimination group
KINGSLEY Bill	SCU3		Arkley Discrimination group
KINLOCH			RSS
KIPPIN Walter	SCU3	G8PL	Hanslope
KRAILING Cob	SCU3	BRS3058	Arkley Discrimination group
LACEY Lt-Col.	SCU3		Arkley
LAIDLER Capt.	SCU12		
LAING			RSS
LAKE Sgt	SCU1		
LAKIN John	SCU3		Arkley Group 2
LAMB Jimmy	SCU2		
LANSLEY R.	SCU8		
LASKI Marchinette	SCU3		Arkley Collation
LAST Derrick	SCU12		
LAVIS Ronald	SCU3	G8DX	Hanslope
LAWLEY Hugo		G62G	Voluntary Interceptor St Neots
LAWRENCE Chas R.	SCU2		
LAWRENCE Vic Sgmn	SCU4		
LEE Leonard		G5FH	VI V/M/51 Oldbury Worcs
LEE Jumbo Capt.	SCU1		Gib. Succeeded by Bamber
LEE Russell	SCU3	G6GL	Arkley
LEEDS Miss Myrtle	SCU3		Arkley Collation
LEES Jack	SCU3	G2IO	Hanslope
LEGGE Harry			RSS
LEITCH			RSS
LENNOX Bill	SCU3		Hanslope
LEONARD Jock	SCU8		
LEWIS Cpl	SCU2		

LEWIS Len	SCU3	G8ML	Hanslope Gp 7 Violet
LEWIS Sol	SCU3		Forfar in 1945
LIMB Wilfred	SCU3	G2DTD	Hanslope (First Op there)
LINGARD Bert	SCU3	G3IR	
LISTER Tom	SCU3	BRS6440	Arkley
LIVESEY	SCU3/4	G6LI	Arkley discrimination group
LLOYD Capt.	SCU3		Arkley Admin (Billeting etc.)
LLOYD J. E.	SCU3	G6SK?	Wymondham DF?
LLOYD Mrs	SCU3		Arkley Collation (Capt. Lloyd)
LONG H. J.	SCU30	G5LO	North Oxford full-time VI (disabled—awarded BEM)
LONG Monty	SCU3	G2CL	Hanslope
LOOK R. P. W.	SCU1		
LOOMES Reg			RSS CQMS
LORNIE Bill			Hanslope (ref G3HEZ)
LOWE Stan	SCU1/8		
LUCKIN Miss	SCU3		Arkley Collation (Manchester)
LUNN R. F. (Rupert)	SCU4		
LUSCOMBE Les H.	SCU3	G8NY	Arkley (Training) & Hanslope
LUSH Bill	SCU3		Hanslope
LYMAN John J.	SCU3	G2AII	Hanslope (source G8VG)
LYNCH Capt.	SCU8		SLU8
MacINTAGGART Sgt	SCU1		
MacKAY D.	SCU3		Forfar in 1945 (from Thurso)
MADGE Bop			RSS
MAGSON	SCU3/4		Italy
MAITLAND T.	SCU3	GI5SQ	Northern Ireland VI
MALPAS Reg			RSS
MALTBY Lt-Col. Ted	SCU3		Hanslope CO—Controller RSS
MARCUSE Gerald		G2NM	Group leader
MARSHALL J. R. C.	SCU3		Thurso DF
MARTIN Boogie	SCU3		Hanslope?
MARTIN J.	SCU3	GI3SG	Northern Ireland VI
MARTIN Capt.	SCU3/4		Arkley Group 2 Discrim
MARTIN Sgt	SCU1		
MARTIN Stan	SCU3	G2IZ	
MARTIN Steve	SCU4		
MARTIN W. H.	SCU3	GI5HV	Northern Ireland VI
MASON F.	SCU12		Hanslope
MASTERS Capt.	SCU12		
MATHESON P. J.	SCU3		Hanslope
MATHEWS Bert	SCU3	G6QM	Arkley discrimination group

MATHEWS Jim	SCU3	G6LL	Hanslope
MATTHEWS Bill	SCU3	G2CD	East London VI group coordinator
MAXEY Jack	SCU2		
MAXWELL J. E.	SCU3	BRS1612	Northern Ireland VI
MAXWELL		G3IAX	
MAY D. P. L.		G2BB	London area
MAY George		VI/HS/407	Thurnley, Leics 1940–42
MAY Alan		G5AL	Glossop area
MAYERS Cliff	SCU12		
MAYHEAD L. V.		G3AQC	
McAFFERTY John	SCU3		DF 1943 St Erth, Lydd
McALINDEN			RSS
McCANN B.	SCU3	GI2KN	Northern Ireland VI
McDOWALL Jack			RSS
McDOWELL F.	SCU3	GI5MZ	Northern Ireland VI
McEACHERN	SCU3		Gateshead op (fm Newcastle)
McEACHERN Sgt Tom	SCU4/10		RSS
McFARLANE Lt-Col.	SCU1		
McGLYNN J. R.	SCU3		Thurso 41–43 Forfar 43–46
McHARG Maj. J.	SCU3		Thurso 41–43 OIC of Forfar 43–46
McINTOSH Capt.	SCU3		Arkley Training
McKAY D.			RSS
McKAY H.			RSS
McKECHNIE A.			RSS
McKEE Harry	SCU4/10		
McKENZIE Jock	SCU12		
McKENZIE Lt	SCU8		SLU8
McKENZIE Tom	SCU3		Hanslope? Sgt
McLACHLAN	SCU3/4		Hanslope? Sgt
McLARTY Ian			RSS
McLAUGHLIN Jim			RSS
McLEAN Jim	SCU3/4		Thurso 41–43 Forfar 43–46 SCU4
McLENNAN			RSS
McLEOD Sgt D.	SCU3		St Erth DF GPO
MEADE Ralph	SCU4		Darlington radio (ex-Merchant Navy)
MEEK Fred			RSS
MEHAREY D.	SCU3	GI2OY	Northern Ireland VI
MELLOR Sgt J.	SLU8		
METCALFE Sgt	SCU1		
MILLAR A. &/or W.	SCU3		Thurso 41–43 Forfar 43–46
MILLER Jack	SCU3	G4MM	Arkley Discrimination

MILLER Kenneth	SCU3	G6QF/G3QF	Hanslope & Lydd
MILLIGAN	SCU3		Arkley joined around D day
MILLMAN Mrs	SCU3		Arkley Collation
MILLS Mick	SCU12		
MILTON Sgt George	SCU3		Hanslope & Thurso DF
MODRIDGE Peter	SCU3	G6PM	Arkley Allocation?
MOGG Doug			RSS (Possibly VI only)
MOORE Kenneth	SCU12		
MORCOM Archie	SCU3	G2FZZ	Hanslope
MORGAN Ted	SCU3		Hanslope Op
MORLEY Sid	SCU3	G3FWR	Arkley Discrimation BRS2780
MORRIS Alan	SCU3		Forfar in 1945
MORTIMER Cpl	SCU1		
MORTON EVANS Ken	SCU3	G5KJ	Arkley Lt-Col. RSS Deputy Controller
MORTON Mary W.S.	SCU3	ATS	Arkley DF (ref G2BTO)
MOSELEY Jack	SCU3	G2CIW	Hanslope
MOSS G.	SCU3		Hanslope
MOXHAM John			RSS
MUDFORD W. F.	SCU3	G6BK	Arkley Group 1
MUDLE Chas	SCU4/10		
MUNSON Fred	SCU3		RSS
MURRAY John	SCU4		
NACHMAN Sid	SCU4		
NEIL F. E.	SCU3	GI5NY	Northern Ireland VI
NERY	SCU8		SLU8 Capt.
NEWBY Allan	SCU3	G8CP	Hanslope (later G3ALN)
NEWMAN A. C. A.	SCU3		RSS
NICHOLL W. J.	SCU3		Northern Ireland VI
NICHOLS	SCU4/10		RSS Capt.
NICHOLSON Kenny	SCU3		Forfar & Arkley (Royal Signals)
NICHOLSON Miss	SCU3		Arkley Collation
NICHOLSON	SCU1		
NIGHTINGALE Ted	SCU3		RSS
NOBBS Danny	SCU3		St Erth (fm Ken Reid)
NOBLET Tom	SCU3		RSS
NORBURY	SCU3		RSS
NORMANTON Fred	SCU12		RSS may be Normington
NORTON Capt. D. H.	SCU3		VI SW regional officer (1940–46)
OAKLEY Stan	SCU4/10		
OAKS Sgt Arthur	SCU3		St Erth
OATENFIELD John	SCU3		Hanslope
O'CONNER Sgt	SCU1		

OLIVER Victor	SCU3	G3XT	Arkley Research Op.
OPENSHAW Gerry	SCU3	G2BTO	Wymondham DF & Group 7
ORCHIN Arthur	SCU3	G8PT	Hanslope
ORR Charles A. L.	SCU3	GM2CPC	Hanslope
ORR James	SCU3	G8JO	Hanslope & St Erth DF
ORR Lt T.	SCU3		Thurso 41–43 Forfar 43–46
ORR Themie	SCU3	G3IV	Hanslope/Arkley
OSWALD Dave	SCU3		RSS
OTLEY Bernard	SCU3		RSS Sgt
OTTERY Kenneth	SCU3	G3ECS	St Erth
OVERTON Fred	SCU3/4		Forfar Nordet
OWEN Stuart	SCU3	GW3QN	Arkley Group 14
PACE Ernie	SCU3		St Erth
PAGE Sgt E. A. W.	SCU3		Thurso 41–43 Forfar 43–46
PAINTER Robert A.	SCU3/4	G3BPF	Hanslope 44–46 DF & Eng. Palestine
PALIN CQMS	SCU1		
PARKER Bernard	SCU4		IDET
PARKES Gordon W.	SCU3	G3NL	Arkley Discrimination CQMS
PARKINSON Dennis	SCU3		Despatch Rider?
PARRENT Kingsley C.	SCU3		Hanslope Group 7—Violet
PARSONS John V.	SCU3	G5QP	Arkley Group
PATTENDEN Audrey	SCU3		Arkley Group 2
PATTERSON J.	SCU3	BRS2798	Hanslope Gp7 Violet
PAXMAN P.	SCU3		Forfar W/T operator
PAYNE A. C.	SCU3		Forfar
PAYNE Bernard Sgmn	SCU8		
PAYNE J. F.	SCU3	G2XP	Arkley
PAYNE Cpl Sam	SCU3		
PEACOCK Capt.	SCU1		
PEAK (Luxford) Ruth	SCU3		Arkley Gp 2
PEARCE M. A. (Jim)	SCU4/10		
PEAT Watson	SCU3/1	GM3AVA	Arkley and SCU9
PEEK Bill	SCU3	G2ZZ	Arkley
PENFOLD Bill	SCU12		
PERRIN Sgt John	SCU3		
PERRY Sgmn	SCU1		
PETRIE Ron	SCU3		
PETTERSON J.	SCU3		Hanslope
PETTIFAR Claude	SCU3	G2DPQ	Hanslope
PICKUP Ron	SCU3		Arkley
PILLING Bill	SCU4		
PIPER	SCU12		

PLYM Ken	SCU6		
POLLARD Maj.	SCU1		
PONTING C. R.	SCU3	G6ZR	Arkley (was VI)
POOLE F/Sgt J. A. R.	SLU8		
POOTS W. R. (Yander)	SCU4/10		
PORTER E.		G8LQ	May not be RSS
PORTHOUSE Dickie	SCU12		
POTTS Cliff	SCU3		RSS
POUNTNEY Syd	SCU3		Hanslope
PRICE Eddie	SCU3		St Erth
PRICKETT Capt.	SCU3		
PRITCHARD Sgt Adam	SCU3		
PROCTOR George	SCU3	GM8SQ	Hanslope & Forfar (original)
PRYOR George	SCU3	G3YX	Hanslope
PYETT Frank Clough	SCU3		Forfar W/T operator
QUINCY Sgt V.	SLU8		
QUINNEY Vic	SCU8		
RADCLIFFE Bernard	SCU4		
RADLEY Maurice	SCU3		RSS
RAMSDEN G. H.	SCU3	G6BR	Arkley (may have gone abroad)
RAMSEY Albert	SCU3	G5RK	Hanslope
RANNER Brian	SCU4		St Erth
RATHBONE Jim	SCU3		RSS
RAYNER Bernard	SCU3	G8BR	Hanslope
RAYNES Lt F. H.	SCU3/4		Gateshead (GPO at Darlington)
READ Eddy	SCU3	G6US	Hanslope
READ Mrs	SCU3		Arkley Collation
REARDON Maj.	SCU4		
REED Ronnie	SCU1?	G2RX	Arkley? Op for deception XX
REES Frank	SCU4		
REEVE Bill	SCU3	G2AA	Hanslope (1st in call book!)
REEVES Len	SCU3	G4CEM	VI 40–43
REGAN R.	SCU3		Hanslope
REID Ken	SCU3		Arkley & St Erth
REID Miss Connie	SCU3		Arkley Collation
RENDALL Bob	SCU3		Arkley discrimination—Group 2
REYNOLDS Dick	SCU3		Arkley Group 1
RHIND Tommy	S C U 8 / SLU8		RSS Major
RHODES Capt.	SCU3		Arkley i/c Allocation
RICHARDSON Ted	SCU3		RSS
RICHARDSON	SCU12		RSS CQMS

RIDDEL	SCU3		RSS
RIDGWAY Harry	SCU3		RSS
RIDLEY J. B.	SCU3		Hanslope (source G8VG)
RIESEN Stan	SCU3	G5SR	Arkley
RIGG Harry	SCU3		St Erth (fm Ken Reid)
RILEY Jack	SCU3		Hanslope
RILEY	SCU3		Arkley Oaklands training Cpl
RITCHIE Roy	SCU3	GM3OYV	Arkley Group 2 N. Africa & Palestine
ROBB Frank	SCU3	GI6TK	Northern Ireland VI
ROBE Stan	SCU3		Thurso DF
ROBERTS Gordon	SCU5/6		
ROBERTS H. T.		GW5UO	
ROBERTSON Jimmy	SCU3		RSS
ROBERTSON Capt. W.	SCU3		Thurso 41–43 Forfar 43–46
ROBERTSON Wm	SCU3	G6WR	Hanslope
ROBERTSON Wm	SCU3	GM6RI	Hanslope
ROBINSON A. C.	SCU1		RSS Corporal
ROBINSON Alan		G3XG	
ROBINSON Dougie	SCU3		DF
ROBSON A. J.	SCU8		RSS CSM
ROBSON Dicky	SCU12		
ROBSON Jock	SCU3		Arkley Collation Sgt
ROE J. W.	SCU3	BRS5303	Gateshead op (fm Blackpool)
ROGERS	SCU12		RSS
ROSS Ken	SCU3		Arkley St Erth (fm Ken Reid)
ROUGHLEY J. P.	SCU3		Hanslope
ROWE Jack	SCU3		Arkley Collation (R.Sigs Regular)
RUSSELL	SCU12		RSS
RYECROFT Doug	SCU3		Gateshead op (fm Leeds)
RYLE Gilbert	SCU3		HTR(with) Arkley Prof of Phil. Ox.
SADDLER Eric	SCU3		RSS
SAND	SCU3	GI6TB	Northern Ireland VI
SANDERSON Leslie	SCU3	G8TN	Hanslope
SANDHURST Ralph S.	SCU3/1		Arkley (Lord) Hatch Manson Wines
SANDISON Jack	SCU3		Thurso DF
SAUNDERS Vic	SCU12		RSS
SAVAGE J. R.	SCU3		Northern Ireland VI
SCOTT	SCU3		Arkley Group 2?
SCOTT	SCU3		Gateshead op (fm Scotland)
SEAL Les R.	SCU3	G2OC	Hanslope (source G8VG)
SEARLE	SCU1		RSS Sgmn

SEAWARD	SCU1		RSS F/Lt
SEDGEWICK Norman	SCU3	G8WV	Hanslope
SHARES Ted	SCU3	G8TV	Arkley
SHARP	SCU2		RSS? function of SCU2
SHAW Martin	SCU1/7/3		Whaddon/Little Horwood/Hanslope
SHAW Capt. Peter	SCU3		Arkley discrimination—Group 13
SHEEN Joe	SCU3		RSS
SHELDON Bill	SCU8		RSS
SHENE L. L.	SCU3	2BRV	Northern Ireland VI
SHEPHERD T. H.	SCU3		Hanslope
SHORT William	SCU3	G2HNP	Hanslope
SILLS Bernard	SCU2		RSS
SIMPSON Bill	SCU8		RSS Sgmn
SIVERS John T.	SCU3		RSS
SLACK Barney	SCU3		RSS
SLY Capt.	SCU3		Arkley Admin
SMALL E.	SCU3	BRS 5318	Hanslope
SMALLEY	SCU12		RSS Capt.
SMITH	SLU8		RSS Sgt
SMITH Bob	SCU3	G6TQ	Arkley Research op.
SMITH C.	SCU3/4		Thurso 41–43 Forfar 43–46
SMITH J. N.	SCU3	GI5QX	Northern Ireland VI
SMITH M.	SCU3		Hanslope
SMITH William	SCU3/4		Arkley St Erth Alex. (fm Ken Reid)
SMITH	SCU12		RSS Cpl
SNAITH Geoff W.	SCU3/4		
SNELL E. (Tubby)	SLU8		RSS
SNOWDEN Roy	SCU3		St Erth (fm Ken Reid)
SOAMES Richard	SCU3		Arkley Lawns training CQMS
SPELLMAN R.	SCU3		Thurso 41–43 Forfar 43–46
SPENCER Sgt Alf	SCU4/10	G3HEZ	
SPENDIFF Harry	SCU3		Hanslope
SPODE A. C.	SCU8		RSS Sgmn
SPRATT Ernie	SCU12		RSS
SPRIGGS George	SCU3	G4KG	Hanslope
SPROULE R. A.	SCU3	GI2SP	Northern Ireland VI
STACEY Claude	SCU4		RSS CSM
STANDERWICK Bob			RSS
STANLEY J. F.	SCU3	G6SY	Hanslope
STANLEY Thomas	SCU3	GW3AX	Hanslope
STANSFIELD	SCU12		RSS

STANWORTH Capt. Walter	SCU3		NW Regional Officer—Preston/ Southport
STEAD Sgt	SCU3		Arkley
STEELE Monty	SCU3/4		Gateshead op (fm Lincoln)
STEVENSON G.	SCU3/4		Thurso 41–46 Forfar 43–46
STEWART Capt. W.	SCU3	G2HAB	
STEWART W. (Bill)	SCU8		RSS Sgmn
STEWART Peter	SCU4		Hanslope then Egypt–Maadi camp
STIGGERS Frank	SCU3		Arkley Group X
STIMPSON CSM	SCU12		
STOBO Alan			RSS
STOCKS Stan	SCU3/4		
STOWE Fred	SCU3		Arkley Discrimination/Hanslope
STREETER A. R.	SCU3		RSS
STUART Charles	SCU3		with HTR Arkley
STUCK Gordon	SCU3	G3AMR	Hanslope
SULLIVAN Alec	SCU4		
SULLIVAN W.	SCU3	GI6XS	Northern Ireland VI
SUMMERS Roy	SCU3		RSS
SUTHERLAND J.	SLU8		
SWANN Gil F.	SCU3/4		RSS Major
SWIFT Peter G.	SCU4		
SWORD L. J. John	SCU8/ SLU8		
TAGHOLM John E.	SCU3		RSS
TANT Capt. H. E. F.	SCU3		Arkley Discrimination 'Auntie'
TARANTO Stan	SCU4/10		
TAYLOR Alfred	SCU3	G8TZ	Hanslope
TAYLOR Bill (W. G.)	SCU3	G2AGX	Arkley discrimination Group 2
TAYLOR E.	SCU3		Gateshead op (fm Stockport)
TAYLOR Eric	SCU3	G3FK	Hanslope
TAYLOR J. E.	SCU3	G6XI	Hanslope
TAYLOR Jim	SCU3	G4QX	Hanslope
TAYLOR John	SCU3		Arkley Research Operator
TAYLOR Keith	SCU3/1	G0XKT	Forfar BP 43–45
TAYLOR Mrs	SCU3		Arkley Collation
THOMAS L. O.	SCU3		Thurso 41–43 Forfar 43–46
THOMAS Stanley	SCU3	GW3AX	Hanslope
THOMAS W.	SCU3		Arkley Group 2 Map section
THOMPSON J. C.	SCU3	2ATC	Northern Ireland VI
TICKLE John	SCU3	GW5TC	Arkley DF or Allocation Sgt
TIERNEY L. J. John	SCU8		

TINNION H.	SCU3	G2HT	Hanslope
TOMKINS Ralph	SCU3		St Erth
TOUGH Alex	SCU3		Arkley and St Erth
TOWNHILL Harold	SCU3	G5XL	Hanslope
TOZER Douglas	SCU2		
TRACY Sgmn	SCU1		
TREEECE Gordon John	SCU3	G3QD	VI 40–58
TREVOR ROPER Hugh	SCU3		Arkley—Lord Dacre
TREWIN Rev. A. B.	SCU3	G2AT	VI only
TRIPPER F.	SCU3		Darlington GPO
TROTT Fly	SCU3		Royal Signals & Arkley Research
TRUMPER Ernest G.	SCU3	G3DAZ	Hanslope/Arkley
TURNER Fred	SCU3	G4AG	Hanslope
TURNER George	SCU3		St Erth
TURNER Harry	SCU3	G6ZT	Hanslope
TURNER Tony Capt	SCU3		Arkley discrimination—i/c Collation
TUTT Capt.	SCU1		
TYLER Wat	SCU3		Hanslope GPO Gloucester
ULLYATT Les	SCU3		Arkley Group 2?
URQUHART Pat	SCU3	G4DR	Hanslope
VARNET Sgt	SCU1		
VARNEY R. Louis	SCU3	G5RV	Hanslope
VEAL W. G. Jack	SCU3		RSS
WAITE D.	SCU3		Northern Ireland VI
WAITE, Jnr, H.	SCU3		Northern Ireland VI
WALES Vic	SCU2		
WALKER Miss	SCU3		Arkley Collation
WALKER Ernie	SCU3		NW Regional VI (employed by Cable & Wireless in Liverpool)
WALLACE Capt. J.	SCU3		Stirling
WALLIS Don F.	SCU3/4		St Erth Trained & MERS
WARD Bert	SCU3	G3WD	Hanslope
WARD Percy	SCU3		Forfar in 1945
WARD Geoff	SCU3		Arkley & St Erth
WARNER H. W.	SCU3	G3BB	Arkley
WARREN George	SCU4/10		
WATERS Bill	SCU1		
WATSON Bert	SCU2		
WATSON N.	SCU3		Thurso 41–43 Forfar 43–46 SCU4
WATTS Arthur	SCU3	G6UN	RSGB President/Group leader
WATTS Frank	SCU3	G5BM	Hanslope
WEBB Ethel	SCU3		Arkley Discrimination Group

WEBSTER Al N.	SCU3	G2DWB	Arkley
WEDDERSPOON Doug	SCU3	G2WZ	Arkley
WELLINGTON Ted	SCU3	G3AEM	Hanslope
WHERRY Reg	SCU3		St Erth
WHITEHEAD H.	SCU3		Thurso 41–43 Forfar 43–46
WHITELEY S. E.	SCU3	G2DAN	
WHITTAKER H.	SCU3	G3SJ	St Erth intercept
WIGG Reginald	SCU3	G6JF	Hanslope (Sent by ME to evaluate)
WILD John	SCU3	G3WG	Hanslope
WILKINS H. V.	SCU3	G6WN	Arkley (Brother to G6RW)
WILKINS Les	SCU3	G6RW	Arkley
WILKINSON Harold	SCU3	G4NW	Arkley
WILKINSON Walter	SCU3	G3VR	Arkley Group 14
WILLIAMS David A. V.	SCU1/3	G3CCO	Whaddon 45–47 Engineer
WILSON	SCU3		Northern Ireland VI
WILSON Les	SCU3/4		(Bradford)
WILSON Mary	SCU3	ATS	Arkley D/F Capt. (ref G2BTO)
WILSON Sgt Tom E.	SCU3	G6VQ	Gateshead Admin Sgt
WINDETT Harold	SCU3		Arkley Allocation
WINDLE Capt. Bill	SCU3	G8VG	Hanslope
WINSTANLEY Arthur	SCU3	G2JA	Hanslope
WISE Leonard	SCU3	G6XF	Arkley Discrimination Group
WITCHER L. M.	SCU4		Gibraltar
WITHERS Horace	SCU3	G6XA	Hanslope (were there 2 Withers?)
WITHERS	SCU3		Arkley Oaklands training
WOOD Harry (NCO)	SCU3		Thurso 41–43 Forfar 43–46
WOOD Ronald	SCU3	G3TK	Hanslope
WOODCOCK Tommy	SCU3	G6OO	Arkley—Tant's Specials ops
WOOLNER George H.	SCU3	G4BC	Arkley discrimination group
WOOSNAM F. C.	SCU3		Hanslope
WRATTEN Ronald	SCU3	G2JV	Hanslope
WRIGHT Paul	SCU3	G3SEM	
WRIGHT Capt. John	SCU3		Arkley Group 2
WYLIE Bob	SCU3		Thurso DF
YULE Leslie	SCU3		St Erth–Arkley Op

Endnotes

Chapter 1

1. Simpson, Lt-Col. Adrian, *Notes on the Detection of Illicit Wireless 1940*.
2. Trevor-Roper, Hugh, *Sideways into SIS* (Note by Lord Dacre of Glanton).
3. *Ibid.*
4. *Ibid.*
5. *Ibid.*
6. *Ibid.*, p. 10.
7. POST56/144.
8. HW34/1.
9. Cort-Wright, P., *The Secret Listeners* (BBC Documentary, 1979).
10. *Ibid.*
11. *Ibid.*, p. 16.
12. HW34/1.
13. Cort-Wright, P. *op. cit.*, p. 16.

Chapter 2

1. KV4/98.
2. *Ibid.*
3. KV4/98, *op. cit.*, p. 21.
4. HW34/1.
5. *Ibid.*
6. WO208/5105.
7. *Ibid.*, p. 24.
8. HW34/17.

Chapter 3

1. Simpson, Col. Adrian., *Notes on the Detection of Illicit Wireless 1940* (MI5 Booklet).
2. *Ibid.*
3. *Ibid.*
4. Cort-Wright, P., *The Secret Listeners* (BBC Documentary, 1979), p. 16.
5. *Ibid.*

6. King, B., *PO Box 25: The Radio Security Service from 1939 to 1945*.
7. Kelsall, Captain R. Signals Testimonial letter April 1946.
8. Fautley, Ray *pers. comm.*
9. Daily Mirror article *'Spies Tap Nazi Code'* Friday 14 February 1941.

Chapter 4

1. Cort-Wright, P., *The Secret Listeners* (BBC Documentary, 1979), p. 16.
2. *Ibid.*
3. Wright, Ray., *pers. comm.*
4. *Ibid.*, p. 42.
5. Cort-Wright, P. *op. cit.*, p. 16.
6. King, Bob., *pers. comm.*
7. *Ibid.*
8. HW34/5.
9. Cort-Wright, P. *op. cit.*, p. 16.

Chapter 5

1. WO208/5098.
2. *Ibid.*
3. FO370/2930.
4. *Ibid.*
5. Cort-Wright, P. *op. cit.*, p. 16.
6. KV2/1936.
7. *Ibid.*
8. *Ibid.*
9. *Ibid.*
10. KV2/1936
11. HW34/5.

Chapter 6

1. WO208/5104.
2. *Ibid.*
3. *Ibid.*
4. *Ibid.*
5. Wright, Ray, *pers. comm.*
6. *Ibid.*
7. *Ibid.*
8. *Ibid.*, p. 75.
9. Wallis, Don, *pers. comm.*

Chapter 7

1. CARS (Chelmsford Amateur Radio Society) note on Plan Flypaper g0mwt.org.uk/newsletter/2006/2006-09-nl.pdf.
2. *Ibid.*
3. Findlater-Stewart, Sir S., *The Government Communications Voluntary Radio Service* (Official Review report of 1945).
4. PRO86.

Bibliography

Aldrich, R., *GCHQ—The Uncensored Story of Britain's Most Secret Intelligence Agency* (Harper Press 2010)

Austin, Dr B., '*EWB Gill—Taking Wireless to War.*' (The Journal of the Royal Signals Institution. Volume XXIX Winter 2010, No. 2, blogs.mhs.ox.ac.uk/innovatingincombat/files/2014/03/Oct10V5.pdf)

blog.jgc.org/2012/03/delilah-secure-speech-system.html

Busby, G., *The Spies at Gilnahirk* (Ballyhay Books 2016)

Butler, D. A., *Memo to Captain HR Sandwith RN in DSD9/Admiralty* 9 December 1940

CARS (Chelmsford Amateur Radio Society) note on Plan Flypaper, g0mwt.org.uk/newsletter/2006/2006-09-nl.pdf

cdmnet.org/RSS/SecretListeners/page2.html

cdmnet.org/RSS/SecretListeners/SCUNLMarch2007.htm

Cort-Wright, P., *The Secret Listeners* (BBC Documentary, 1979)

Curry, J., *The Security Service 1908–1945* (Report published by PRO in 1999)

Daily Mirror article 'Spies Tap Nazi Code', published 14 February 1941

Ellison, K., *SCU Units in France*, Chapter 8: Special Counter Intelligence In World War II Europe, 2015

Fautley, R., 2018, *pers. comm.*

Findlater-Stewart, Sir S., *The Government Communications Voluntary Radio Service*, official review report of 1945, pages 1-9, 154-170, & 356-35

Hastings, M., *The Secret War: Spies, Codes and Guerillas 1939–1945* (William Collins, 2015)

Hinsley, F. H. and Simkins, C. A. G., *British Intelligence in the Second World War, Volume 4: Security and Counter-Intelligence* (Her Majesty's Stationery Office London, 1990)

Kelsall, Capt. Royal Signals. Testimonial letter (ref RSC/0/18) for Sgt Bill Peek 18 April 1946

King, B., *Box 25: The Radio Security Services from 1939–1946*, personal copy

MacIntyre, B., *Double Cross: The True Story of the D-Day Spies*. (Bloomsbury Publishing House 2012)

McKay, S., *The Secret Listeners: How the Y Service Intercepted German Codes for Bletchley Park* (Arun History Press, 2012)

Morton Evans, Lt-Col. Private correspondence with Bob King 1/3/1995 (ref ME1); Private correspondence with Bob King 13/6/1995 (ref ME8); Private correspondence with Bob King 1996 (ref ME13)

newscientist.com/article/mg21428672-700-alan-turing-codebreaking-and-code-making/

Particulars regarding Special Enlistment for Interception and other Technical Duties in the RSS (Confidential Note)

Pigeon, G., *The Secret Wireless War: The Story of MI6 Communications 1939–1945* (Arundel Books, 2008, prestige-press.com)

Simpson, Col. A., *Notes on the Detection of Illicit Wireless 1940* (MI5 Booklet)

Tatly, S., *Agent Garbo: The Brilliant, Eccentric Secret Agent who Tricked Hitler & Saved D-Day* (Houghton Mifflin Harcourt, 2012)

Taylor, J. A., *Secret Sisters of Bletchley Park: Psychological Warfare in World War II* (Magic Flute Publications, 2015)

The Polish Heritage Society Proceedings, 2nd International Military History Conference. '*The Polish Section of SOE and Poland's Silent and Unseen*' 1940–1945 Conference Papers Saturday 11 June 2016, polishheritage.co.uk

Trevor-Roper, H., *Sideways into SIS*, note from Hugh (Lord Dacre of Glanton)

West, N., *GCHQ: The Secret Wireless War 1900–1986* (Weidenfeld & Nicolson, 1986)

Wright, P., *The Secret Listeners* (Radio Communication article, December 1980)

Archives

CAB 301/77

FO370/2930

FO850/256

HW19/331

HW25/36

HW34/1 Miscellaneous manuscript notes on RSS History. Covering 1938-1946. Opened 5 April 2001 including memo (MI8/A.1433 on 13/5/1941) highlighting transfer of RSS to MI6

HW34/16

HW34/17

HW34/19

HW34/2 February 1946 RSS(I) Administration Files – Comparison notes between RSS and *Funkabwehr*

HW34/28

HW34/3 RSS war records. CO/2A Traffic Reports December 1942 to August 1944

HW34/4

HW34/5

HW34/6

HW34/7

HW51/26

HW51/56

HW51/84

HW69/15

KV 2/211

KV2/1936

KV4/98 Security Service and SIS relations and coordination of interests in RSS organisation. Volume 2

POST56/144

PRO106 Future of the GCVRS 99/1 & Interception Miscellaneous – GCVRS IX B2/3 1948-1956

PRO86 1xB2/3 File XII 1/9 1946 Policy: Transfer of RSS Functions

WO208/4970 The History of CSDIC (UK)

WO208/5096 MI8 War records Q/3428 – RSS Policy (high level)

WO208/5097

WO208/5100

WO208/5104

WO208/5105 MI8 War records Q/3441. RSS – Lord Swinton on the Security Services, 1941

Index